COGNITIVE-BEHAVIORAL REFLECTIONS ON SOME DIMENSIONS OF PERSONALITY

Matt E. Jaremko
University of Richmond

University Press of America

Library of Congress Catalog Number: 79-6602

To:

Donald L. Whaley,

An inspiring model of excellence

TABLE OF CONTENTS

APOLOGIA

I started out to write this book as a textbook for the undergraduate course in personality. I wanted to teach students to view the area of personality from a "scientific" perspective. I was under the impression that my approach to personality was "scientific." It took me three years to realize that the book I was writing was not the scientific approach, but was merely one of many approaches that are contained in the scientific approach. I was trying to produce a comprehensive work that would provide the last word on all of the unanswered questions of personality research. I soon realized that such a task could not be done.

After receiving some feedback from colleagues, I came to realize that what I was, in fact, doing was recording some of my own views and values about what was important in some areas of personality research. My "reflections on some dimensions of personality" have a highly filtered quality to them. I have filtered the content and method of personality research through a set of influences that are sometimes scientific, many times theoretical and speculative, and all too often, dogmatic.

In many respects the models and conceptions I have offered can be considered cognitive-behavioral. By that I mean that the content areas of personality are addressed in terms of how three interacting "channels" of behavior are described and explained. At various times I have tried to analyze the overt behavioral, the covert emotional and cognitive, and the physiological aspects of human experience. The work is most influenced by the writings of radical behaviorists: B. F. Skinner, Donald L. Whaley, and Richard W. Malott. The work of cognitive-behaviorists, Michael J. Mahoney, Donald Meichenbaum, and Albert Bandura, may also be recognizable here. I hasten to add, however, that the ideas of these psychologists have been hopelessly filtered through my system of values, priorities, and pet theories. I apologize to any of them, or others whom I may have misquoted or misinterpreted. I am afraid that the final responsibility for this set of speculative reflections rests with me.

I offer this book as an emerging way to approach certain questions in personality analysis. I no longer consider it, as I did when I started, a comprehensive treatment of all the vastness of personality theory, research, and application. At best, it is one interested observer's view on issues relevant

iii

to human personality. The single most scientific aspect of the book is that I have tried to show that empiricism of one form or another is a good arbiter in the definition of reality. Considerable information can be obtained by subjecting speculation to empirical validation. Much of what is presented here is speculation that awaits verification (or falsification). It is offered now in a spirit of tentative acceptance and empirical evaluation.

I would like to acknowledge several people who have helped to bring this book to its present form. The following colleagues provided thoughtful reviews of selected chapters: Harriet Aronson, Sigrid Glenn, Kevin Kennelly, and Wes Wenrich, all of North Texas State University, George Kish of Roanoke College, Mike Nelson of Xavier University, Paul Taylor of the Medical University of South Carolina, Dick Whettstone of James Madison University, and Marvin Zuckerman of the University of Delaware.

Linden Jaremko and Betty Baker have been kind enough to do preliminary editing on my shameless grammar. Gloria Sapp, Betty Baker, and Doris Allen were dedicated typists. Jim Tromater was helpful in letting me teach the personality course several times in succession. Several students aided my progress by reviewing the psychological literature on selected topics. The University of Richmond Faculty Research Committee has been kind enough to support some of the monetary costs. All of these people were helpful in the completion of this project, but any errors and inconsistencies remain my own responsibility. And finally, Linden and Annie were a constant source of motivation to finish work.

CHAPTER 1

WHAT IS PERSONALITY?

Kim and Jeannie sat in a booth at the Student Union coffee shop eating their usual cheeseburger and greasy fries. Their conversation, too, was pretty typical.

"That Bill has such a strong personality. Last night, we were talking, and he practically <u>forced</u> me to agree to go to the concert with him. I really had no choice but to give in," Kim related to her friend.

"I know what you mean. He's in one of my classes and he takes up more time talking than the teacher. But he <u>is</u> nice looking." Jeannie answered, thoughtfully.

"Yeah, maybe....I just don't like someone who comes on so strong. Now, Peter--he's really neat. You know? What a personality! He smiles all the time and is always so nice."

"But he's so busy. At least Bill's around." Jeannie sipped her syrupy coke.

And so it goes...

What "Personality" means

The two young women were talking about people and the way people are. We all use terms like "strong personality," "good personality," and so forth. But what do we mean by them?

One thing we mean is assertiveness. Kim describes Bill as a strong personality--meaning that he makes it his business to get what he wants. He lets his feelings be known. He behaves in a certain way. Another thing "personality" means when it is used in informal conversation is likability. Peter is nice and is liked by many of his fellow students. He has a "great personality." He behaves in a specific set of ways.

There are many other popular usages of the concept of personality. A weak personality refers to a person's timidity and shy behavior. An open personality describes someone who talks a lot about personal things. A friendly personality obviously refers to someone who is friendly. The list could go on.

1

This book is about personality. Since we all talk about different "personalities," we should know something about them. We will take a look at the <u>dimensions of human personality</u> from a scientific point of view. Popular notions and usages of the concept are fine for student union building informal discussion and late night bull sessions. But for a true understanding of what human personalities are, how they are formed, and what effects they have, we are better off playing it by a set of scientific rules. The reason for this is important.

Reification

The trouble with the popular notions of personality (and some scientific notions, as well) is that they are <u>reified</u>.

****

(John's fifth grade teacher was talking with his mother.) "Why does your son fight so much in my class? He's always pushing, shoving, and biting."

"Well, Miss Snodgrape," Mrs. Feasdale replied, "John is a very aggressive youngster." (He has an aggressive personality.)

"You are certainly right about that. I wonder why he has such an aggressive personality?"

"That's obvious. He's always fighting..."

****

To reify means to regard an abstract idea as material or real. It is the process of turning a relationship between two real things into a real thing itself. So when we talk about nice "personalities," "strong personalities," etc., we make the mistake of implying that "personalities" are real things. They are not. No one really has a "personality." Anyway, the real cause of a person's aggressiveness, likability, or assertiveness is not a "personality." Gordon Allport, one of the first personality psychologists, discussed the problem of reification many years ago (1966). We need to solve this problem by playing by scientific rules.

REIFICATION: The process of turning a relationship between two real things into a real thing itself.

The trouble with reification is that it explains nothing

2

(Carr & Kingsbury, 1938). Some people who have talked about personality have reified it and then gone on to use it for explanatory purposes. For example, why is Bill so hostile? Because he has an aggressive "personality;" Why does he have an aggressive "personality?" Because he is hostile all the time. In the end, these people have explained nothing. We will avoid reification and the circular reasoning it breeds by always looking to the many factors that make someone act the way they do. Our approach, the dimensions of personality approach, will help us do that.

This book will enumerate the major dimensions of personality and describe them by a consistent set of scientific rules. In the end, we will have covered the list of popular "personalities," but it may be considered that we will have put together the person in a more sensible, meaningful, and scientifically-sound way.

1. How do most people look at the notion of personality?

2. What is reification? Define it. Cite an example.

3. Why is it bad to reify "personality?"

The Nature of "Personality"

"Personality" is not a thing. "It" refers to the way people act--what they do, how they think, what they feel. Their behaviors, both outward and inward (thinking and feeling), are what is being described when the word "personality" is used.

But more than behaviors, "personality" refers to how a person's behavior fits together. How does this set of behavior combine to result in a unique "person?" (Guilford, 1959). When we say Bill has a strong personality, we mean that he exhibits certain behaviors that go together--he says what he wants, he knows his desires, he manipulates people, and so forth. So to know about "personality," we have to know about how people are different and how they are the same. Even further, we have to know how one person (the "person" in the "personality") can be different at different times and how he can be the same at different times.

I once attended a concert that can serve as a good demonstration of the differences among people. A few days after the concert, I asked someone I knew had been there how he liked it.

3

"Boy, it was terrific. I have never been so moved in my life. Kenny Loggins (a "pop" singer of the 70's) was really alive. I always have liked him anyway, and he really got the place jumping. I hope the student union has more of those concerts."

On the same day, I asked another who went what she thought.

"Oh well, you know. It was okay. I mean, I had a good time. I really like Kenny Loggins, but I thought he was silly, and the people were so weird... I don't know, I wasn't all that impressed."

Two people, the same concert, different reactions. Why? Because one was male and the other female? Because one was friendly and the other introverted? Because one had a good date and the other didn't? It could be all of these. The point is that people differ from each other on certain behavioral dimensions. These can be called individual differences (Eysenck and Rachman, 1965). However, people also differ within themselves from moment to moment.

INDIVIDUAL DIFFERENCES: The notion that people differ from each other on certain characteristics.

****

"Ronnie is so weird. (She's my roommate, you know.),"
Jill was saying to her friend, Sally, as they walked to biology lab.

"She is probably one of the nicest girls I have ever met; I'm really lucky to have her as a friend. She always helps me with my stat and can cheer up the other girls in our suite. But when she gets around guys, she's something else. We went to a party last night, and she was very cold and catty to me. I really believe she's sincerely nice, but she gets so weird when she's around men."

****

Does Ronnie have two "personalities"--one with girls in the dorm and one with guys? Remember, there is no such thing as a personality. Ronnie's behavior demonstrates the situational specificity of behavior. Situational specificity refers to the fact that the same person behaves differently in

4

different situations, depending upon experiences in similar situations in the past (Mischel, 1976).

SITUATIONAL SPECIFICITY: The point of view that situations determine how people will behave. A person can behave different ways in different situations, depending upon his or her experiences.

With the two ideas of individual differences and situational specificity, we can define personality.

"The thing" defined.

There are two ways people differ: from each other and from themselves. What personality refers to is how a person behaves in a consistent manner across situations (Malott & Whaley, 1976). While no one is entirely consistent, certain commonalities exist. If you behave in a friendly way in many situations, then you have a "friendly personality." If you aggress toward people in many different situations, you are an "aggressive personality".

Since some people are aggressive and some not, some curious and some not, some assertive and some not; then the word personality also refers to the behavioral differences among people. By combining the two notions of situational specificity and individual differences, we get a definition of personality.

PERSONALITY: Those behaviors a person does that (1) are fairly consistent across different situations, and, (2) differ from the ways many other people behave in those same situations.

An example will clarify. If you knew someone who helped people in many different situations, you could call him "altruistic" because he differed from other people who didn't help others as much in the same situations. One person has an "altruistic personality," the other doesn't. (However, in order to avoid reification, we would say that one had altruistic behavior, the other didn't.)

This is a logical and consistent way to look at human personality. It is referred to as an integrative approach by professional personality psychologists (Bryne, 1974). It is the definition that lays the groundwork for the dimensional approach to personality.

But first, some qualifiers:

5

*4. What are individual differences?

*5. What is situational specificity? Give an example.

*6. Define personality.

THE SCIENCE OF PERSONALITY

The Role of Theory

Most of the psychologists who have studied personality have used "theories" to help them in their understanding. Some very famous psychologists have provided "theories of personality." While most approaches to personality study theories, there are some problems with that approach to the study of personality (Hunt, 1965). A theory is a set of general principles formulated to explain a set of related facts. It is a way to put an order on things--to explain why they relate. It is often a very helpful tool of science, but can easily be overused (Skinner, 1969).

The problem is that theories often go beyond data. That means that they are speculations about how things might be rather than how they are. In and of itself, there is nothing wrong with speculating. It   generate and organize knowledge. But theory building should come after we have a significant amount of data, not before it. In personality, much theorizing has gone on. At the same time much data collection has also gone on. However, it may be that too much "press" has been given to the theory and not enough to the research. In this book, we will take the position that speculating is okay, but it should be kept to a minimum until the research facts about many basic questions concerning human personality have been dealt with. To some, this position may seem biased, but the scientific approach of focusing on the data may be a more accurate one (Block, 1968).

Another problem about personality theories is that they suggest an order and coherence in behavioral patterns that many psychologists and lay people alike are not ready to accept (Gergen, 1973). There is an order to behavior, that is, it is determined by some combination of variables. But people are not as cohesive and consistent as some theorists would have us believe. By being too global or theoretical, some psychologists have led us to believe that personality is a mysterious higher order thing--an entity in itself. However, things may not be that way. We will try to be more conservative and realistic about what personality is and what it isn't.

6

This does not mean that we will ignore the great think-
ers in the history of personality--people like Sigmund Freud,
Carl Rogers, Abraham Maslow and others. They had enlighten-
ing things to say. Some of those ideas will be presented in
this book. We will attempt, however, to place those ideas
where they make more sense. An attempt will be made not to
lead you to believe that there is a consistency and order to
personalities when there isn't. The approach of this book
will be to make sense out of behavior, not a reified concept
like "personality." In some ways this approach does limit us,
but it has other advantages not found in the theoretical approach. The most obvious advantage is that we will be exploring more closely what current personality psychologists do--
research.

Behavior, Behavior, Behavior

We keep talking about behavior--what does that mean?
Let's look in on a fictitious class to see if it will help...

****

Dr. Reynolds was lecturing on the first day of personality class to his upper level undergraduate students.

"The question that concerns us today is 'what do personality psychologists study?' Many things have been said about
this question. Only in the minds of a few psychologists has
it been answered. What do you think? What is the subject
matter of personality psychology?"

"Psychology is the study of the mind," one bold student
volunteered.

"Thoughts," another said.

"Feelings are what I'm interested in," answered a third.

"Doesn't psychology really study the way people act?" A
voice from the back meekly offered.

"That's correct." replied Dr. Reynolds, "In fact, everything you said is correct. Psychology--and especially personality psychology--is concerned with all those things."

"There are, however, more things that need to be said
about our subject matter. We need to specify things further.

7

What do we mean by 'mind', 'feelings', 'thoughts', and so forth? Let's talk about typologies...."

As Dr. Reynolds lectured on and on, the students wondered if they would get out of the first day of class a little early. They didn't.

****

There are three ways to classify behavior that seem to clarify and specify what the object of our study is (Rachman, 1975). First, behavior is overt action--writing a book, talking to friends, reading, riding a bike, studying, etc. Second, behavior is physiological response--hearts beating, heads swelling, butterflies, palms sweating, and so forth. Finally, behavior is private, conscious experience--what we say to ourselves, how we assess our feelings, our commentary to ourselves about what's going on outside of us and inside of us. All three of these types of behavior are of interest to the personality psychologist.

The above is a typology of behavior: A system for classifying things according to certain criteria. Criteria are very important in science. The three classes of behavior--overt, physiological, and consciousness--will be looked at according to the rules of science. So we have a typology of behavior that we'll use from now on...playing it by the rules of science.

*7. Name two reasons why theory is sometimes a problem?

*8. What is an advantage of a research approach to personality?

*9. What is a typology of behavior?

*10. Describe the behavioral typology used in this book.

SOME RULES OF SCIENCE

The attitudes of science

An attitude can be characterized as a general orientation toward an object that is composed of three facets: values, beliefs, and actions (Malott & Whaley, 1976). A value refers to the rewards and punishments that are meaningful to a person--likes and dislikes. A belief is something a person holds as true or untrue. An action is, of course, something a person does or does not do. All of these combine to form attitudes.

8

****

Roger had already run ten fifty-yard sprints. His legs hurt, he was thirsty, he had a blister on his toe. When the whistle blew, all the others at basketball practice stopped running and went to the showers. Roger ran two more 50's and shot free throws for half an hour.

As Coach Jiles was leaving the gym, he remarked to the trainer, "Roger's got a good attitude. If he keeps hustling, he'll be getting a lot of playing time in."

"Yeah, he'd like that...," the trainer turned away to gather the basketballs...

****

Roger is a good example of holding an attitude. Playing during the game is a reward--a value. He believes that hard work will make him good enough to play--belief; therefore, he works hard--action. He has a good "attitude."

ATTITUDE: The combined effects of values, beliefs, and action.

Scientists have attitudes, too. These attitudes are also based on values, beliefs and actions. Three of the attitudes of science are determinism, empiricism, and scientific manipulation(Whaley & Surratt, 1967).

Determinism

The scientist believes that the things he studies have some order to them (belief). He acts accordingly--trying to uncover the order (action). And it is rewarding when some order is found in the research that is conducted (values).

Personality psychologists are of the opinion that there is rhythmn and reason to personality dimensions. Certain patterns of behavior are preceded by predictable events. There is an answer, even in the complex vagaries of human behavior. It may seem incredibly difficult at times to understand why some people are the way they are. Why, for instance, does a man drink and then beat his wife? Or why does a person take his own life? Psychologists hold the attitude that there is an answer--a lawful, orderly answer. It may take a while to find it but we will eventually uncover the mystery.

Empiricism

Many years ago, it was believed that the shape and contour of a person's skull was an important predictor of the person's behavior. Phrenology, it was called. The study of skull configurations and how they related to mental faculties. If you had a bulge on the front part of your skull, you were probably eloquent of speech. When someone finally got around to checking it out scientifically, frontal bulges were found to have no relation to eloquence. Today, phrenology is called a pseudoscience--not really a science.

The attitude of empiricism was at work when the claims about skull contour were investigated. This attitude drives the scientist to look and see whether his/her ideas are true. To be empirical means to derive answers from materialistic or experimental procedures. That's what psychologists are doing when they test their guesses. We will be careful to make sure our statements are empirical. To be able to say something from an empirical stance is a value. To have proof makes us feel good (value). We believe it is the only way to be a good scientist (belief), and so we do experiments to test our ideas (actions). If we don't have an empirical orientation, we are probably not scientists.

Scientific manipulation

I guess everyone has heard the story about the person whose next door neighbor sprinkled salt around the edge of his yard every day at sunset. One day, the neighbor was asked why this strange thing was done every day.

"Well,"the neighbor replied, "I'm trying to keep elephants off my lawn."

"Elephants! That's ridiculous! There aren't any elephants around here."

"I know--it really works great, doesn't it?"

Of course, the neighbor violated the attitude of scientific manipulation. He didn't test his idea under controlled conditions. He would have had to refrain from sprinkling salt for a couple of weeks to know whether the salt was responsible for the lack of elephants. That's called experimental control.

Psychologists, too, have to use experimental control pro-

cedures to make sure they are reaching the right empirical conclusions. When we do this, we are operating under the attitude of scientific manipulation. We believe the right conclusions are important (belief); therefore, we take pains to
use experimental control (action); and it is rewarding to be
correct in our conclusions (value).

Those are the global attitudes which will be used to approach the subject matter in the rest of this book. The object of our study is orderly and understandable (determinism),
we need to base our ideas on observed facts (empiricism), and
we observe behavior under controlled conditions (scientific
manipulation).

*11. Define attitude. Give an example.

*12. What is determinism?

*13. What is empiricism?

*14. What is scientific manipulation?

Methods of experimental control

In order to behave according to the attitudes of empiricism and scientific manipulation, personality psychologists have
used three main forms of experimental control: correlation,
experiments with groups, and intensive study of one person.

All of these methods have been shown to be very helpful
in answering the questions raised by our deterministic attitudes. It is usually felt that reliance on any one of
these methods to the exclusion of the others is unwise (Barber,
1974). It's best to be familiar with each and to use each in
answering our questions. Let's briefly look at them.

Correlation

Correlation may be most useful at beginning stages of
experimental inquiry. Roughly, this refers to the amount two
variables are connected to each other. Let's say you wanted
to see if people who were depressed were also self-conscious.
After defining the two variables--depression and self-con-
sciousness--you would devise ways to measure them. You might
use already established measures, such as the Beck Depression
Inventory, developed by Dr. Aaron T. Beck and his associates
at the University of Pennsylvania (Beck, 1961). Or you might

11

make your own measure, as a group of us at the University of Richmond did with self-consciousness--the self-analysis scale (Jaremko, Noles, & Williams, 1979). (Incidentally, there are many ways to measure a personality dimension. We will be discussing these methods as the book progresses.)

You would then administer the two scales to a group of people. Each person will have a depression score and a self-consciousness score. By using a set mathematical formula, you then compute the amount of correlation between the two variables. A high positive correlation means that a person high in depression tends to also be high in self-consciousness; whereas a high negative correlation reflects the opposite-- a low depression score goes with a high self-consciousness score. A lack of correlation indicates that there is no predictable pattern between the scores.

This technique is helpful in revealing major relationships, but it does not reveal which variable caused which. Did depression cause self-consciousness or did self-consciousness cause depression? More specific analyses of causality require experiments.

CORRELATION: Any relationship between two variables. Change in one variable is associated with change in the other, although causality cannot be inferred.

Experiments

Suppose you wanted to know if being stared at makes people anxious. You could use the correlation method to answer the question, but an experiment would enable you to make statements about causality. For example, you could measure the anxiety of a group of people being stared at in an elevator. Expose a different group to the same circumstances--same elevator, same person, same measurement--only this time, no one being stared at. If the anxiety scores of people in the two groups are different, then you can conclude that staring does lead to anxiety, at least under those conditions.

Experiments are observations under controlled conditions. Usually an experimental group is compared with a control group. It is assumed that both groups are the same except for one variable--the treatment given to the experimental group (staring, in the above experiment). These studies can and do get quite complex. We will be describing some of them in the pages to come. But even experiments have a problem. What if only 80% of the people in the experimental group got anxious when stared

12

at? What about the other 20% Are they non-human? Do we not consider them? No, but it does show that we need to look at a final type of analysis.

EXPERIMENT: A series of observations carried out under controlled conditions. Usually, a tentative statement about causality can be made after an experiment.

Intensive analysis on one person

Probably one of the most important methods of analysis for the personality psychologist is intensive analysis of one person. We are trying to know people and must, therefore, account for the total person in each case. In order to get to know them, intensive study is required.

The methods of intensive study are not as well honed as the other methods. Some guidelines are presented under the rubric of "within subject" designs (Leitenberg, 1973). But probably the major effort at understanding personality at this level is in the psychotherapy or counseling room. Because of the unique relationship between client and therapist, much is learned about the client. That is why many of the examples used in this book will be of clients I have seen in counseling. I know these people well and have made a study of their positions on the personality dimensions. This approach is not always as well controlled as the experiment but is thorough and detailed. And it can be very helpful in generating ideas about how people are. These ideas can then be subject to experimental analysis. Taken together the three methods of experimental control can tell us much about the behavior of personality.

INTENSIVE STUDY: An informal method of finding out about personality by interviewing or talking with one person for a long period of time.

Mentalistic explanations of behavior

One final scientific rule is important and should be discussed. When asked why someone does something, most people give mentalistic explanations (Jaremko, 1979). This is especially the case with clients who seek the advice and counsel of a professional psychotherapist. A former client is a very good example.

Nancy came to the counseling center during the early part of her sophomore year of school. She was quite upset about an

13

inability to form close relationships, particularly with men. Since she had been to many other psychologists and psychiatrists, she thought she was very good at knowing the cause of her problem. She even told me that she already knew the cause-- she just needed help in overcoming it. Emotional suppression was the cause. "I've got all these feelings bottled up inside me, and I can't seem to let go of my fears. I don't get close to people because of these fears."

While I allowed Nancy to hold to this explanation for a while , I went about asking her what her experiences had been when she had gotten close with men. There had not been many, but the experiences she had were negative. They were marked by broken promises and unfulfilled expectations. The real cause of her lack of close relationships was outside of Nancy, in her environment. It was unsuccessful experiences at interaction with men rather than emotional suppression, something inside of her, that was the "cause of her problem."

The treatment we decided on involved a graduated series of social encounters with Nancy being successful at each one. First, she learned a better way to deal with a problem she had with her roommate. It seems that her roommate's boy friend frequently stayed over in the room. This bothered Nancy, but she was unable to reveal her concern. By learning some new skills, she was able to tell her roommate her feelings. The roommate understood and became more respectful of Nancy's feelings. Then, it was arranged for Nancy to go to an informal social mixer at a campus event. She had a good time there and met a few people. Shortly thereafter, she was asked on a date. She practiced how to make conversation while remaining calm and relaxed. Her effort paid off because she had a good time on the date. Such successes continued until she became more and more active, and she was able to tolerate more and more unsuccessful encounters. She now has quite a few friends and is getting along quite well.

If I had assumed that Nancy was reluctant to get close to others because of emotional suppression, I might have spent time trying to talk her out of being afraid. Her experiences, however, proved to be the controlling factor.

Mentalistic explanations refer to events within the person as being causes of behavior. While these events occur, the real control is outside the person. A child doesn't throw temper tantrums because he is angry. Even though he may "feel angry," he throws them because such tantrums have yielded favoable results in the past. His mother gives in, his brother gives him the toy, and so forth. It is in the events outside of the person that we will find the controlling influences of human behavior. What happens after a person does something, the result of one's actions, is the most fruitful place to look for explanations of "why."

There is no objection to analyzing cognitive behavior. Internal cognitive behaviors are important but can be better looked at as parts of complex behavioral chains. The influence of internal behavior as a cause is not especially useful. It is difficult to explain a behavior with another behavior. The question still remains as to where the cognitive behavior came from. On the other hand, cognitive behaviors can and do serve to lead people into maladaptive behavioral sequences (e.g., the negative self-statements of depressed persons might precede lethargy and unproductivity). In this sense these behaviors "cause" other behavior, that is, go before it. It is, however, in the analysis of the origin of cognitive behavior that the non-mentalistic approach provides assistance.

Noted behavioral psychologist, B. F. Skinner (1953, 1974) provides the basis for a description of mentalism. A distinction should be made between describing a behavior (what Skinner (1974) calls "structuralism") and explaining why it occurs. As long as we remain aware that descriptions of private behavior are not causes or explanations, the search for the original environmental (or operational) origins will continue. Such a search is very significant in really understanding why people behave as they do. In order to make psychological knowledge useful, there is a need to identify precise relationships between behavior and its external environmental causes. It is further necessary to specify the relationships between environments and private cognitive behavior. For example, what sort of "verbal community" is (or has been) responsible for a person's negative self-statements? A mentalistic approach will make answers to such questions inaccessible. The reason for this is contained in the notion of what mentalism is.

Mentalism refers to the notion that behaviors are caused by internal events. It may be said, for example, that a man goes to college because he wants a degree, a professor writes articles because he wants tenure, a young man courts women because he wants a wife. These are simple examples from the non-professional. Others come from professional sources, e.g., "hate, as a relation to objects, is older than love. It derives from the narcissistic ego's primordial repudiation of the external world with its outpouring of stimuli," (Freud, 1965). The emphasis in a mentalistic approach is placed on purposes, needs, wants, or instincts of the person as causes. It has the

15

effect of discontinuing the search for what can be called
"operational causes." If we have a "cognitive computer" to
explain why Johnny learns, we don't need to analyze the complex factors in his history that lead to (or failed to lead to)
complex learning. The difference is more than just words.
Pat answers like cognitive computers are not useful unless
more precise descriptions of behaviors are provided. These
mental phenomena no doubt exist, but only as intermediate steps
in complex chains that originate because of the person's personal history. To use these intermediate steps as explanatory causes does not further our understanding.

Skinner (1974) describes why mentalistic explanations a-
rise. It seems that a violation of an attitude of scientific
manipulation may be at the root of adherence to mentalism.
The person with whom we are most familiar is our own self. As
we behave, we often have feelings or purposes occurring immediately prior to or simultaneous with our behavior. We therefore attribute our behavior to those feelings. As Skinner suggests, we operate on the principle of post hoc, ergo propter
hoc (after this, therefore because of this). We assume that
others feel the same as we do when they behave as we do, then
their behavior must be caused by those same feelings. Where
do the feelings come from? Where do the cognitions come from?
How did the computer get there? The point is that two things
do not necessarily cause each other because they occur together.
Another set of explanations is indicated (and available).

The operational approach appeals to events outside the person as causes of behavior. Among other things, behavior is controlled by its consequences. A graduate student goes into an
academic position not because she wants to, but because she
has been rewarded for professorial behavior. She may "want"
to be an assistant professor, but the operational approach
places emphasis on the consequences of such private behavior.
It further investigates the origin of the "want" by analyzing
the past history of the person. The history is the key. Because of its obscurity (it is in the past), mentalistic explanations overlook it. The feelings are in the present and
therefore seem to exert control. But the history is really
the cause just as natural selection caused the development of
the species (Skinner, 1969). The search for causes in the
operational approach stops at the action of the environment.
Things are more verifiable since the unit of analysis is ob-
servable. The occasion of a behavior, the behavior itself,
and the results of the behavior (whether these are private or
public) are all specifiable.

16

Cognitive behaviors are seen as just that--behaviors. They don't "cause" any more than any other behavior. They are concomitants of overt behavior. Their influence is only in terms of being part of some of the person's environment. They originate as verbal behavior from a verbal community. One of the concerns of personality should be to analyze the aspects of these verbal communities (Skinner, 1957). We will try to do that in this book. Thus, we might be able to see that the origin of cognitive behavior is outside of the person, in the verbal community. By making sure that behavior is viewed as a result of a chain of events initiated by an external environment, we place a focus on "environmental programming." Changing or arranging environments is as important as reducing maladaptive emotions or teaching skills. The mentalistic approach often has the effect of minimizing the role of the environment. This, of course, is a less than desirable state of affairs.

But remember, this does not mean that the person doesn't do anything inside. Most of us spend more time behaving "within ourselves" than we do outside. But the control of such internal behavior still remains outside of us. We will present many examples of mentalistic explanations of behavior throughout this book and show the origin of such control. We will always use "operational explanations of behavior." That is, explanations that refer to events outside the person--the operations of the environment. It's important to do so because the implications of changing the behavior are more direct in the operational approach. If indeed, the real causes of behavior are the operations of the environment, then we can devise better ways to change such behavior.

MENTALISTIC EXPLANATIONS: Explanations of behavior referring to events inside the person, such as purposes, desires, motives, etc.

OPERATIONAL EXPLANATIONS: Explanations of behavior that refer to events outside the person, such as results of behavior and situations.

*15. What are three types of experimental control? Give examples.

*16. Give an instance of a mentalistic explanation of behavior.

*17. What is a major problem with mentalistic explanations?

*18. Define operational explanations. Give an example.

17

*19. Why do mentalistic explanations arise?

*20. What is the best way to view internal cognitive behaviors?

THE DIMENSIONS OF PERSONALITY

Now that we have the definition of personality in focus, know what we are studying, and how to most effectively study it, we can describe the approach the rest of the book will take.

A dimension is a measure of spatial extent, especially width, height, or length. It is the extent to which something can vary. For example, if we were concerned with how much people could vary in anxiety, we would be talking about an anxiety dimension of human behavior. On one end of the dimension, people could be very non-anxious--nothing bothers them, they don't get uptight, they can remain calm in most settings. Other people, however, are tense all the time; they jump at the drop of a pin. The anxiety dimension, therefore, is how people can vary in anxiety.

DIMENSION: The extent to which something can vary.

There are quite a few facets to the human being--dimensions we will call them. These dimensions of personality will be defined and described. By studying the major ways in which people differ, we are looking at the dimensions of personality--the consistent ways a person behaves that differ from the ways other people behave--you can see that this is what we do with the dimensional approach to personality. We look at the ways of behaving consistently. Any one person can be placed somewhere on each of the dimensions. After placing a person somewhere on each dimension, we will have described the person. This book explores eight dimensions of human personality.

Questions

With regard to each dimension of personality, we will be interested in asking the same set of questions. This will increase our knowledge of how much we can compare across dimensions. It will also provide a structure making it easier to remember the dimensions.

The first question is <u>what is the dimension in question?</u> We will describe the range of behaviors (actions, thoughts, feelings) that comprise each dimension.

18

The second question: how do you measure the dimension?
In this section, we talk about already established methods of
measurement as well as new possibilities. Measurement problems and inadequacies are also presented.

Development is our next concern. How do the behaviors
of the dimension develop? For example, what early experiences are needed in order for a person to be very altruistic?
What physical or constitutional factors are required? By
knowing how a person comes to be where he is on a certain
dimension, we learn much about the dimension and how to change
it or develop it further.

Change is important. That's our next question--how is
certain dimensional behavior changed? What are the repercussions of change?

We are also interested in how the dimension behaviors
relate to survival. How likely is a person (and a species) to
survive if he possesses behavior of a certain type. In other
words, what are the effects of each behavior with regard to
survival?

So now we have all the tools for investigating personality. The rest of the book attempts to be a consistent "cognitive-behavioral" treatment of the research on human personality. The approach is "cognitive-behavioral" because we will
try to describe and explain the interaction of cognitive or internal behaviors and external behaviors. Such an approach
seems to provide a more complete account of human behavior
(Meichenbaum,1977; Lazarus, 1976).

********************'

Rex and his friend, Vinny, were having a beer after their
first test in graduate achool. Their professor, Dr. Nestor,
was with them.

"What's the most important thing to learn in graduate
school, Doc?" Rex asked.

The answer was simple, "To know how to ask the right
questions."

*21. Define dimension.

*22. What is a dimension of personality? Give an example.

*23. What questions are important to ask about each dimension
of personality?

CHAPTER 2

SOME BASIC CONTINGENCIES OF REINFORCEMENT

Psychology as a science has been around for close to seventy years. In that time much has been learned about human behavior. Many basic facts and relationships about how behavior comes to be learned and unlearned have been established (Whaley & Malott, 1971). For the most part, psychologists agree on these "principles of behavior," although they disagree as to the range of these principles. Some say that there is more to psychology than is covered by the field of learning (Mahoney, 1974). Others would opt to add basic physiological processes to the "principles" list (Geen, 1976). But by and large, serious, research-oriented psychologists can agree on the importance of the "contingencies of reinforcement." This chapter examines some basic principles of behavior--the contingencies of reinforcement.

In our study of personality it is important for us to be familiar with these principles because in the pages to come we will use them to explain complex behaviors that are the topics of our discussions. In some ways the principles (or contingencies) are like a language--a jargon. In order to become conversant in a science you must first master the technical language, the jargon. Many students bemoan such a hurdle, saying that the ideas covered in the principles of behavior could be understood in "common sense" terms. While this may be true in some cases, common sense often lets you down. It's like the mentalism problem we have already discussed. Common sense explanations are rarely complete. People sometimes think they know more about behavior than they do. Science steps in (complete with its jargon) to clarify the issues and to complement common sense. That's what this chapter is about and why it's important. We will go over a number of common sensical aspects of behavior. However, we will also learn about some not-so-obvious contingencies or principles that help explain behavior. In the end, it is hoped that you will have a greater appreciation of the place of systematic effort in explaining behavior. Science can thus be used as a powerful tool in understanding human behavior--one of the toughest jobs any science has ever undertaken.

*1. What is "jargon?"

*2. In what way is science better than common sense?

21

DEFINITION OF "CONTINGENCY OF REINFORCEMENT"

The title of this chapter uses the term "contingencies of reinforcement." You may ask what those words mean. This phrase is one of those technical terms that the science of behavior uses for precision. If you can understand it, you are on your way to understanding the role of the environment in shaping behavior. As you may have noticed thus far in this chapter, the words "contingencies" and "principles" have been used together. Contingencies of reinforcement refer to the principles by which the environment influences behavior.

Dr. B. F. Skinner, one of the most influential psychologists of our time, introduced the concept. He said:

> An adequate formulation of the interaction between an organism and its environment must always specify three things: (1) the occasion upon which a response occurs; (2) the response itself; and (3) the reinforcing consequences. The interrelationships among them are the contingencies of reinforcement. (1969, p.7).

Thus, the contingencies of which any given behavior is a function refer to how these three factors interact: the situation, the behavior, and the consequences. If one of these three is changed, the behavior is changed. The situation or setting of a behavior was touched on in Chapter 1. You behave differently at a commencement program than you do at a basketball game even though they both are in the same university auditorium. Change some aspects of the setting, and the behavior changes. You are likely to behave differently when your friends are around than when you parents are present--different settings. You behave differently before an exam than you do after it. The settings of your actions are obviously important. There are many thousands of things present when you behave that make up the situation, both external to you and within you. The remaining chapters of this book specify the impact of many of those things (or "cues" as psychologists call them.)

CUES: The wide range of internal and external events that can be present when a behavior occurs.

It would be a drastic understatement to say that behavior is important in the contingencies of reinforcement. But to understand how behavior relates to the environment, we must

specify the behavior. The concept of contingency of reinforcement is important because it makes us specify the environment; and specifying the environment helps us understand better how behavior works. Science is a search for order; to find order we must specify things. In describing the
contingencies of reinforcement we do that. In analyzing the
behavior part of the contingency we look at its difficulty.
Some responses are harder to make than others. When the other
parts of the contingency are equal, the easier response will
turn up. We also look at the "topography" of a behavior.
Topography refers to the physical form of a response. Running
is a topographically different from sitting. It involves
different physical movements and since it involves different
movements, it has different effects. The effects of talking
nasty are different than being nice because of topographical
differences. So we also look at the topographical aspects of
a behavior when we analyze the contingencies.

TOPOGRAPHY: The physical form of a behavior.

*3. Describe what a contingency of reinforcement is.

*4. What is a cue?

*5. Why do we need the concept of contingency of reinforce-
ment?

*6. What two things are considered when looking at the behav-
ior part of a contingency?

The effects or consequences of a behavior are the last
part of the contingency. It has been said that behavior is
controlled by its consequences. In a moment we will see how
this statement has been supported by psychological research.
But the point is that we continue to do those things that have
favorable results, and we discontinue doing those things that
have no results or have unpleasant ones. We also do things
that gain us relief from unpleasant or punishing results.
Consequences have been divided into two types: natural and
artificial. The natural effects refer to what happens after
a behavior due to the very nature of the behavior. The
natural result of copulation is genital stimulation and sometimes conception. A natural result of war is destruction.
Artificial consequences are created by humans to back up rules
or obtain important behavior whose natural consequence is lacking or delayed, for example, the result of thievery is a jail
term if you are caught--a manmade consequence. The distinction

23

between natural and artificial consequences will become important in later chapters. But consequences can effect behavior in different ways. When one action is rewarded and another is not, the first will continue, the second will drop out. The effects of a behavior are an important part of the contingencies of reinforcement.

However, the definition Skinner gives to a contingency emphasizes the interrelationships among the three factors in a behavioral sequence. These interrelationships are why the concept of contingencies is so useful in specifying the behavior of the personality dimensions. Such behavior is often quite complex. The contingency allows us to clarify the complexity. Let's take an example. Jean is a friend whom I have known for close to ten years. She is a complex and interesting woman. When I am with her as co-worker, the effects of being light-hearted and silly are summarily discouraged. She's all business, and she does not cater to foolishness. On the other hand, when we are at the same social event--a party or some such, she will discourage "shop-talk" but will generously reward having fun. For me, two different sets of behavior interrelate with the occasions in which they occur, and the consequences that follow. Work is the setting for receiving rewards when I act task-oriented. Play is the setting for rewarding light-heartedness. So the setting, behavior, and results all interact to influence my "personality." (At least in Jean's eyes--she often remarks on how consistent I am in being task-oriented.) The fact is that she is greatly responsible for having influenced me in this direction. The contingencies of reinforcement specify the influence of the environment on behavior.

CONTINGENCY OF REINFORCEMENT: The way the setting, behavior, and consequences interact to influence how a person's environment affects his or her behavior.

*7. Behavior is controlled by its _____.

*8. Describe artificial and natural consequences.

*9. Why is the interaction among the three parts of the contingency important?

*10. Define contingency of reinforcement.

The remainder of this chapter will present some of the basic contingencies of reinforcement that will be used in the rest of the book to explain the dimensions of personality.

First we will give an example of the contingency, then define it, provide supporting evidence, and then give another example. Hopefully you'll be able to see the points at which common sense and science converge and depart.

SOME CONTINGENCIES OF REINFORCEMENT

HECTOR, THE KISSING CAT: Operant Conditioning.

Imagine a cat who is the pet of some friends of yours. Cats are said to be independent creatures (a reification if ever I heard one!) and usually spend a lot of time outdoors. Since much time is spent outdoors, we can assume that being outdoors is a "reward" for a cat. Now when you visit your friends you notice that their cat will sniff around the house, scratch the door, leap up on the table by the door, and look to its master. Your friend goes over to the door, puts his hand on the door knob, and bends down. The cat stands up on its haunches and "kisses" its master. Your friend then opens the door, allowing his cat to go outside. You may say that the cute cat "wanted" to go outside. Since this would be mentalistic, a better explanation is that <u>operant conditioning</u> was at work.

I actually had a cat once who would "kiss" to go out. His name was Hector. I used operant conditioning to teach him the series of behavior just described. Knowing that being outside was probably a reward for Hector, everytime I saw him on the table by the door I would open the door and out he'd go. After a few weeks of this training, I began to grab Hector's neck gently and bend down to touch his snout to my lips (cats are clean animals, you understand). I gradually withdrew my grasp in subsequent episodes and made Hector touch his snout to my lips on his own. Each time Hector did what was "required" of him, I opened the door and he went outside.

The process described above is operant conditioning. In it, a behavior ("kissing") is followed by a reward (going outside)--more technically called a "reinforcement." When a behavior is followed by a reinforcer it increases the probability of the behavior occurring again in the future. In fact, a reinforcer is defined by its effect. When the thing that follows a behavior increases the behavior, it's a reinforcer. If there is no increase, then it's something else. Even if you or I <u>think</u> that an event will be a reinforcer, unless it increases the behavior it follows, it is not a reinforcer.

OPERANT CONDITIONING: A change in the likelihood of a response that is followed by certain results.

REINFORCER: An event(s) occurring after a behavior that res-
sults in an increase in the likelihood of that
behavior.

During the course of this book we will discuss many examples of the effect of reinforcement. It is my opinion (one
shared by many other psychologists) that reinforcement is a
critical event in behavior. If you want to know what makes
a person tick, look at the reinforcers that are operating
on that person. There is plenty of research support for the
potency of reinforcement. One study of a four-and-a-half year
old child showed that attention from an adult could be a reinforcer (Harris, Wolf, and Bear, 1966). These researchers
counted for five days how many times the child played with a-
dults and how many times with other children. The results
were dramatic. Within six days the child was playing with
other children around 60% and 20% with adults. The teacher-
attention procedure was withdrawn (that is, changed back to the
same conditions before the study) and the percentage of interaction changed accordingly (15% - other children; 40% - adults).
Finally the teacher attention was reintroduced, and the rates
of playing changed back to more time being spent with the
children. Obviously teacher attention as a reinforcer is quite
powerful in influencing behavior.

*11.   What happens when a behavior is followed by a reinforcer?

*12.   What is meant by the statement that a reinforcer is de-
       fined by its effect?

*13.   Define operant conditioning.

*14.   Define reinforcement. Give an example.

There are two types of reinforcement. Both increase the
rate of the response they follow. One is positive (the presentation of an event-right after a response. The event is usually
pleasant) and the other is negative (the termination of an
aversive and unpleasant event right after a response). We have
talked of positive reinforcement. Negative reinforcement is
just as important. In fact some writers think that more of our
behavior is maintained by negative reinforcement than by positive (see Beyond Freedom and Dignity by B. F. Skinner, 1971).
I'm inclined to agree, and we will see many examples of it in
personality in the pages to come. But what is negative reinforcement? As a reinforcer it increases the likelihood of a

26

response. This occurs, however, due to the action of results that serve to stop a painful situation. Let's look at an example.

If you take a small laboratory animal--a white rat--and put him in a cage which has an electrified floor so that a tiny shock can be applied to his feet, he can be taught through negative reinforcement. Suppose further that there was a small bar in the cage which the rat could push down and thereby turn off the electric charge if it were on. As we turned on the juice we would see the rat hop around, stand up, defecate, urinate, engage in other "emotional" acts. If he accidentally presses the bar, the shock goes off. We turn the shock on again; he accidentally hits the bar again in his scurrying about the cage. Soon the rat will immediately press the bar when the shock comes on. He has learned through negative reinforcement that the behavior of bar pressing resulted in termination of the unpleasant event, shock. Skinner and many other researchers have repeatedly shown this process. It is a basic contingency of reinforcement that creatures, including humans, are negatively reinforced by avoidance and escape from painful events.

Everyday, human examples are easy to find. Consider what your father does when your little brother is "pestering" him for some money. When your dad gives him the money, the nagging stops. Your dad is negatively reinforced for giving the money--that is, he is more likely to give it in the future when your brother nags. Or perhaps an example closer to home is more appropriate. It's Friday night; you're alone and bored with nothing to do. As you walk down the hall for some action, a suitemate offers you a few "hits" of marijuana. You get to feeling disoriented and self-conscious, but at least it's interesting--you're no longer bored. You have been negatively reinforced for smoking marijuana because it stopped the boredom. We will consider many other examples of negative reinforcement in the chapters that follow.

NEGATIVE REINFORCEMENT: The strengthening or increasing of a behavior due to the fact that it is followed by the termination of an unpleasant event.

*15. Negative reinforcement _____the behavior that it follows.

*16. Define negative reinforcement and give an example.

27

Extinction.

What would happen if your behavior was followed by no meaningful consequence? What would happen if everytime you started a conversation with someone, they merely yawned and walked off? Or what would happen if all your brilliant comments in a class were met with a quick shrug of the professor's shoulders and then off again to some other topic? Psychologists use the term "extinction" to describe the process of withholding consequences for a behavior which has previously resulted in positive reinforcement. What is likely to happen is that the behavior will decrease. It will stop occurring. It will "extinguish.

This process was demonstrated in a study with a two-year-old child who had tantrums just before he was to go to bed (Williams, 1959). The tantrum was mainly manifested in crying. The child cried so much that the parents had to stay in the room until he went to sleep. Since the crying continued and even increased in frequency, it was determined that the parental attention of staying in the room was maintaining (positively reinforcing) the crying. Extinction was chosen as the procedure to reduce the crying. The plan was for the parents to put the child to bed calmly, leave the room, and not reenter when the child started to scream. He cried 45 minutes the first night. (To a parent, that's a long time!) The next night he didn't cry, the next night--10 minutes, and the crying kept decreasing until he was no longer crying. Extinction had worked.

A famous man once said, "If at first you don't succeed, try, try again." He was talking about something called resistance to extinction. When someone is only occasionally reinforced for some behavior, that behavior is more likely to take longer to extinguish when all reinforcement is withheld. This is a basic contingency of reinforcement that influences behavior. It's kind of like being spoiled. The rich kid up the street that always got everything he wanted could be seen as being on a continuous reinforcement schedule--that is, he was reinforced everytime he did something. When he left the nest, times got harder but he wasn't prepared. His behavior wasn't very resistant to extinction--so he gave up on a lot of things. He became depressed because he was not a very effective person-- he had not learned to hang in when times got tough. Naturally he had a "low self concept." The person as a child who had to scratch for all he got and often didn't even get it is better prepared for the real world which only occasionally reinforces people. The point here is that resistance to extinction is an important idea to remember.

28

EXTINCTION: A reduction in response frequency that occurs
when the response no longer yields reinforcement.

RESISTANCE TO EXTINCTION: When a response has only been occasionally reinforced, it will take
longer to achieve extinction when
reinforcement is withheld.

*17. Define extinction. Give an example.

*18. What does it mean that a behavior is only occasionally
reinforced?

*19. Define resistance to extinction. Give an original example.

Punishment

There is a way other than extinction to reduce the frequency of a response. That procedure is called punishment. It
involves reducing the likelihood of response by applying
an unpleasant event after its occurrence. An example is when
you are given a parking ticket for parking in a loading zone.
The idea is to reduce the likelihood of parking in the wrong
place by punishing it. But it should be remembered that punishment, like reinforcement, is defined by its effect. If the
ticket doesn't reduce your parking behavior, then it was not
punishment. In this example, the contingency is weak. That
is, the punisher (ticket) does not follow parking but follows
returning to your car. Therefore, it doesn't work well.
Many intended punishments are like that. They are applied
by people who think they will work, but they don't. In a section on aggression, we'll discuss the effects of just such a
state of affairs.

PUNISHMENT: A procedure that decreases the rate of a response
by applying an unpleasant event immediately after
its occurrence.

*20. Define punishment and give an example.

Operant Conditioning: a summary

We've talked of four types of operant conditioning, all
of which change a behavior because of what follows it. Look
back at the definition of operant conditioning to see what I
mean. Two of the varieties of operant conditioning increase
a behavior; positive reinforcement and negative reinforcement.
The other two are designed to decrease a response: extinction

29

and punishment. If you think of a procedure in terms of its
effect, either increasing or decreasing a behavior, you'll
have no trouble with these ideas.

*21. Review: What two procedures are designed to increase
      behavior? What two decrease?

*22. What does it mean to look at a procedure in terms
      of its effects?

Differential reinforcement

      We have talked about conditioning in a very circumscribed
way--only one behavior occurring at a time. This is seldom the
case. We usually are performing many acts in rapid succession
or even simultaneously. The acts that stay around--that are
maintained--do so through differential reinforcement. This
is a procedure whereby one act in an array of other acts is reinforced and the others are not (that is, the others are extinguished). My daughter learned to grasp things through this process. As an infant she would flail her arms wildly. Occasionally,
a certain movement that was topographically controlled would result in her touching an object in her crib. Manipulation of a
novel object was a reinforcer, and the wild uncontrolled arm and
hand movements were not rewarded so they soon dropped--extin
guished. My daughter had learned to "reach" by differential
reinforcement. Differential reinforcement results in response
differentiation. That is, the tendency for one response to occur and the others around to not occur. A response becomes differentiated through differential reinforcement. Reaching was
the response that had become differentiated in my daughter's
case. Differential reinforcement is the procedure (how to do it)
and response differentiation is the result.

DIFFERENTIAL REINFORCEMENT: The procedure of reinforcing one
                             response but not any others. It
                             results in response differentiation.

RESPONSE DIFFERENTIATION: The tendency for one response to
                           occur and others similar to it to not
                           occur. The result of differential
                           reinforcement.

      An interesting study of differential reinforcement in the
behavior of psychotherapists was conducted by Judith Conger in
1971. Thirty graduate students acted as counselors and inter-

30

viewed one of two "clients." The clients were really experimental confederates (working for Conger). Fifteen of the counselors were differentially reinforced for present tense verbs. That is, everytime the counselor used a present tense verb, the "client" would reinforce that behavior by eye contact, smiling, leaning forward, or some other expression of interest. The other fifteen counselors were reinforced for past tense verbs. The results showed that response differentiation had occurred. The present tense group was more likely to use present tense verbs, the past tense group more likely to use past tense verbs. The principle of differential reinforcement and response differentiation are two of the important ways in which we learn differentiated behavior out of the vast number of potential responses we make.

*23. Define differential reinforcement. What does it result in?

*24. In the psychotherapist study what response was differentiated? Why?

*25. Differential reinforcement is the _____.
Response differentiation is the _____.

Shaping

I remember one year some friends and I drove to a nearby town to escape the "blackout" of a professional football game. Since the game was being played in our city, it was not being televised. We couldn't get tickets but still wanted to see the game. So we drove about 100 miles to another town, rented a hotel room and proceeded to watch this vital game. My friend's daughter, Christy, was along on the trip. Since Christy was only three-and-a-half, she hadn't developed a passion for the game. Consequently she was creating quite a disturbance by going from adult to adult expecting (and usually getting)attention. This, of course, interfered with our watching the game. We tried to find a way to solve the problem of Christy.

As a young psychologist I felt that I had a solution--Shaping. The idea of this procedure is to teach a new behavior not yet in the person's response repertoire (group of potential responses). Christy was not presently watching the game. We needed to "shape" her game-watching behavior so that we could have some peace and quiet and watch the game with Christy, the new fan. I, therefore, devised a plan in which Christy was at first to be reinforced for looking at the T.V. with an

31

adult. As Christy sat with me, the others and I applauded her
and told her what a good "sitter" she was. After the sitting
behavior was occurring at a high enough rate, Christy was rewarded for pointing to the T.V. screen. When she was pointing
enough, reinforcement for pointing was withdrawn and she was
reinforced for looking at the T.V. without pointing. Well, it
took until half time before Christy was "shaped up," At half
time we all went outside to the pool and stretched our legs.
At the start of the second half Christy was to use her new
found skill. We all went in the room saying, "Let's go watch
the football game, Christy." She enthusiastically ran into
the room, sat down facing the screen, pointed, and watched
for a full five minutes! The rest of the half was spent
"coaxing" her to watch with us. So we didn't see much of the
game, but I did get to tell you this story about an attempt at
shaping.

SHAPING: The procedure of teaching a new response in which any
            response that approximates the final new behavior is
            reinforced. Then a response nearer to the final res-
            ponse is reinforced. The procedure is continued
            successively until the final desired behavior is a-
            chieved.

     Shaping explains many more serious behaviors than foot-
ball-game watching. It is perhaps one of the more important
contingencies of reinforcement we will speak of. In fact, most
of the behavior of the dimensions of personality that is pre
sented in this book comes about through a process of shaping
that has occurred earlier in the person's history (Dr. Freud
was correct about one's past being very influential in the
present). Shaping actually consists of a series of differential reinforcement procedures in which behavior successively
closer to a "target" behavior becomes differentiated. It is
probably one process that occurs when children learn language.
Consider: the infant makes a sound that is somewhat like
"Daddy," The proud father picks her up, loves her, attends to
her. This increases the child making the sound--"Da." Eventually, "Da" is not enough, so the baby says "Da-Da" which is
also amply reinforced until its occurrence is stable. The
next step is the differential reinforcement of a more "articulate" sound--"Day-Y." Finally, reinforcement is only given for
"Daddy", but not for other"baby-talk,"

*26. What is a response repertoire?

*27. Define Shaping. Give an example.

*28. Shaping is a series of _____ _____ procedures.

*29. Using the learning of a language response, explain how shaping is a series of differentiated reinforcement procedures.

Sometimes called the method of "successive approximation," we see the pervasiveness of shaping in the example of the outgoing or extraverted person. As a child the parents reinforce talk and social interaction. Everytime baby says something, the parents pay attention to him/her. Even when guests are visiting, the child's interactions with them are reinforced by attention and "being the center of the group." When the child is exposed to other playmates, he/she has the favorable experience of having fun sharing and playing with others. In nursery school, the teacher reinforces him/her for "speaking out." He/she is elected to be a leader in the grade school student government. He/she is given great recognition for being "Joseph"/"Mary" in the Christmas play. In high school, his/her friends always look to him/her for companionship. He/she even gives classes in Sunday School and is reinforced. All his/her life, being outgoing is "shaped up." He/she is an extravert. Needless to say, shaping is important.

Stimulus control

So far we have talked mostly about the response and the consequence part of the contingency of reinforcement. Now it's time to examine the situation part. Behavior does not occur in a vacuum, it is usually accompanied by a great many things: person, places, conditions, times, etc. These are called stimuli (stimulus is the singular form). Some of these stimuli gain control over our behavior in the sense of setting the occasion in which a behavior is likely to be reinforced. This is called stimulus control. Let's look at a laboratory example.

A hungry rat in a cage can be reinforced to press a bar by the presentation of a food pellet. This is the positive reinforcement aspect of operant conditioning. Suppose we put a light in his cage. When the light is on and he presses the bar, he receives food. When it is off, his bar-presses lead to nothing. (That is, they are not reinforced.) It will simply be a matter of time before the rat presses only when the light is on and does not press when it is off. The light is said to have "stimulus control" over the bar-pressing because in the presence of the light, bar-pressing has been reinforced, and an increase in the rate of pressing will follow. When

the light is off nothing happens. This results in extinction
and the response will drop out under those conditions. The
following diagram demonstrates the points just made:

LIGHT ON⟶ BAR PRESS⟶FOOD: INCREASE IN PRESSING
LIGHT OFF⟶ BAR PRESS⟶NOTHING: EXTINCTION

This demonstrates another one of the experiments done by
Skinner in the 1930's. It shows the precise role of stimuli
in behavior. Almost any stimulus can come to control almost
any behavior by the basic process described above. The stimulus that comes to control the behavior is called the discriminative stimulus (Cue is another term for the same thing). It
sets the occasion on which some particular response will be reinforced.

STIMULUS CONTROL: When a response occurs in the presence of
                   a stimulus that has been present when that
                   response was reinforced in the past.

DISCRIMINATIVE STIMULUS (CUE): A stimulus in the presence of
                                which a response is likely to
                                yield reinforcement.

Take a more complex example. Assume that a friend of yours
has a "history of reinforcement" in which attention from others
has been forthcoming when he talked "bad self-talk" (put himself down,pouted, and so forth). However, he only received
this attention when his wife was out of town. At other times,
his bad self-talk was merely ignored (that is, it was extinguished when his wife was present). Under these conditions,
his wife's absence will become a cue for your friend to be depressed and talk bad. It's just like the rat in his cage.
Your friend has been reinforced for bad talk when his wife
is gone--stimulus control. People resorting to mentalistic
explanations might say that your friend was lonely or had a
hard time being alone. We know, however, that the environment
influenced him by way of stimulus control.

*30. What is stimulus control?

*31. How is stimulus control established?

*32. What is a cue?

*33. Give an example of how a mentalistic explanation can be
      used for a case of stimulus control.

34

Sometimes a stimulus that is similar to but not exactly like the original cue will also exert stimulus control. This is called stimulus generalization. Another example concerning my daughter is a fitting case. My wife taught her to use the sounds "Ma-moo" to label her grandmother. The presence of my mother-in-law is a cue for my daughter to be reinforced for saying "Ma-moo." It works great; in fact, my daughter labels all kindly-looking elderly women "Ma-moo." She generalized . That is, she fails to make a discrimination between two similar stimuli. Future experience (differential reinforcement) will teach her to discriminate just any older lady from "Ma-moo."

STIMULUS GENERALIZATION: Behavior that occurs in the presence of one cue also occurs in the presence of a cue that is similar to the first.

The cues that come to control behavior can be almost anything, external or internal. Things outside of your body can set the occasion for behavior to be reinforced--things such as other people, the time of day, the season of the year, the weather, pay-day, movies, bills, letters, books, facial expressions, clothes, just to name a few. Internal events can also come to exert stimulus control such as muscle aches, stomach fullness, adrenalin flow, "brain activity," "gas," butterflies, sinking feelings in the stomach, and other physiological processes. The point is that a full and active external and internal environment will come to influence your behavior.

*34. Define stimulus generalization and give an example.

*35. List some external cues.

*36. List some internal cues.

Epilogue

In this chapter we have dealt with eight of the basic contingencies of reinforcement that have been discovered: positive and negative reinforcement, extinction, punishment, differential reinforcement, shaping, stimulus control, and stimulus generalization. We have learned that these principles have been discovered through research experimentation and human experience. The concept of the three part contingency has been used to specify the role of the environment in its relation to behavior. By using these concepts, we can explain (and sometimes even predict) a wide range of human behavior. However, there are some even more complex types of behavior in which

humans engage. In order to understand such behavior, we need
to learn about some of the more complex contingencies of reinforcement. For that we turn now to the next chapter.

CHAPTER 3

SOME COMPLEX CONTINGENCIES OF REINFORCEMENT

In the last chapter we explored the basic contingencies of reinforcement. These notions are crucial for our continued understanding of the complex subject matter of personality. However, our view of the human being was probably overly simple. Human beings are very complex creatures. There are several features about the human being that make a simple analysis incomplete. If we want a full understanding of the nature of personality, we must consider these complexities. The present chapter is an attempt to do that. In this chapter we will deal with some of the contingencies of reinforcement that influence the most complex aspects of human personality.

There are two basic reasons why the basic contingencies of reinforcement are not enough to cover the complexity of human affairs. First, most human behavior occurs in groups, classes, or chains. As might be expected, such groupings complicate things considerably. We'll see how that works. Secondly, humans have the ability to be verbal. This verbal behavior greatly enhances the human's range of experience. I can be here talking with you one minute and my imagination can take me a thousand miles away to a Mexican desert talking with a wise Yogi next. Verbal behavior makes the human the most complex and flexible creature known to us. We will explore the parameters of this capability as well. In the end, you'll come to know a little more about how science sees you. The analysis presented here is short and compact, and it is derived from a number of sources. Space limitations prevent us from a detailed analysis of these complex contingencies of reinforcement. Later chapters of the book will, however, apply the contingencies presented here to the personality dimensions.

*1.   What are two reasons we need to look at the complex contingencies of reinforcement?

Response Classes

When a little infant learns to use language, is only one separate response conditioned or does she learn a whole group of responses named language? The truth is that "making sounds," a number of specific responses, is operantly conditioned. Not only is my daughter reinforced for "Da-Da", but

also for "Ma-Ma," "Light," "Shoe," "Eye," and so forth.
These sounds are early attempts at language and are therefore reinforced by parents who are reinforced by having a
verbal child. The specific responses are different, but
they are the same in that they are all sounds. When a
group of responses have at least one thing in common, they
can be called a response class.

RESPONSE CLASS: A group of responses that have at least
one characteristic in common.

Most of the behaviors we learn belong to a response
class (a response may even be in more than one response
class-i.e. "thank you" is in the response class of verbal
behavior and in the response class of social behavior.)
An important thing about members of a response class is
that they are "connected." When a response class is established and one member of that response class is reinforced (or punished), there is a tendency for the other
members to be likewise affected. When you receive an "A"
on a term paper in French because you worked very hard in
French, you are also more likely to work hard in Psych.
Or if you have been reinforced for reading the newspaper,
this book, and your friend's term paper, you're more likely to read a ovel. Of course, the more responses of a
response class that have been reinforced, the stronger the
chance that you will engage in the other not-yet performed
responses of that class. That is, responding will become
generalized within a response class. This is called response generalizaiton.

RESPONSE GENERALIZATION: The tendency for an entire class
of responses to occur.

As you can see, the range and types of response classes
are great: talking, reading, playing, sexual behavior,
working (school and otherwise), religious practices, interaction, eating, sleeping, drug use, and on and on. Each response class is composed of many members or elements that have
at least one thing in common (often more than one). The
common element could be their effect (eating satisfies your
hunger), their typography (exercise involves vigorous movement), or their effort (work is difficult). By looking at
behavior as classes, we can see more complexity and diversi-
ty in human affairs. At the same time we can see how behavior is more simple to analyze. You and I learn tendencies
to respond in classes. Therefore, a lot of what we do is
understandable in terms of membership in response classes.

Each of the dimensions of personality to be addressed in subsequent chapters represents, in fact, a response class. For example, the dimension of anxiety (Chapter 7) is a class of responses that have a number of common characteristics: physiological responses, responses to threat, and so forth. We can conceive of the dimensions as response classes because of the shared characteristics each dimension has. Since we know some of the ways in which response classes are affected (differential reinforcement, shaping, etc.), we know something about how the dimensions of personaltiy are affected. The notion of response class will be quite helpful in our analysis of the dimensions of personaltiy.

*2. What is a response class? Give an example.

*3. What happens to the other members of a response class when one response from that class is reinforced?

*4. What is response generalization?

*5. What are the three common elements that can bind a response class together?

Stimulus Classes

Just as responses can be grouped into classes, so can stimuli. The "chair" is a simple example. There are many different kinds of chairs (I even saw a giant bowling ball chair once), but they all have a certain dimension in common, a place to sit on. People are another example. People can be short, tall, fat, dark, light, old, and so forth, but they're all people. Just as stimulus control and generalization can happen with a separate stimulus, it can happen with stimulus classes. When someone is called an "antisocial person," we usually mean that he is responding to all people in the same way, coldness or avoidance. The stimulus class of people has stimulus control over his antisocial behavior.

STIMULUS CLASS: A group of stimuli that have at least one characteristic in common.

Stimulus classes can be grouped together on a number of dimensions: physical appearance, effect on our lives, physical properties, and so on. Any of the basic contingencies of reinforcement which we have discussed can be applied to stimulus class. By dealing with classes of stimuli rather than a separate stimulus, we add to our understanding of complex behavior.

As applied to personality analysis, the notion of stimulus class has utility because we can begin to see some consistency in human behavior that previously appeared inconsistent. For example, some people respond to stimulus A (a dirty joke) with response B (laughter), while others respond to stimulus A with response C (anger). It's easier to understand such inconsistency by saying that stimulus A (dirty joke)is a member of the stimulus class "comedy" for the first person, but is member of the stimulus class "insults" for the second person. By using the idea of stimulus class, we can explain some inconsistencies in human personality and see how they are really consistencies. In a like manner, it often happens that stimulus A (kind words) leads to response B (appreciation) in person one but in a second person, stimulus C (being yelled at) leads to response B. The inconsistency can be explained by assuming that "kind words" are a member of the stimulus class "someone caring for you," for the first person but "being yelled at" is a member of that stimulus class for the second person. By viewing events, people, and other things around us as stimulus classes, we can better understand the complexity of human affairs.

*6.   What is a stimulus class? An example?

*7.   What are some of the ways stimulus classes can be grouped together?

*8.   How does the notion of stimulus class help explain apparent inconsistency in human personality?

Behavior Chains

A final notion that adds to the understanding of complex behavior is that of behavior chains. Often what we do requires a series of acts before we reach a final payoff. For instance, writing a term paper involves a very long and complex chain of behaviors. First you pick a topic which sets the occasion for finding some references. Then you're ready to make an outline which is followed by writing the parts of the paper and typing it. All this occurs before you get the payoff--a grade, reinforcing comment from your teacher, or a feeling of a job well done. Even writing a sentence is a behavior chain. In it you have to do one behavior before you can do the next thing--organize the thought before choosing a subject, verb, and finally, the object. That's how behavior chains work. The completion of one behavior sets the stage for the next behavior and so on.

BEHAVIOR CHAIN: A series of behaviors that must be done in a set order before an outcome is reached.

When you think about it, even our simplest acts are behavior chains. But the usefulness of the concept of behavior chains is most evident in complex situations. Take, for instance, a person who displays a dogmatic attitude. This person is exposed to a situation in which his opinion is sought. He gives the opinion, which sets the stage for supporting why he thinks that way, and that sets the stage for defending his opinion when it is questioned. The stage is then set for him to devalue the one who questions his opinion. The entire chain is maintained by the dogmatic person "coming down on" his opponent. This effect has both positive and negative reinforcement qualities. You can, therefore, see that personality dimensions are more accurately viewed as behavior chains. Such chains can provide another aid in understanding/observing complex behavior.

*9.   What is a behavior chain? Give an example.

*10.   In a behavior chain one behavior is a _____ for the next behavior.

*11.   Behavior chains are maintained by what?

*12.   Thought Question: Why is the effect that maintains a dogmatic behavior chain both negatively and positively reinforcing?

Conceptual Behavior

If you are like most people you have had the experience of"just knowing something" on an intuitive level. For example, you probably have a fair grasp of what is right and what is wrong. In like manner, you know good art when you see it. These are examples of conceptual behavior. Conceptual behavior is generalizing (responding the same way to) a group of stimuli within a stimulus class but discriminating (responding differently to) stimuli from other stimulus classes. You respond in a similar way (generalize) to all

41

members of the stimulus class "good" by approaching them and you respond differently to (discriminate) members of the stimulus class "bad" by avoiding them. Since another name for stimulus class is concept, you are said to be engaging in conceptual behavior. The idea of conceptual behavior is very helpful in understanding and identifying the origin of the stimulus classes people hold.

CONCEPTUAL BEHAVIOR: Generalizing within a stimulus class (concept) and discriminating between or among stimulus classes.

Psychologists R. J. Hernstein and D. H. Loveland (1964) performed an important experiment that showed us how conceptual behavior originates. As you might expect, the consequences of the behavior are important in the development of concepts. A hungry pigeon was placed in a cage and various pictures to which the pigeon was to respond by pecking the picture with its beak were presented. The pictures either contained humans or did not. When the bird pecked a picture with a human in it a piece of grain would be made available. Pecking a picture with no human resulted in the bird receiving no grain. The sequence was like this:

HUMAN PICTURE(CUE) $\longrightarrow$ PECK(BEHAVIOR) $\longrightarrow$ GRAIN(REINFORCER)
NON-HUMAN PICTURE $\longrightarrow$ PECK(BEHAVIOR) $\rightarrow$ NO GRAIN(EXTINCTION)

You may recognize these procedures as those involved in establishing stimulus control. However, several similar stimuli having a common characteristic--humans--represented the "cue" for being reinforced for responding. Conceptual behavior, therefore, is stimulus control with stimulus classes as the "cue." After exposing the bird to ten to twenty pictures, Hernstein & Loveland found that it would only peck at the pictures of humans and do nothing when given a non-human picture. This occurred even when the pigeon was given pictures it had never seen before. The bird had learned the concept of "human."

*13. Another name for stimulus class is _____.

*14. Define conceptual behavior and give an example.

*15. Describe an experiment that shows how conceptual behavior is formed.

*16. Conceptual behavior is _____ _____ with concepts.

Let's look at a human example of how conceptual behavior is learned before we leave this section. How do you learn what is "sexy?" "Sexy" is a concept. As you go through life you get exposed to many stimuli, some of which elicit sexual responses which we will define as stimulation of the genitals. Now, the sexual or genital arousal can be caused by the fact that you are simply turned on by something or it may be that other people told you that something is a turn-on. In any case, when exposed to an object or situation that turns you on, you are liable to say, "Wow, that's sexy." Chalk one up for the "sexy" concept. You see Robert Redford without his shirt on, chalk another up. You see the cover of a Penthouse magazine with a Christmas elf who has more than Santa on her mind, chalk another up. You see your sixth-grade teacher in a swim suit. This isn't a "turn-on," and, therefore, is not in the "sexy" concept. Eventually you become a normal, healthy, red-blooded, American person generalizing within the sexy stimulus class and discriminating between it and other non-sexy stimuli. Now when you go to a porno movie, you can tell the seedy old man at the ticket counter that you are merely engaging in conceptual behavior.

*17. Describe how an original (one we have not discussed) concept might be learned (for instance, "beauty".)

Many of the personaltiy dimensions we will discuss involve concepts that have been learned in much the same way that the pigeon learned about the human concept. However, the pigeon could not talk about his concept. His was a non-verbal concept. Humans, possessing verbal behavior, can talk about and label concepts. In fact, most of the concepts human beings have are verbal in nature. We will return to verbal behavior shortly, but first let's look at the way in which conceptual behavior adds to the complexity of human personality.

The Stream of Consciousness

Through many years of experience, each person has formed a wide variety of concepts in much the same way as the pigeon in the concept formation experiment, that is, by exposure to similar consequences when the various elements (specific stimulus) of a stimulus class were present. Anytime one element of a stimulus class is presented, the other elements are more

43

likely to be present also. Since some elements are in more
than one stimulus class, the presence of a specific stimulus can set off a chain of "conceptual activity" that will
lead to a completely different stimulus class and behavior.
As an example, assume that you are at a party talking with
fridens about an upcoming political election.   Now part of
your concept of politics is lawyers. Lawyers is also in the
stimulus class of "Joan" who was a previous girlfriend,
who had gone away to law school and fell in love with someone
else. One of the elements of the concept of "Joan" is "jealousy" because of the competition she presented to you. Assume further that jealousy is also in the concept called
"self-doubt" because when you are in the competitive situations of jealousy you doubt your own ability. The self-
doubt concept contains the negative self statement, "I am
a worthless person," which is also in the concept of "things
that make you depressed." This last concept controls depression in you, you become sad, feel worthless, and want to
withdraw from people.

As you leave the elections conversation to prepare another drink, you think of lawyers, which makes you think
of "Joan", which makes you think of jealousy, which makes
you say the negative self statement to yourself, which
leads to feeling depressed and sad. Since you aren't enjoying the party, you go home and continue to be miserable.
Figure 3-1 is a diagram depicting the flow of events in the
above example.

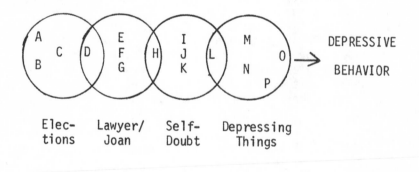

				DEPRESSIVE
Elec-	Lawyer/	Self-	Depressing	BEHAVIOR
tions	Joan	Doubt	Things	

D = Lawyers;   H = Jealousy   L = Negative Self-
                                        Statements

FIGURE 3-1. The conceptual flow of thought

We can analyze the concepts that a person has and come to know a lot about his personality. We can also learn about how the complex chains of thoughts, situations, and behaviors operate to make each of us unique people. A number of researchers who view personality from a cognitive-behavioral viewpoint are involved in analyzing this type of conceptual activity (Bower, 1979; Langer, 1978). Such activity is at the core of human personality. We can call it the "stream of consciousness" (James, 1961). It is a verbal activity and it is to verbal behavior we now turn.

*18. Give an original example of how overlapping concepts account for what we can call the "stream of consciousness."

What is verbal behavior? What is language? To start with, humans have the genetic and physical "wiring" that allows them to emit complex vocal sounds. In addition, humans have highly developed dexterity of the hands and can manipulate writing tools. These behavioral potentialities come with the human creature and are important in understanding language because language is behavior. Language is learned just as any other behavior is learned, by its effects. Just as we can learn to walk upright because of some genetically determined behavior potentialities, we can learn to emit sounds that convey meaning. Meaning is defined by effect as well. When a child emits the sound "Da," it means nothing to the infant. But the response from the child's father lays the groundwork for the development of meaning. Each time the infant emits "Da," the father responds by reinforcing the child with attention. It is this effect that comes to give "Da" its meaning. Each of the words you are now reading on this page have come to mean something in the same way, that is, through their effects. These words, it could be said, have stimulus control over your behavior of "understanding." Understanding can be seen as a complex and varied response class. The words on this page are a stimulus class that control understanding. Because of your history of being reinforced by responding in the presence of words, stimulus control has been established and you understand what I'm saying (I hope!). Let's look at a more simple example.

*19 What are the behavioral potentialities involved in language?

45

*20. Language is learned by its _____.

*21. What is meaning?

*22. Explain the statement "Understanding is a response class."

     Your little brother is in the classroom during his first
year of school. His teacher says, "Sit down, Billy," When
those words control his behavior of sitting, he receives a
negative reinforcement--avoids getting the aversive results
of having to write on the board, "I will mind the teacher"
500 times. The teacher's words were a cue in the presence
of which appropriate behavior was reinforced--stimulus control.
Verbal instructions from us to someone else (or from someone else to us) are a special case of stimulus control. We
are reinforced by following instructions and those instructions come to control our behavior.

VERBAL INSTRUCTIONS: Verbal behavior from someone else that
                      has a stimulus control over our "fol-
                      lowing" behavior because of the past
                      reinforcing effects.

     A traffic signal is a simple set of verbal behaviors.
It has three possible meanings, each of which controls our
behavior in different ways. Red is a cue to stop (and be
reinforced for stopping by avoiding a collision or a ticket),
green is a cue (verbal instruction) to continue or resume and
yellow is a cue to slow down and "be careful." Another
example is the smile of a person to whom one is attracted.
The smile is a verbal cue that the setting is right to be reinforced for "coming on." Why? Because in the past that
kind of smile indicated that the other person was responding
with like attraction. In other words, its meaning is defined
by the effects it now has or has had. But wait, you say, a
smile isn't verbal. Well, it isn't vocal. But it is verbal.
Verbal behavior includes a wide class of "symbolic" activity,
as we shall see in a moment.

*23. Review: What is negative reinforcement? Give an exam-
      ple.

*24. How are verbal instructions cues that have stimulus
      control over us? Give an example.

     First let's look at something interesting about verbal

behavior. It is both a cue and a response. The words I am writing are a response from me but may act as a cue to you. When I re-read my words, they become a cue to me, setting the occasion for reading. We have seen how verbal behavior as a cue comes to have control over us (verbal instructions). As a response, verbal behavior gains prominence because of its effects. If you are thirsty and you say, "water," someone gets water for you. You have been reinforced for verbal behavior and are more likely to respond like that again. Communicating your needs via verbal behavior is very reinforcing. You are able to get what you need. You can get what feels good or what stops unpleasant feelings. We'll see later how people with whom one comes in contact control our verbal behavior through the differential consequences they provide. Such groups of people are called verbal communities and are quite important. The point so far is that verbal behavior can function as both a cue and a response and is controlled by its effects.

*25. How is verbal behavior as a response maintained?

*26. Verbal behavior is both a _____ and a _____.

Types of Verbal Behavior

Verbal behavior isn't just talking. It's many other things as well. Let's look at some.

(1) WRITING

Writing has the same effect as talking. Your words become cues for someone else. The medium is different but the effect is the same--other people are controlled by your words. Writing is maintained in the same way as talking. It's a response that is generated and maintained by its consequences. If enough people read this book and tell me it's not good, I'll stop writing. Likewise you will stop talking about your political feelings if everytime you do so, you are punished. A final thing about writing is that the time frame between when the behavior is performed and when it is consequented is longer than in talking. In talking we get almost immediate feedback. In writing, it takes longer to get feedback. Such a delay may make writing more resistant to extinction than talking.

*27. What are the consequences that maintain the behavior of writing?

47

*28. Why may writing be more resistant to extinction than talking is?

(2) READING

Reading is the written equivalent of listening. It is the receiving of written material just as listening is the receiving of spoken verbal behavior. Spoken verbal behavior (instructions) has stimulus control over our reactions. Reading printed words also has control over our actions. And the control it exerts can be quite powerful. As a science fiction addict, I am always amazed at the way written words control that class of behavior called "imagination." These written words can have such control that I can become absorbed in completely different realities. For example, I can be on "Segundus" (a fictitious planet from a Robert Heinlein novel) even before we as a species have the capabilities to travel to Mars. Reading is a case of written words having control over actions. Sometimes that control is a remarkably powerful one.

*29. How does reading control the response class of "imagination?"

(3) THINKING

Some people aren't able to tolerate being alone very well--a condition we will talk about in Chapter 6 on interpersonal relationships. But when you really "think" about it, we are neve alone. We always have ourselves to talk to. And we almost always do it. Ever notice a person stopped at a traffic light moving his/her lips? He/she is probably talking to him/herself. Such behavior can be called thinking. Sometimes thinking is explicit verbal behavior or sometimes it's "intuitive." That is, we are engaging in conceptual thought for which we don't have labels for each of the elements in the stimulus classes or concepts that are occurring to us. Thinking, therefore, can range from explicitly talking to oneself to "automated" concept manipulation. Psychologists are only beginning to study the automated conceptual thought (Bower, 1979), and our understanding of it is quite limited. However, in all cases of thought, we are still referring to verbal behavior--private verbal behavior. It is maintained by the same consequences that maintain any behavior chain. Suppose you are presented with a problem. A friend tells you that the dance on Friday is

48

semi-formal. You go around "thinking" about what to wear.
'I could wear my blue chiffon dress or my paisley shirt."
"Ron doesn't seem to care for my orange jumpsuit. What can
I wear that's cool and attractive." You go like this,
exploring possibilities, until you make a choice of the
green tent dress. When you go to the dance, you get one of
the payoffs that maintain this "thinking" chain. "Wow, that
looks super," Ron says. Thinking as private verbal behavior
of talking with yourself is maintained like other overt
verbal behavior. (Incidentally, along the way you probably
gave yourself rewards or punishments for certain thoughts.
We'll see how this works shortly.)

*30. Give an example of how private verbal behavior (think-
     ing) is maintained.

(4) NON-VOCAL VERBAL BEHAVIOR

     Many of the things we do with our bodies in space are
verbal cues to other people. The smile we talked about earlier is an example. It can be intentional on the part of
the smiler and mean the same as "I like you" or "It's nice
to see you." Or it could merely be an automatic thing that
you do, but you don't "mean anything" by it. In that case,
the receiver is making the behavior verbal. He/she takes it
to mean something. In both cases it is controlled by its effects. Other types of non-vocal verbal behavior exist.
Body language may often be meaningful to the receiver but
not to the sender. A facial expression can often be worth
a thousand words. Touching can communicate a great deal of
verbal meaning. I'm always reminded of the poet's lines...
"for me some words come easy/but I know that they don't
mean that much/compared with the things that are said in a
lover's touch." (Browne, 1973). Many psychologists have
said that there is no such thing as "not communicating."
Many a "pregnant silence" has given its originator away.
That's verbal behavior.

*31. How is some non-vocal verbal behavior only verbal
     behavior for the listener?

*32. Give some examples of non-vocal verbal behavior.

*33. Review: What are four types of verbal behavior?

Classes of Verbal Behavior

Now that we have seen the types of verbal behavior and how they are all controlled by their consequences, let's look at the <u>classes</u> of verbal behavior. The distinction I am making <u>between</u> types and classes is simple. Types refer to the form of the verbal behavior: written, spoken, etc. Classes refer to the function of the verbal behavior, whether it denotes action, whether it lables or qualifies, and so forth. There are four classes with which we should be familiar. Each one is characterized by verbal behavior which has a different function. Notice that function implies effect. Therefore, these classes of verbal behavior have different effects.

(1) NOUNS

The noun "table" is a verbal response that is symbolic for any of a variety of physical structures. A "date" is a label used for heterosexual interactions that are planned, or it can be used for a specified point in time. A "headache" symbolizes the pain we get in our head, although there are probably great variations among people as to what they actually feel when they use the label of "headache."

<u>NOUNS</u>: Verbal labels that symbolize objects in the world

Nouns are learned by discrimination training. Baby and Mother are together at the beach. Pointing to a man passing by, Baby says, "Boy," "That's right," says Mother. Pointing to a seagull, Mother says, "And what's that?" Baby says, "Kit-ty-tat." "No, that's a bird. Can you say 'bird ?'" "Bird." Eventually Baby learns to discriminate the labels of different things in her world.

*34. What is the difference between "types" and "classes" of verbal behavior?

*35. Nouns_____things. How are they formed?

(2) COMMANDS

Some verbal responses attempt to get other people to do things for us. "Water" is a verbal behavior designed to get another person to get us something to drink. Sometimes we intend to get something, but that intention is not the

50

cause of our verbal response. The cause is that we get or
have gotten the water or whatever it is that we are lacking.
The intention, as we will see later, is an additional verbal
behavior. Commands come in all varieties and forms but are
maintained by the effect of producing the things for which
we are asking.

*36. What is a command?

*37. Why is a command not caused by an "intention?"

COMMANDS: Verbal behavior that results in having a request
          fulfilled

(3) VERBS

     The class of verbal behavior called verbs refers to
the labels we give for actions. A verb is like a noun except
the label characterizes an action--something someone is doing--
rather than a thing. "The sun sets," is a sentence in which
two labels are present--one a noun (sun) and the other a
verb (sets). Verbs came into being because of the effect
such labels have in dealing with the world. It is advantageous to be able to label what others are doing. In this
way you can ask what others are doing as well as tell
others what you are doing. All are important functions in
life.

VERBS: Labels for types of action.

*38. Verbs label _____.

(4) QUALIFIERS:

     Adjectives and adverbs are the major groups of this
class of verbal responses. They qualify an already produced
label. "Professional swimming" is different from "swimming."
Or "happy man" is different from "man." The function of
qualifiers is to specify further the nature of the world.
Just think of all the qualifiers you use in an ordinary day!
These qualifiers are learned and maintained by the effect
of being more specific. There are many instances in which
it is more reinforcing to use qualified nouns or verbs. Saying that a student "worked hard" on a paper is more expres-
sive than to say she "worked." To call a professor a "teacher" is less likely to be reinforced by him than calling him/

51

/her a "good teacher." Once again, this class of verbal
behavior is maintained by its effects.

QUALIFIERS: Verbal responses that change the nature of a
noun or verb by specifying it further.

*39. Qualifiers are learned and maintained by the effect
of being more _____

*40. Name four classes of verbal responses.

Now that we have an understanding of verbal behavior,
where it comes from, what forms it takes, and its functions;
we can now integrate these ideas to try to understand the ways
in which verbal behavior is shaped and maintained in daily
life. The notion of the verbal community is important for
these purposes.

VERBAL COMMUNITY

Each of us belongs to several groups; some groups are
more important to us than others. The family is a group with
which most of us interact for the major part of our lives.
Family influences help shape what we are, what we do, and how
we think. Your class in high school or college is another
group with which you interact and are influenced. A sorority
or fraternity also has the same effect. A close circle of
friends (peer group), roommates, fellow subject majors,
church and club members are all other groups to which we belong. But the question is: How do these groups influence
us?

The answer to that question comes in the form of one of
the basic contingencies of reinforcement which we have already
discussed--differential reinforcement. These groups provide
us (whether they intend to or not) differential reinforcement for behaviors (verbal and otherwise) that are "acceptable" to them. Wearing a string bikini is not likely to be
reinforced at the church picnic, but it may get you some
"strokes" (literally) at a fraternity spring beach party.
Talking about prices of marijuana and the potential of para-
quat poisoning may be an issue in the dorms but not likely
to be paid off by your parents. These groups provide positive reinforcement, negative reinforcement, punishment, or
extinction for different behaviors that are condemned or con-

52

doned. As a result, your behavior is shaped and influenced.
(Sociologists call this a role.)

When differential reinforcement is provided for your
verbal behavior, the group is then a verbal community. What
you say to, around, or with one group can differ from what
you say to the next group. The difference can be wide or
small depending upon the values and taboos of each group.

VERBAL COMMUNITY: A group of people with whom you interact
                      that differentially reinforces your verbal
                      behavior.

*44. What are some of the groups we belong to?

*45. Define verbal community.

The verbal community can influence quite extensively.
This fact is nowhere better demonstrated than in a case in
which a major verbal community changes. Going off to college
is often such an instance. A person we can call Bob exemplified the case well. He had spent his entire academic
life in religiously affiliated private schools--fourteen
years! He had been differentially reinforced for adherence
to belief in a supreme being, high moral standards, thoughtful reflection, moderation in all things, and a few
other "saintly" characteristics. Bob wasn't a prude, but he
was conservative and under good self-restraint. He had been
in a seminary for five of those fourteen years studying to
be a Catholic priest.

In his second year of college he decided that the life
of celibacy was not for him. He dropped out of the seminary,
moved to another town, and enrolled in a large state university. Like many others before him, Bob was lost--socially,
physically, and idealogically. But being an adaptable fellow,
he surveyed the situation and decided that joining a social
fraternity was a smart thing to do (Bob had been reinforced
in the past for being in close-knit groups of men). Between the fraternity and his academic life, he felt he
would fit in just fine. And he did. He was well-liked
by frat brothers, professors, and student-colleagues. However, after about six months to a year in this new enviornment, Bob began to feel out of place and confused. He was
saying and doing things that he had never done before:
talking like a sailor, drinking to excess, being promiscious,

He even was beginning to question the existence of God at times!

While these changes were mildly upsetting, he was having such a good time and was so busy that he had no time or inclination to analyze what was happening. He merely endured the disorientation until it came time for him to go back to his hometown after the term was over. That's when things blew up. Bob was no longer the fellow his parents had known when he left for the state university. There were conflicts, accusations, and finally a split from the family, Everyone felt bad. To this day the "coming of age" of Bob is a sore spot for the family.

Bob got a handle on what happened to him when he was introduced to the notion of verbal communities. His verbal communities had changed. Where he was once reinforced for seminarian behavior, he was now reinforced for hedonistic skepticism. The transition was silent and quick. Such is the power of reinforcement. Imagine what would have happened if Bob had talked with frat brothers about "spiritual life." Or with professors and students about the ultimate control of a deity. Bob was smart; he did seminarian-like actions once or twice, was guffawed or ignored, and picked up on different ways to act. The differential reinforcement of the verbal community had done a job on Bob.

Bob's story is not unlike many other people who change verbal communities. The personalities of these people change in every real sense. They are no doubt different creatures after such experiences. Another line from a favorite composer of mine is appropriate: "In '69 I was twenty-one and I called the road my own/I don't know when that road turned onto the road I'm on..."(Browne, 1971). Even more tragic are the folks who can't take such a big break so they drop out or develop maladaptive compensatory behaviors. What psychologist Dr. Richard Malott says is certainly true--"You are who you're with." (Malott, Tilema, and Glenn, 1978).

*43. Relate a human interest story about the effect of the verbal community.

Two Questions...

Even though differential reinforcement is the way that verbal communities exert an influence, there is another way that combines with differential reinforcement to make the effect all the more powerful. Verbal communities ask two types of questions of each of us that require us to produce verbal behavior that can then be differentially rein forced. B.F. Skinner has frequently discussed the role of these two questions (1969, 1974, 1957). The first question is "What are your doing?" It comes in many forms: your parents ask about grades, you are involved in informal self-disclosure at a party, friends of the family inquire about your life goals, and even the IRS (every year around April 15) does its share of inquiry. The answers that are reinforced vary depending upon the values and goals of the particular verbal community. Herein lies the influence of the verbal community. For example, what would your dad do if when he asked about what you had done this school year, you said, " "Cut class, stayed stoned, and joined the SDS?"

The second question results in even greater variety of potentially reinforceable verbal behavior. "Why are you doing it?" In order to answer this question you have to come up with reasons, which, of course, you get from the verbal community itself. You might say that you are dropping out of school because you feel that life is too short for "artificial learning." You want to learn by experience. Even if you got by the first question on this one, I doubt if the anwer to the second question would be acceptable to some verbal communities (although it might be higly reinforced in other communities). In either case, what you say, think, feel, and do is influenced by the verbal community in the two ways we have described: differential reinforcement of answers to the two questions. (Whaley, 1979).

*44. What are two questions verbal communities ask us?

*45. Give examples of these questions and state why they work to influence our verbal behavior.

*46. In what two ways is verbal behavior influenced?

It may have occurred to some readers that they are individuals and not greatly influenced by others. Sorry about that, but the very fact that you would say something like that probably indicates influence by a verbal community in which "individualistic" answers are paid off. There should be no shame in being influenced. Your behavior has to come from somewhere. It may as well be from those around you.

Those readers who are persistent may even say that they influence the verbal community, that they are part of it. This is exactly right. You are someone else's verbal community. In this way you, too, help control and influence the others around you. What you say and what you reinforce is important for how others think, feel, and act. If you reinforce "bad talk," those around you will either leave or talk in negative ways. Such reciprocal influence is one of the specialized functions of verbal behavior to which we now turn.

*47. How does a person become a "rugged individualist?"

Specialized Functions of Verbal Behavior

There are four   specialized functions of verbal behavior we will touch on only briefly; however, they will come up throughout the course of the book.   The first is the reciprocal influence that verbal behavior allows.   In an article by Albert Bandura (1978), it was argued that humans are special because they influence the environment as much as it influences them.   Bandura called this "reciprocal determinism". What he means is that the enviornment determines what we are as much as we determine the environment.   We are able to determine the enviornment because of verbal behavior.   This behavioral capacity allows us to construe the world in many different and sometimes distorted ways.   If we belong to a verbal community that has taught us to label sex as sinful, then we will have created an enviornment in which sexual thoughts and behaviors are punished.   However, the ability to change the enviornment through our personal perception of it comes   itself from the external environment, the verbal community.   Verbal behavior, which stems from a verbal community,   allows man to create "separate realities."   A casual glimpse at the varieties of human opinion and preference attests to this fact.   Each human is, in some sense, living in his own private world and has his own truth.   The nature and function of such belief systems will be a frequent topic in the chapters to follow.

RECIPROCAL DETERMINISM: The idea that the human creates the environment as much as the enviornment creates the human.

*48. What is reciprocal determinism?

*49. Why is it important?

The second specialized function is what I call historicality. This refers to the fact the humans possess a sense
of time. They are aware of a past, future, and present.
Without verbal behavior, this would not be possible. Verbal
communities teach us from early on how to "tell time." We
learn to wait and hope for the future as well as learn from
the past. All of this is verbal behavior. Existential
psychologists, such as Rollo May (1967), make the point
that this time perspective is one of the essential aspects
of being human. Since the human responds to time stimuli,
he is always able to label his own end, that is, his death.
Dr. May says that the essence of humanity is to know you will
die but to go on living in spite of it. Such an ability is
dependent on historicality, which is dependent on verbal behavior.

HISTORICALITY: The awareness of a time frame in which a
creature lives consisting of past, present,
and future.

Knowing that I existed yesterday, do so now, and will
tomorrow has survival value for the human species. As far
as we know, we are the only creatures that have this characteristic. And that fact is both a blessing and a curse as
we shall see in later chapters.

*50. What is historicality?

The third specialized function of language is the ability to imitate others. Imitation is a special case of stimulus control in which the cue and the response the cue controls
are topographically similar. When I say to my infant daughter,
"Do this", as I touch my nose, that is a cue for her to perform the act of touching her own nose. I will then reinforce
the the correct imitative behavior. From the time we are
born we begin to be reinforced for imitation. As the number
of different times and cues for which we are reinforced increases, so does the likelihood that imitation will become
generalized. That is, we will imitate many things without
even having to be reinforced for them. An example is when
youngsters use the four-letter words they've heard their
parents use.

IMITATION: Responding under stimulus control in which the
stimulus (or cue) is topographically like the
response it controls.

GENERALIZED IMITATION: Imitation of behaviors which is non-
dependent on reinforcement. It comes
about because many different instances
of imitation have been reinforced in
the past.

Dr. Albert Bandura (1965) maintains that imitation is
"verbal mediated" which means that it requires verbal behavior, or at least is facilitated by language. Early instances
of imitation are probably not verbally mediated, but pretty
soon after generalized imitation is established, a good deal
of our imitation is verbal. As an example, let's consider
the issue of self-reinforcement. As we live in the world,
we observe others doing things. One of the things they do
is reinforce us for "good" actions. This reinforcement is
usually verbal. For example, "That was a nice thing to
do, John." Since we imitate, we are likely to begin rewarding ourselves in the same verbal manner when we do one of
those "good" things. So self-reward can be conceived as
imitation. This imitation would not be possible without
language. In this way, imitation can be seen as another
way our verbal communities influence us. We see others
behaving in specified ways, we model what they do, and are
differentially reinforced for it.

*51. What is imitation? Give an example.

*52. What is generalized imitation?

*53. How is imitation another part of our verbal community?

*54. Explain how imitation could be verbal mediated.

The final specialized function of verbal behavior is
what B. F. Skinner (1969) calls rule-governed behavior.
It is the tendency to be able to follow a rule without ever
having had to experience the consequences the rule describes.
A rule is a statement about what will happen if you do something. "A stitch in time saves nine" is a rule stating
that timely effort will result in time-saving later on.
"Store beer in a dark place" is a rule that implies negative
results if you do not obey the rule. Rule-governed behavior
is the following of rules. It comes about because you have
been reinforced in the past for following a number of different rules, usually given to you by your parents. "You were
a good boy to mind me and stay out of the street." "Thank
you for not playing with your food." After a number of re-

inforced instances of rule-following behavior, the process becomes generalized. From then on, all that needs to be said is the rule and you will follow it. In that way, you don't have to experience the direct consequences of many things in order to learn. You know crossing the Interstate at 5:00 p.m. is dangerous even though you've never done it. You know jogging is good for your health even though you've never had a coronary from not exercising.

RULE-GOVERNED BEHAVIOR: Responding to a rule without ever having had direct experience with the consequences the rule involves.

Rule-governed behavior allows us to learn by the experiences of others. Rule-governed behavior is possible through language. In the chapters to come, we will see numerous examples of the process.

*55. What is a rule? Give examples.

*56. Define rule-governed behavior.

*57. Why is rule-governed behavior important?

Complex Contingencies: An Epilogue

We have presented several of the complex contingencies of reinforcement in this chapter. These tools will allow us to understand the dimensions of personality that we are about to investigate. The presentation has been merely a brief overview. Much more is understood about the principles of complex behavior than what we have covered. However, this introduction should suffice for our purposes. The reader interested in further analysis of this mateiral is urged to consult the sources cited in this chapter, especially Skinner (1953, 1959, 1969); Malott, Tillema, & Glenn (1978); and Whaley & Malott (1967).

CHAPTER 4

THE "SELF" SYSTEM OF BEHAVIOR

In this chapter we will discuss the "you" in personality. You and I both know that we exist. I differ from you,
and you differ from me. My uniqueness extends to more than
just my physical body. It also encompasses other aspects
of "self." The "self" is the term many psychologists have
used to talk about what is uniquely me or you (Sullivan, 1953)
Since the phenomenon of "self" is so close to home (it's you),
many times what has been said about the self has been steeped
in mysticism as if the "self" is something sacred. But right
off the bat it's easy for you to see that the "self" is a
reification. There is no such thing as the "self." It refers to a complex and remarkable set of behaviors possessed
by most of us. We will try not to talk about the "self"
since it is reified, but we will talk about a self-system
or self-concept. What is this self-system? Where does it
come from? How does it work? How is it changed? These are
questions we will address; but you must remember that "it"
really isn't an "it." The self-system is not something
like your liver is something. The self-system is complex
conceptual behavior.

*1. Why is "self-system" or "self-concept" a better term
     for the set of behaviors usually labelled "self?"

*2. The "self" is _____.

WHAT IS THE SELF-SYSTEM?

Characteristics of the Self-System

A self (short from now on for self-system or self-
concept) is characterized by some interesting properties.
The first is that the self is phenomenologically isolated
(Rogers, 1961). No other person can know another in exactly
the same manner as one knows oneself. Likewise, a person is
limited in his/her ability to empathize with another. A
line of song lyrics from Jackson Browne expresses it well,
"No matter how close to your's another's steps have grown/
in the end there is one dance you'll do alone..." (Browne,
1973). A person is incapable of assuming the perspective
of another in any complete degree. This notion is an important one because it creates problems for the measurement

60

of the self-system of behavior. If I can't completely
get into "where you are at," it will be hard to assess
what you are. The solution to this problem involves the
idea that the verbal community instills the words, labels,
and characteristics that are used in developing the self-
system. In that way we can measure a self by measuring the
features of the verbal community.

The characteristic of phenomenological isolation also
raises personal issues. It means that we are "alone"
in the world (May, 1967). Even though the interdependent
social influences of the verbal community can't be denied,
the fact is that we are separate individuals. We shall
see, however, that we aren't really that unique, that we
often only perceive oursleves as being such. But we nonetheless believe that we are unique. That belief can cause
great havoc with our place in the scheme of social harmony.
Since we are primarily social animals, the only true "meaning" we can have is in juxtaposition with others (Adler,
1931). But our perceived uniqueness makes the struggle
difficult. We still try to be individuals. We try to "make
it on our own." Both are impossible because we have to be
with each other. Our self-systems of behavior would be
non-existent without others. The struggle for individuality
versus social harmony is real for a lot of people because
they believe they need to be unique individuals. A case is
made here that "maturity" is in part believing that you are
a social being.

PHENOMENOLOGICAL ISOLATION: The idea that the self-system
                            of behavior as known by self
                            perception is isolated or dif-
                            ferent from other self-systems.

*3. What is phenomenological isolation?

*4. How does it make measurement of the self-system difficult?

*5. Describe the issue of social harmony and individuality.

A second characteristic of the self-system of behavior
is that it possesses awareness. Awareness refers to the
fact that the person can make verbal statements about what
he or she is, what is happening, and so forth (Malott &
Whaley, 1976). The awareness is selective in the sense
that a person is only aware of a small fraction of what goes
on around him or her. What we will be aware of depends on
what the verbal community differentially reinforces us to

61

attend to. At a social function we are usually aware of
"who's there" but are not likely to be aware of the size
of the beer mugs. Awareness comes about because we have
been taught the labels and concepts for things present
in the world. Manipulating these verbal behaviors is
usually reinforced by being advantageous. Awareness is a
marvelous feature of our species, one that we often take
for granted. If we weren't self-aware, it wouldn't matter
because we would not be aware that we weren't aware. At the
same time, the fact that we can be influenced to be self-
aware is both a blessing and a curse. It is one of the
unique characteristics of our species. It is also one of
the main reasons we attribute an autonomous quality to
ourselves.

*6. What is awareness?

*7. Where does it come from?

Another thing about the self-system is that it probably does not possess the consistency we often think it
does. The self-related behaviors we engage in are more
often than not likely to be inconsistent. The standard
justification for our erratic behavior--"I wasn't myself
today"--is probably just a lot of hot air. If your "self"
was consistent from day to day and hour to hour, it would
be the exception rather than the rule. In a review of
the literature on this topic, Gergen (1968) concluded
that the notion of a consistent and unified self-concept is
inaccurate. The self-system of behavior is subject to
being influenced by many aspects of the enviornment, such
as the other people one is with, the length of relationships
with them, the task demands of the situation, and the reinforcing qualities of attention from others. Gergen
suggests that it would be better to conceptualize the self-
system as consisting of multiple selves that are elicited
by differing characteristics of the enviornment. The notion
of multiple selves is a good idea since people are so
divergent from day to day. However, it is still a reification to consider multiple selves as if there was something
that operated when you were in the dorm and another thing
that existed when you had to get a hard job done. The reification is not needed. We can understand the diversifica-
tion of the self-system by looking at it as conceptual behavior.

*8. The self-system is/is not (?) consistent.

*9. List four things that influence self-behavior.

*10. Why is the notion of "multiple selves" a good one?

*11. Review: List three characteristics of the self-system.

Self-Conceptual Behavior

An infant is playing in his crib. There are a number
of brightly colored toys and mobiles hanging overhead. As
he plays, our little friend accidentally grabs his toe, puts
it in his mouth, and bites. Ouch! A physical discomfort. In like manner, he chomps on a baby toy given to him
by Grandma. No ouch. A few months later, the infant is
a toddler walking around the house. He passes a mirror
and notices motion. He stops, looks at the reflection,
moves his own arm, and notices that the thing in the mirror
moved too. Mommy comes along and asks, "Who's that?" Baby
grins (and notices the image "smile") and says nothing.
Mama says, "That's Bobby. That's you!" A week later Bobby
is running rampant through the house and Smack! right into
the wall. Ouch! Later Bobby passes that mirror again and
stops and looks at the figure. He blinks, it blinks; he
smiles, it smiles; he stoops, it stoops. He is engrossed
in this thing. Mama comes along again and labels it for him,
"That's you, Bobby. Say 'Bobby.' Say your name." Bobby
says a sound like his name, and his mother hugs him, saying,
"I love you, Bobby."

What's happening to Bobby? His self-concept is being
developed. Remember what conceptual behavior is? Generalization within a stimulus class and discrimination among stimulus
classes because of similar consequences for "self" stimuli,
Bobby is beginning to discriminate "me" from "non-me."
Eventually he will respond in similar ways (generalize)
to all the things in his world that are "self", and he
will act differently toward (discriminate) those things not
"self." At the same time, his verbal community (mom) is
telling him the label for this concept--"you." She even
reinforces him for behaving conceptually in this manner.
Much of the self-concept is learned in childhood, but differential reinforcement for conceptualizing the self is provided by verbal communities throughout your life. All of
the things you call "you" are grouped together because they

63

have similar consequences.

<u>SELF-CONCEPTUAL BEHAVIOR</u>: Generalizing stimuli that have
"self" in common and discriminat-
ing these from "non-self" stimuli

So the "self" isn't a thing, it is behavior. Self is
not what you are, it is what you <u>do</u>. The self-concept is
composed of different elements. An element is one of the
things a stimulus class has in common. For example, one
of the elements of the stimulus class "chair" is that it
has a place to sit on. In like manner one of the elements
of the "self" concept is that it has physical characteristics.
There are other elements. We will now turn to a description
of those elements.

*12. How is the "self" really conceptual behavior?

*13. Describe how a self-concept might be formed.

*14. The "self" is not what you are, it is what you_____.

*15. What is an element in a concept?

<u>Physical Self-Concept</u>

Bobby, you, and I conceptualize the physical element
of the self early in life. In fact, it is the start of the
self. "You" and "non-you" begin and end with the physical
phenomenon of the body. Throughout life you are consistently consequated for discriminating and attending to your body.
Nourishing, washing, and exercising are only some of the
reinforced behaviors that relate to and are grouped into
this element. People differ with regard to how much they
conceptualize the physical part of the self-system. They
also differ with regard to how conscious they are of that
physical part. People who are obese are generally more
aware of their physical bodies than people who are not.
If you are overweight, for example, and may have had twenty
years of trying to fightweight problems, you'll be more
likely to notice weight issues in your world. You'll
count calories, think about what happens when you drink a
beer, and be more likely to notice when others bring up
the subject. In like manner, a person who is physically
glamorous has been positively consequated for attending to
the body. Someone without such a history is less likely to

64

notice physical characteristics because detection of the
body or concern for it has not been reinforced.

Dr. Seymour Fisher of Syracuse Medical School has studied
how people learn to perceive their bodies (1972). His results support the notion that the physical self-concept
emerges because of differential reinforcement. Women, for
example, are more aware of their bodies than men. Consider
how much more women have to contend with their bodies in
terms of clothing, menstruation, and so forth. Psychiatric
patients have a tendency to perceive their bodies as smaller
than other people's, a fact likely derived from the insig-
nificance these people are afforded as members of society.
Fisher also says people in general have distorted views
their bodies. Since is it sometimes not considered o.k.
to talk about another's physical features, and thus provide
feedback for an accurate body image, the distortion is
understandable. The verbal community is not specific enough
in giving precise feedback about what you look like.

The physical "self" is always changing but the change
in awareness may not be as rapid as the physical change itself. The "feedback loop" for updating the physical
element of the self-concept is sometimes long in terms of
time. For example, you have bags under your eyes before
you know it. Awareness of the physical changes that take
place in a person comes from two sources. First, the verbal
community gives feedback about changes and differentially
reinforces us to attend to the changes: greying hair, weight
gain, wrinkles, and so forth. Secondly, the person him
or herself notices the changes and "talks to oneself"
(Meichenbaum, 1977) about the differences. Self-reward and
self-punishment are administered for these changes. It's
important to note, however, that such self-reinforcement
originally derives from the verbal community (Chapter 3).
Aspects of the physical self concept continue to change
throughout life as these two sources change. But there may
be a time lag in the "feedback loop."

*16. Explain this statement, "The physical self-concept
      emerges from being consequated for attending to one's
      body."

*17. List three sources of data from Dr. Seymour Fisher
      that support the notion that the physical self-concept
      comes from differential reinforcement.

*18. Why are you usually the one least aware of your true
      physical features?

Psychological Self-Concept

     The term "psychological self-concept" refers to the
"I" element of the self-concept. What is "I?" It is a label that the verbal community gives you for yourself. It's
shorthand for all of the self-conceptual behaving we have
been talking about. The psychological self-concept can contain two classes of behavior: feelings and attitudes. These
two aspects of behavior are why we have the tendency to
reify the psychological self-concept when we talk about ourselves. B. F. Skinner notes that feelings are very closely
aligned with the self; the self, therefore, appears autonomous (1974). The feelings make the "self" appear to be an
originator, but the feelings are not what cause behavior
(Jaremko, 1979). Other things such as the contingencies of
reinforcement in one's environment are responsible for both
your behavior and your feelings. We'll come back to feelings.

*19. The psychological element of the self-concept contains
      what classes of behavior?

*20. Why is this element mostly responsible for the reifica-
      tion of the self-system?

     First, let's return to the "I" (of "me") in the self-
system. It is clear that this element of the self emerges
from verbal communities which give labels for the concept
of self. Consider the tribe of Arctic Eskimos who don't
have any words in their language for "I" or "me" (Valentine
& Vallee, 1968). Why? Does this mean that they don't
have "self-concepts?" No, it means that they don't have well
developed psychological elements in their self-systems. They
don't need to. Each person's existence depends on each individual's effort in procuring the necessities of life. Survival doesn't depend on mutual effort as in our culture.
It is when the verbal community needs a label for "you"
in order to aid survival that "I" comes about. Think of the
utility of "I" or "me" in our culture. You can be told what
to do, you can be asked for things, you can be held responsible. In this way, the jobs that require doing for the
culture's continued existence get done. Those remote Eskimos may not see another member of the culture for six months
at a time. They have to make it on their own. They don't

<u>need</u> to label the self like we do (Smith, 1978). All this is a way of saying that the verbal community gives us the labels for our "self-concept."

Now we can turn to attitudes and feelings--those special types of behavior that make it look as if the "I" is an autonomous thing. The "I" is not an autonomous thing, it is merely a label. But it does hold attitudes and it does have feelings. What do these words mean? We have considered attitudes in another chapter (Chapter 1) and have seen that they refer to the interaction of values, beliefs, and behavior. They come from the verbal community as well. You tend to adopt thsoe attitudes and views your verbal community holds (Bryne, 1974). The sum total of these attitudes (which change depending on whom you are with) may be seen as part of the psychological element of the self. You may have a positive attitude toward education. You may have a negative attitude toward politics. These are <u>you</u>-- ways of behaving that are incorporated into the self-concept.

*21. How is the "I" part of the self-system related to survival?

*22. How do attitudes contribute to the identity of "I?"

Feelings are also understandable in terms of the verbal community. First, it's very important to remember that feelings are behavior also. Just as with attitudes, your feelings are ways of behaving that form part of the psychological element of the self-concept. They can't cause other behavior, but they can be a part of behavioral chains. You don't visit a sick friend because you feel sorry for him. You visit because such behavior has been reinforced in your past when you were told what a nice person you were for visiting the sick. You probably do feel sorry for your friend, but the behavior of "feeling" sorry is another behavior altogether. The feeling is a statement of self-awareness about the temporary physiological changes that are occurring as you are thinking of your sick friend. Let's take another example because this is an important point.

We humans respond to things in our world with physiological responses such as increased heart rate, "butterflies," sinking feelings in the stomach, and so forth. It's Friday night, your date called a couple of hours ago and said he

67

couldn't make it. Everyone is gone. You're alone and "feel" depressed and lonely. The "feeling" is a verbal behavior that you are aware of the sinking feeling in your stomach which has been caused by being alone. It's a verbal behavior given to your by your verbal community. Just as an infant breaks a toy and is informed by his mom that he should "feel" bad, you have been informed that the sinking feeling in the stomach when you are alone is "depression." So you make the self-aware verbal response and have a feeling.

Since feelings are verbal community-generated they are by necessity vague. The verbal community can't see exactly what physical changes are going on in you. But it gives you a label nonetheless. So the physical changes associated with the feeling of anger in me may be different than they are for you. That's why feelings are vague. We, as members of the verbal community, don't know exactly what the other person feels and neither does he. He thinks he does, but since his labels come from others who are not sure what the physical changes are in the first place, he really doesn't "know" the feeling. He has a self-aware-ness of something, but it is likely to be inexact (Malott & Whaley , 1976).

FEELINGS: Self-awareness verbal behavior about what physical changes are going on in the presence of events or things in the world.

These "feelings" that you have in response to events in your world are part of the "I", which is part of the psychological element of the self-concept. One's feelings are a quite important aspect of a person's personality. From the cognitive-behavioral point of view, we will view per-sons' feelings as parts of the chains of thought, behavior, and feelings that are caused by the various contingencies of reinforcement in the person's life (Jaremko, 1979). In this way we will be able to see how the feelings have a part in making up the self-system. We will also see how people come to learn to attribute the causes of their be-havior to themselves.Such causal attributions are a major focus of psychological research (Wiemer, 1978).

PSYCHOLOGICAL SELF-CONCEPT: Set of conceptualized behaviors unique to a person and labeled "I" or "me." These behaviors include feelings and attitudes.

68

*23. Explain how feelings are merely parts of a behavior chain and don't cause other behavior. Give an example.

*24. Define feelings. Give an example.

*25. How are feelings verbal community-generated?

*26. Why are feelings, by necessity, vague?

*27. Define the psychological self-concept.

The Thinking Self-Concept

In Chapter 3, we talked about thinking being the verbal behavior that occurs when a person is presented with a problem. This element is considered in the self-concept because our verbal community also teaches us that the "I" is thinking. This is the element of the self-concept that consists of being aware that one is thinking. There are some who say that this is the most important and pervasive aspect of the self. William James, one of the pioneers of modern psychology, called this the "stream of consciousness" and further stated, "The very core and nucleus of our self, as we know it, the very sanctuary of our life, is the sense of activity which certain inner states possess" (1910, in Gordon and Gergen, 1968, p. 43). A famous philosopher, Rene Descarte, put it more simply when he said, "I think, therefore, I am."

James and Descartes are probably right; being aware that we are thinking is probably a major part of the behavior of the self-concept. We figure, we plot, we scheme, we plan, we explore, we investigate, we test; all could be called thinking. One point to remember, however, is that sometimes we do it without being aware of it. Is it part of the self then? No, I don't think so. It's just another "non-self" behavior at that point. The thinking self-concept is reserved for being conscious or aware that we are thinking, have thought, or will think

THINKING SELF-CONCEPT: The set of behaviors characterized by awareness that one is "thinking."

*28. What is the thinking self-concept? List some of the specific behaviors that make up this element.

The Social Self

This set of behaviors is the awareness that you are
a social being. You exist in a world with other people
and deal with those people quite frequently. An entire
chapter of this book is devoted to interpersonal relationships. The influence of the verbal community comes about
through the set of interpersonal relationships that one
possesses. Being aware that you interact with others is
what this element of the self-system is about. We compare
ourselves with others, we model others, we have reference
groups for a variety of purposes. We work with others and
are concerned with how they evaluate us. We live with
and love others. Others love us or perhaps nobody loves us.
The range of social interaction is large, and is a large
element in the overall self-concept. There are even subsets
of the social self-concept. One behaves differently with
work colleagues than with family. The wide range of behavior that encompasses the social self-concept is grouped together because it deals with other people. Harry Stack
Sullivan (1953) said it well: "...personality is the
relatively enduring pattern of recurrent interpersonal
situations which characterize human life." (p.111).

SOCIAL SELF-CONCEPT: Self-awareness that a person behaves
in relation to and with other people.

*29. List some of the behavior that makes up the social
self-concept.

The Ideal Self

Throughout your life you hear about and are told that
some things are good and should be goals set for one's self.
All of these interactions with the verbal community will
lead to the development of a set of ideals or goals. Ruth's
mother says, "You know, Ruth, you should really be careful
about your temper. You need to control it, or it'll get
you in trouble." If this suggestion is repeated and reinforced, Ruth will form an ideal. "You know, Mom," she says,
"I want to try and be even-tempered ." Mom, of course,
differentially reinforces this behavior. One of the aspects
of Ruth's ideal self-concept is established. Other ideals
goals, and dreams are learned in the same way. Occupational
plans, family plans, emotional ideals, wishes for success
and fame, monetary goals, religious aspirations, and expecta-

tions of the right way to act all become part of your self-system of behavior. You may even specify time deadlines for when you hope you will have achieved a certain goal or way of being. All these ideals are grouped in the ideal element of the self because they have the common characteristic of being in the future--what you want to do and be. Carl Rogers (1959) has stated that the ideal self is perhaps the most important part of the self-system.

IDEAL SELF-CONCEPT: The element of the self-system that is characterized by ideals, goals, and expectations of what a person wants to be in the future.

*30. List the aspects of the ideal self-concept. Where do these come from?

Closely aligned with the ideal self-concept are the evaluations we do of ourselves. It has been shown in a number of experiments that humans compare their behavior to the ideals that have been established by the verbal community (Festinger, 1954). If there is a big enough discrepancy between present behavior and the ideal, a number of things can happen: 1) The person can "correct" the behavior by bringing it in line with the ideal, 2) The ideal can be changed, 3) Or the person can do neither of these but react emotionally. He may become depressed, emit a lot of self put-downs, and reduce his general productivity. The person may even react with the emotion of anger at himself or other people. The motivating and self-correcting function of self-evaluation is a major human characteristic.

In fact, Dr. Frederick Kanfer, a clinical psychologist at the University of Illinois, has developed an explicit model for understanding how people evaluate and regulate themselves (1970). Briefly, Kanfer's framework includes performance criteria (or ideals as we called them) and three stages of behavior that determine whether the criteria are being met. First, we self-monitor; that is, observe or attend to our own behavior. Next, we self-evaluate; that is, match what we are doing with what we ought to be doing. This is essentially a discrimination process. And finally, we self-reinforce ourselves for having met the performance criteria. If we haven't met the standards, we correct our behavior until the discrepancy is slight (or

71

at least acceptably small). The process is usually
fairly deliberate and conscious but could also be automatic
and seemingly "nonconscious." Other researchers have shown
that people with emotional behavior tendencies like depression are harshly self-critical or don't reinforce
themselves when standards are met (Rehm, 1977). This dis-
rupts the process of self-regulation and these people
develop or maintain behavior problems.

The ideal self-concept has the function of keeping
us growing and improving. People, of course, vary with
how active self-evaluation behavior is or how harsh performance standards are; but most of us spend a good deal
of time engaged in this class of behaviors. Some people
even spend too much time evaluating themselves, as in the
case of overly self-critical people (Kringler, 1965). However, what a remarkable characteristic self-observation is.
We even observe ourselves "looking at ourselves." All of
these activities emerge from verbal communities that encourage self-evaluation and regulation by asking us what
we are doing and why we are doing it.

*31. What three things can happen when a discrepancy
exists between an ideal and present behavior?

*32. Describe Dr. Fred Kanfer's model of self-regulation.

*33. Where does self-regulation come from?

Self-Preoccupation

Before turning to the other questions we will ask
about the self-system, we should consider one other important issue, self-preoccupation. (Johnston & Jaremko,
1979). This is not an element of the overall self-concept,
but it may be considered a dimension of personality, and
as such, is one of the reasons why the self is considered
in a book on the dimensions of personality. Have you ever
been in a public place, a bar or discoteque, and seen a person look at him or herself? It may have been a young man
glancing down at his unbuttoned shirt exposing his chest,
a woman stealing a visual check on the position of her
skirt, a sunbather monitoring that bronze epidermis, a quick
check-me-over as one passes a mirror. These instances may
be considered cases of physical self-preoccupation. For a

72

moment, the person is occupying himself with his own body.
The assumption made here is that people are preoccupied
with the various aspects of their self-system, and that
they differ from each other on how self-preoccupied they
are. Some situations may bring self-preoccupation behavior
out more than others, such as at a singles' bar. But even-
so, there is some reason to believe that across situations
people differ in the extent to which they engage in
this behavior(Jaremko, Noles, & Williams, 1979).

SELF-PREOCCUPATION: Awareness behavior that consists of
a person attending to aspects of the
self-system. People differ on this
dimension of personality.

Dr. Irwin Sarason (1975) of Washington University has
discussed self-preoccupation as a possibly important issue
in human behavior. Little experimental work has been done
on it, but Sarason feels that it's time to start scrutini-
zing it scientifically. He is primarily interested in
what he calls "anxious self-preoccupation;" that is, the
extent to which a person who is anxious is engaging in
self-preoccupation;   "What do others think of ME?" "How
am I going to do all this?" and so forth. However, Sarason
states that there are other ways to be self-preoccupied
that are not negative. A person can be self-preoccupied
about how he is going to solve a problem. Or someone may
be preoccupied about his/her sexuality. Thus, research
into the nature and extent of self-preoccupation may also
be aimed at trying to understand the person who can become
preoccupied with external events. Knowing the opposite
of self-preoccupation (the ability to concentrate external-
ly) may tell us something about self-preoccupation itself.

Sarason suggests further that self-preoccupation may
interfer with a person's behavior at three points. First,
in his attention to the world the self-preoccupied person
may pick up on the things that would not be noticed by a
person lacking self-preoccupation. For example, a self-
preoccupied student worried about failure on a test will
pick up cues in the enviornment relating to negative evaluation whereas a student lacking in self-preoccupation will
pick up cues about how to do well (Wine, 1971). Secondly,
what the person does with the information he has attended
to can be influenced by self-preoccupation. As Sarason
exemplifies, when given pills by a physician some people
worry about its side effects, others get angry about costs,

73

and still others don't give it a second thought. Lastly,
what the person does is likely to be influenced by whether
self-preoccupation is present. Someone high on this dimension may choose to escape a harmless situation because
of the distortion present at the first two points.
This may be what happens when a person avoids social
situations because he is overconcerned about his physical
appearance.

Admittedly, research on self-preoccupation is lacking,
whereas speculation is readily available. However, due
to the importance and research potential of this notion,
we can expect to see more and more work done on it. Some
of the following questions about self-preoccupation should
be addressed. If people differ from one another on this
dimension, how can that be measured? (Fenigstein,Scheier,&Buss
1975)? The question of consciousness also seems to be
important. In order to be self-preoccupied, one must be
conscious of some aspect of himself. How does this consciousness come about? Related to this, what do the verbal
communities that generate self-preoccupation do in order
to achieve that outcome? Perhaps, people influenced
by such a community are differentially reinforced more
frequently for "I" statements. What are the types of self-
preoccupation (Jaremko, Noles, & Williams, 1979)? We've
mentioned physical self-focusing and concern over evaluation
of self. What about mere concern about yourself versus
concern over what others think of you? Finally, self-
preoccupation may relate to emotional behaviors other
than anxiety. The depressed person may be too wrapped
up in him/herself. Or the self-preoccupied person may be
less tolerant of pain. All of these questions will be
addressed as researchers become more and more sophisticated
in this area. Consequently, we will learn more about the
self-system when we have come to understand self-preoccupation.

*34.   What is self-preoccupation? Give an example. How
       is it a dimension of personality?

*35.   According to Sarason, at what three points can self-
       preoccupation interfere with behavior?

*36.   Ask at least five research questions about self-pre-
       occupation.

MEASURING THE SELF-SYSTEM

For a scientist, the first step in studying a phenomenon is to measure it. Personality psychologists have been interested in measuring the dimensions of personality right from the start. There are, however, many problems in trying to measure human characteristics (Anastasi, 1972). Throughout the rest of the book, the section of each chapter on the measurement of each personality dimension will be devoted to specifying these problems and what can be done about them.

Measuring the self-concept is also not easy. In fact, it may be more difficult since each person's self is phenomenologically isolated. It is very hard to measure you as a unique creature in any complete way. Nonetheless, we still try to overcome the problems as best we can. In this section, we will explore three instances of measuring the self-system: the Q-Sort, self-esteem scales, and a measure of self-preoccupation. There are other issues and methods in self-system measurement, but these three provide ample representation.

Q-Sort

The Q-Sort is a way to measure a person's self-perception (Block, 1961); that is, how one sees oneself. The idea is to rank a series of statements along two dimensions: like me--unlike me and like my ideal--unlike my ideal. The discrepancy between the two rankings will yield a measure of "self-value" or self-esteem. The statements can vary but are usually things like: I feel adequate, I am a good mixer, I express my emotions, I am contented, I put up a false front, I am confused, I usually feel driven, and so forth. In other words, if you ranked "I feel adequate" number one on the "like my ideal" continuum and number ten on the "like me" continuum, a large amount of discrepancy is demonstrated. You are, therefore, likely to be low in self-value or esteem.

The Q-Sort has been used mostly for research purposes and has been shown to be reliable (that is, will yield the same score from test to test) and valid (truly measures the construct of "self"). For example, it has been used by Carl Rogers and his colleagues in assessing changes in self-esteem before and after therapy (Rogers, 1967). A pro-

blem with the Q-Sort is that is is a self-report device.
That is, the person reports about him/herself. The researcher must allow for bias in the rankings that an
individual gives himself. This bias is an example of
social desirability; that is, the tendency to want to make
oneself look good, to put oneself in the best light.
Nevertheless, while some people succumb to the desire to
make themselves look good on the Q-Sort, they only constitute a small percentage of people who take the measurement.
When a large number of people take the Q-Sort, the tendency
toward social desirability averages out. This is why it
is good for group research purposes. Using the Q-Sort in
assessing one person, however, should be viewed with some
skepticism because the person may give biased answers.

*37. Describe the Q-Sort measuring device. What is a
      major disadvantage in its use?

Self-Esteem Scales

        Self-esteem scales are another form of self report.
In this case, the person indicates whether a particular
statement is true or false concerning himself. For example, the person who answers true to "I think I'm able to
handle most situations" is likely to have more self esteem
than someone who answers false to the same statement. A
large number of people are given the scale and a distribution is obtained. A distribution is a graph of the frequency of scores at each numerical value of the test. Most
personality traits are assumed to be normally distributed.
That is, most scores are in the middle range of the personality scale and increasingly fewer scores are obtained
at the low and high ends of the range. In a 1 to 100 range,
about 60 out of a 100 people will be between the scores
of 16 and 84. Only about 20% of the people will be above
84 and 20% will be below 16. People high in the distribution are assumed to have more self-esteem than those lower.

        Two such scales that have been developed are Cooper-
smith (1967) and Barron (1953). Both of these scales
can be helpful in discriminating people who are down on
themselves from people who feel good about themselves.
It should be kept in mind, however, that these discriminations
are very general ones. For instance, what's the difference
between someone with a score of 43 on the Barron ego strength
scale and someone with a score of 40? Not much, but you

might be able to make a statement about two people who differ by 30 points. Once again, we see the limited utility of self-report devices. A solution is to actually count the number of times the person engages in a "self" behavior; e.g., how often in one day does someone have a negative self-thought. We'll talk some more about this method of measurement in a later chapter.

*38. Describe a self-esteem inventory.

*39. Describe a normal distribution.

Self-Preoccupation

So far we haven't talked about measuring the different elements of the self-system. We have only talked about measuring self-evaluation, just one part of the self-system. In a self-report scale designed to measure self-preoccupation, Jaremko, Noles and Williams (1979) have been able to measure different <u>factors</u> (elements) of the self-system on the dimension of how preoccupaied a person is in each area. In that scale, in which people indicate whether a statement is true or false of them on a seven-point scale, the person responds to statements about the physical, the social, the evaluative, and the psychological self-concepts. This <u>factor analytic</u> approach to measuring the self-system seems to be more complete than the more usual way of meauring self-esteem alone. However, the self-preoccupation measure is still experimental and is subject to the problems of self-report scales. It appears that a perfect measure of the self-system will continue to elude us. In many ways <u>you</u> are the best and only real measure of your self-system. The entire phenomenon of "you" is more important than any score on a questionnaire.

*40. List the factors of the self-preoccupation scale.

*41. What advantage does this scale possess over other types of self-concept measures?

*42. What is the best measure of the self-system?

DEVELOPMENT OF THE SELF-SYSTEM

We have already outlined the general influence of

77

verbal communities in the development of behavior (Chapter
3). In this section we will specify that influence on
the development of the "selves" of a person. It should
be kept in mind that the self-system is constantly emerging,
and that the developmental process continues throughout
life.

The import of the verbal communities of which a person is a member is enormous. The two questions that the
verbal community asks ("What are you doing" and "Why are
you doing it") require that the person differentiate him
or herself from others. If the verbal community asked what
we were doing, it would be a different story. But it
doesn't, it asks what you are doing. That sets up a discrimination between you and non-you which will be differentially reinforced. Thus, the self-concept gets developed.
This process is especially true in a culture that stresses
individuality the way our's does. The individual is the
most important thing, each person has inaleinable rights.
What if the sign said "Uncle Sam wants Someone?" Instead
it cashes in on individuality and the control that comes
when you are a differentiated concept--"Uncle Sam wants
You." There are countless examples of this process of
making the person focus in on himself. Signing a check with
your signature, filling out bureaucratic forms, having a
unique social security number, getting your driver's
license, putting your name on the test paper are all examples of the very basic nature of this process.

*43. How does the verbal community's two questions work
    to develop a differentiated self-concept?

Different verbal communities influence the development
of different self-systems. This notion is one discussed
by B. F. Skinner (1974) and is not only at the heart of
the development of the self-concept, but is also at the
very core of personality development. "Self" concepts differ from each other on the personality dimensions we will
be discussing. One person is extroverted, and next is shy
and retiring. She enjoys being helpful to others; he minds
his own business. These are self-concept differences and
personaltiy dimension differences. The system of consequences, the models, the labels, the verbal behavior of
the community which influence someone to be extroverted
are all different from a community that encourages and
fosters introspection. "You are who you are with."

78

Of course, things are not as simple as this sounds
They never are. You are a product of a number of verbal
communities. These communities continue to change you
throughout life as they change. Our nation used to contain
a number of war supporters. In the 50's and early 60's
we were ready to fight to defend ourselves. The verbal
community changed in the late 60's and 70's, therefore, many
of us changed. There were more "doves" or peace supporters.
The influence is oftentimes startling. As a boy, I
remember fantasizing that I was a war hero. Now, I would
want to stay as far away from war as possible. So the verbal communities change, and we change with them. A major
influence on each person is the verbal community operative
when we are children, our family. Personality researchers
have talked about the lasting impact of the family. There
are some research findings that we will present here that
demonstrate the importance of the family. There is much
more empirical data available about verbal community influences, but the research on the effect of parents on self-
concept will give you an idea of how it works.

*44. Explain and elaborate on this statement, "Different
      verbal communities influence the development of
      different self-systems."

*45. Do verbal communities change? If so, what happens
      when they change? Why?

      Much of the work on parental influences has been cor-
relational. For instance, a significant correlation has
been found between a person's self-acceptance and his perception of what his parents thought about him (Jourard and
Remy, 1955). When completing a self-concept questionnaire
as they believed their child had answered it, parents of
children in therapy saw their children more negatively than
even the children saw themselves. These children, of
course, had lower self-esteem than a group of non-treated
children (Piers, 1972). How the parent sees the child, therefore, influences the child's self-esteem. In the same way,
discrepancies between how the two parents view a child is
related to lower self-esteem (Wyer, 1965). A child getting
different information from each parent will suffer negative
consequences in the self-evaluation element of the self-
concept. Likewise, children from broken homes have lower
self-esteem when the disruption causes a decrease in their
acceptance by others (Kaplan and Pohorny, 1971). Since

79

these data are correlational, it is hard to tell whether
the lack of parental acceptance caused the low self-
esteem or whether the child's low self-esteem caused the
lack of parental acceptance. Other experimental research
would need to be done to show the direction of the cause.
In addition, research is needed on specifying the verbal
communities' effect on the other elements of the self-
concept; e.g., the physical, social, etc. We can also
be concerned with the additive or cumulative effect
of the many verbal communities a person is influenced by
as he/she goes through life. I think you can see that
research on the core of human consciousness, the self-
system, is only in its infancy.

*46.   Give some empirical support for the idea that lack
       of parental acceptance causes lower self-esteem in
       children.

CHANGING THE SELF-SYSTEM

This section will deal with how some influences
change a person's self-system. We will explore briefly
two of the elements in the self-concept to see some of
the important variables in changing these dimensions. Change
in this context is defined by either increasing or decreasing
the consciousness or scope of the elements of the self-
concept.

Physical Self-Concept

We have seen that there is a delay in how long it takes
a real change in a person's physical appearance to result
in a change of the person's perception of the physical self-
concept. Obviously, some kind of change needs to occur
in the real body before change in the physical self-perception can occur. The reason for the delay is that the
perception won't change until the verbal community provides
feedback to the person. Suppose you used to be fifty pounds
overweight and have lost it all. It may be six months before
you incorporate into your physical self-concept that you
are thin. Some people never change the self-perception because they don't get enough feedback, or they discount the
feedback they get. Most of us know formerly overweight
people who still "feel" fat, or someone who was a late
adolescent-developer who still considers himself a "short runt"
(Nepoleon Complex). These examples show the importance
of the verbal community in changing the physical self-image.

80

Psychological Self-Concept

What "I" am changes as my feelings and attitudes change. There have been a number of experiments that have shown the variability of this element of the self-system. We will review some of these in the next chapter on locus of control. Here we will look at the influence of evaluation by others and its place in changing the "I." In one study (Videbeck, 1960) students who recited poems were given either positive or negative feedback. Prior to their recitations, there was no difference in their Q-Sort discrepancy scores. After the evaluation, however, those who received positive feedback accepted themselves more, while those receiving negative feedback accepted themselves less. The same result was found with having a successful experience on a date (Coombs, 1969).

The psychological self-concept also changes when you are engaging in behavior that is different from what you have done in the past (Kiesler, 1971). Imagine that you hold a moderate attitude toward helping others. Due to particular circumstances, you are put in a position in which you must help someone. After you have done this behavior of helping, your attitude of helping will be likely to change. Some researchers found this occurred with people who donated kidneys to others (Fullner and Marshall, 1970). Another example of changing an attitude in this way would be what happens when you stop dating someone you previously liked and start dating someone you have been less friendly with. In this case, you devalue the first person and begin to value the second person. These are examples of changes in attitudes or feelings (the behaviors of the psychological self-concept) that get changed with new behavioral experiences.

*48. Cite an empirical example of a success or failure leading to changed self-esteem.

*49. Cite instances of behavioral experience changing attitudes or feelings.

Self-Management

Before leaving this section, let's explore the question of how the person goes about changing him or herself. When I change it appears that I am responsible for the change.

81

Researchers have called this "self-management." We have
seen how it works when we discussed Fred Kanfer's work (1970).
Essentially you manipulate and vary the things in your life
because such manipulation results in favorable outcomes.
As I write this chapter I set myself a condition that if I
do three hours of work I can go out to the beach and enjoy
the afternoon sun. "I" have managed "myself" by arranging
a positive event to follow a less positive (or more difficult) task. The reason I do such self-management is that
I have been rewarded in the past for arranging or manipulating variables. I got the chapter finished; I completed
grading a number of test papers; I mowed the lawn--all behaviors that have desirable long-range outcomes. The management of "self" by "self" is a class of behaviors which
is maintained by its effects.

Irwin Sarason (1975) suggests a six-part program for
changing anxious self-preoccupation that is a good example
of how the "self" can change itself. The program involves
manipulating variables in the following categories:
(1) Information--by educating yourself about what you are
doing, you get a better idea of what to change. Therefore,
you may ask others about yourself, read literature,or observe others. (2) Modeling--by observing others who are
performing a task, you get information on how to do the task
and are less likely to be self-preoccupied. (3) Self-moni-
toring--by systematically observing what you do, you can
see what needs changing. (4) Attentional training--by
training yourself to attend to only certain task-relevant
cues, you get better at performing the task. (5) Relax-
ation--teaching yourself relaxation will result in less
task disruption due to tension. (6) Practice--using the
skills when doing the real task will insure that you become
more proficient at them. Manipulating variables in a systematic way will result in a changed self-concept. Such
manipulation will not occur, however, unless there are
favorable outcomes for doing it.

*50. What is "self-management?" How is it maintained?

*51. List six categories of behaviors involved in the
self-management of anxious self-preoccupation.

THE SELF-SYSTEM AND SURVIVAL

The final section of this chapter will consider the
question of the survival utility of the self-system. Is

82

it good or bad to possess self-consciousness? That is a complicated question that will not be answered here. The best thing we can hope to do is to uncover the rationale and arguments for each side. The human is the only creature we know of that possesses self-awareness (which requires the "self" which we have been discussing). The reason for that fact is unknown. We know "how" humans can be self-aware, through verbal behavior. But the "why" is less clear. From an evolutionary point of view, you can expect that a self-system evolved because it was advantageous for the species. It may have been that the differentiation of self emerged due to the interdependence that began to emerge in primordial tribes. There are those that maintain that the development of self-awareness may have had relatively immediate survival value, but that in the long run, it was an "evolutionary mistake." That is, the very self-awareness that once aided survival may someday threaten it. Self-consciousness (and the human species along with it) may be a blind alley in the overall process of evolution. To our knowledge, no other species does things for the good of the individual rather than for the good of the species. Humans are the only species that perform "selfish" acts. This may mean the downfall of the species. Let's look back at the specifics of both sides of this issue.

*52. Outline a discussion about the survival merits of the self-system.

On the positive side, there are many things about the self-system that enhance survival. On the individual level, high self-esteem has been shown to be related to better response to threat, better memory, assertiveness, and more adaptive reactions to failure (Bryne, 1974). In addition, we have looked at the role of self-regulation in improving oneself. On a cultural level, the ability to be aware of ourselves has enabled us to correct maladaptive things that we have done, a good example being the self-regulatory behavior of the ecology movement. On the species level, we may well survive major natural catastrophy because of the ability to project ourselves into the future. For example, the harnessing of solar power for energy purposes now may save the species from annihilation when other sources of energy are consumed.

*53. List the individual, cultural, and species advantages of a self-system.

83

The other side of the issue is as convincing. The anxiety of modern life expresses itself because of anxious self-preoccupation, robbing many people of productive lives. Depression, which is reaching epidemic proportions in modern life, also is characterized as an aberration of the self-system in which negative self-statements and pessimism about the self play a prominent role (Beck, 1976). Culturally, the effects of "self-serving" are reflected in many of the crime statistics. Additionally, it may be that anger and hostility are self-preoccupied behavior chains. Self-interest obviously threatens the survival of the species. A nuclear holocaust may come about because of the motives of a few self-preoccupied people and would have important repercussions for the survival of the rest of our species.

*54. List the disadvantages of the self-system.

The self-system, then, is one of our greatest strengths as a species while at the same time being one of our major deficits. Dr. B. F. Skinner makes the important point that self-awareness is advantageous only under some circumstances. It is only good, he says, when it aids in meeting "the contingencies of reinforcement under which it has arisen" (1971, p. 184). In other words, whether or not self-awareness is good depends upon its effects. Some forms are good, as in the self-analysis involved in scientific achievements. Other forms are not advantageous, as in the self-preoccupied ramblings of a paranoid assassin. Good and bad are notions that can be judged in terms of the individual, culture, and the species. It is bad if it doesn't do that or if it enhances survival for the individual but not the culture or species.

It should be apparent that assessing the survival utility of the self-system is a difficult process. Survival issues are important questions to consider, but it may be that only time will be able to answer them. As long as humans have awareness, however, both the risks and potentials will be there. If answers are found before the risks are realized, then self-awareness will be judged in history as "good." If the reverse happens, there will be no history as we now know it. The question, as they say, is an empirical one. What will happen, will happen.

*55. What is "good?" From where will the answer about the self-system's "goodness" come?

THE SELF-SYSTEM: AN EPILOGUE

This chapter has been somewhat speculative, somewhat empirical analysis of the phenomenon of "self." It's hard to believe that so little is known about an aspect so integral to us. Mystery and myth continue to shroud scientific work in understanding the self-system. The present chapter has provided a unified and consistent, if somewhat radical, way of looking at this pervasive aspect of humanity. More questions have been raised than answered but this, too, may be a function of science.

CHAPTER 5

LOCUS OF CONTROL

"What are you doing?" Charlie asked June as she struggled to remove the receding sand from the bottom of the pit.

"I thought I'd have a go at making a tunnel through this dune."

"You must be crazy. You can't make a tunnel out of dry sand. That's almost as crazy as trying to convince President Henrich that co-educational living would be healthy for State College."

"Oh, I don't know. I've never seen a tunnel in the dunes; but I don't know that it's impossible. Besides, Henrich almost bought the idea. Even though he didn't, we were able to make strides in other areas of student life. Getting a pub on campus is a pretty good deal, don't you think?"

Charlie shook his head in amused bewilderment. "Don't you ever give up, June?"

"I wouldn't be here with you, the most attractive and talented male this side of Layton Hall, if I gave up, would I?" June replied.

"Aw, shucks," Charlie mumbled as he started to dig.

****

It was the eighth referral Ted had seen that day. They were all alike and were beginning to get depressing. "Now, Mrs. Smith, you say here that you haven't had any heat in your apartment for two weeks. It's been pretty cold; how have you survived?"

Silence

"You also indicate that you ran out of milk for your baby three days ago. What has the child been doing for nourishment?"

Silence

86

"Does your husband work, ma'am?"

"No husband, sir. Just me and the children. I don't
know what to do. I got laid off last week at the bottling
company. I don't know what to do. The electricity man says
the lights go off tomorrow. We got a sack of potatoes left
and no money for more. I just don't know. I'm ready to
give up," Mrs. Smith sobbed quietly.

"It must be pretty rough trying to live like that. Have
you tried any other agencies?"

"It doesn't matter if I try; we're going to starve if we
don't freeze to death first." Tears flowed freely now.

Ted just wanted to scream, he felt so helpless. "We'll
try to take care of things, Mrs. Smith. Don't worry."

WHAT IS LOCUS OF CONTROL?

Locus of control is a term that is used to describe
a major orientation present in people's lives. Some people, like June, believe that they can do anything and consequently they try many things. Others feel completely helpless. One psychologist calls these people "pawns" (De Charms,
1968). No matter what happens, their major belief is that
they have no control over it. Locus of control refers then
to the place (locus) a person perceives the control of his
life to be. Though most of us are somewhere between the
extremes, on one end is the internal who feels that the place
of control lies within himself. He can do what he wants or
needs to do. On the other end is the external, someone
like Mrs. Smith. The control is outside of her. She feels
she has no say-so over what happens. Psychologist Julian
Rotter (1966) has called this personality dimension "perceived locus of control," the belief that what happens to
you is a function of what you do (internal) or is a function
of chance or what others do (external).

LOCUS OF CONTROL: A dimension of personality that specifies
the belief that what happens to you is a
function of what you do (internal locus
of control) or the belief that what happens to you is a function of chance, what
others do, or things external to you
(external locus of control).

87

This chapter will explore this dimension of personality
and attempt to explain its origins and characteristics.
The entire notion of locus of control rests on the idea
of expectancy. In the first section, an understanding of
expectancy will help greatly in viewing locus of control.

*1. Define perceived locus of control.

*2. What is an "internal?"

*3. What is an "external?"

     Expectancy is the term some psychologists use to
label a cognitive behavior characterized by what the person believes will happen under certain conditions. For
example, Rotter, Chance, and Phares (1972) state that expectancy is "the probability held by the individual that a
particular reinforcement will occur as a function of a
specific behavior on his part in a specific situation or
situations" (p.11). In other words, if the person believes
no reinforcement will come about by studying for the final
exam in Organic Chemistry, the probability (expectancy of
reinforcement) is zero. On the other hand, the person who
believes hard work will allow her to pull an "ace," has
a"strong" expectancy.

     An expectancy can be seen as the same thing as a rule.
Remember that a rule is a verbal statement about a setting,
a response in that setting, and the effects of that response.
Rules are by necessity verbal, but they can lead to what
is called intuitive controlled behavior (Malott, Tillema,
and Glenn, 1978). Intuitive control is the control of
behavior by direct reinforcers and punishers rather than
by rules. An example of rule-governed behavior gradually
fading into intuitive-controlled behavior is that of learning to drive a car with a standard transmission. At first,
you recite a sequence of rules about clutching, shifting,
and accelerating. But as time goes by, you drop the rules
(verbal statements) and "do it naturally." Your motor acts
are controlled by the direct consequences of getting the
car to go rather than by the step-by-step rules you started
with (Schneider & Shiffrin, 1977).

INTUITIVE CONTROL: The control of behavior by direct re-
                   inforcers and punishers rather than by
                   rules.

Having an expectancy is rule-governed behavior. When you study hard (behavior) for a test (setting), you will get a good grade (result). The expectancy involved in locus of control is a rule stating that some of your behavior in a given situation will result in reinforcement (internality) or that no behavior you are capable of makes a difference (externality). So the expectancy involved in locus of control stipulates a setting, a behavior, and whether or not you will receive reinforcement for it.

*6. What is intuitive control? Give an example.

*7. What is the expectancy involved in locus of control?

A helpful example is what animals do at feeding time. A hungry dog will perform preparatory behaviors like jumping around, wagging its tail, etc. when placed in a situation in which it has been fed before. You've seen this in your house pet. The animal "expects" food. But the animal's behavior is not verbal. Since an expectancy is a cognitive (verbal) behavior, how is it that the non-verbal animal has an expectancy? The answer is that the dog is engaging in <u>intuitive</u> behavior. The dog's behavior is controlled by the direct consequences of being exposed to reinforcement. The dog's preparatory acts are controlled by direct exposure to the consequences. But it is still an "expectancy" because the food bowl (setting), jumping about (behavior), and food (result) are all present. In humans the process merely gets labeled. So don't confuse expectancy with verbal behavior. Some "expectancies" are verbal (rules), some are intuitive. Both types refer to a history of being reinforced in a particular setting.

EXPECTANCY: The probability of an occurrence happening within a certain situation. This probability can be explicitly labeled (a rule) or it can be experienced directly (intuitive). A setting, behavior, and result are specified in an expectancy.

*8. What is an expectancy? Give an example.

As we mentioned in Chapter 3, rule-governed behavior becomes established because we are reinforced for following rules. An expectancy is formed because we do a particular act, are reinforced, and describe a rule that states the conditions of the expectancy. In locus of control, the expectancy of whether or not we are reinforced will come about because of having been reinforced (in the case of internality) or not having been reinforced (in the case of externality). When the expectancy is generalized, as it is in locus of control, there have been a number of different situations in which action has been reinforced and a rule derived to describe the sequence of behavior and reinforcement. A rule held by the internal person may be that hard work will pay off in many activities. That rule or expectancy became generalized because the person was reinforced for hard work in school, at home, on the job, while playing, and in a number of other situations. Generalized expectancies are rule-governed behaviors that apply across a number of situations. Internal and external locus of control is a generalized expectancy about whether your behavior will be reinforced. One other thing to remember is that the expectancy can be verbally coded (rule-governed) or non-verbally coded (intuitive).

*9. How is a generalized expectancy developed?

*10. Give an example of how an internal locus of control develops?

We have been talking about beliefs, expectancies, and other cognitive behaviors, but what is the real significance of locus of control behaviorally? The major point that we will see time and time again is that internality relates to trying. Externality relates to not trying. June tried anything; she was internal. Mrs. Smith was through trying; she was external. Behaviorally, locus of control relates to how much a person tries to do things.

*11. Behaviorally, locus of control relates to _____.

We should also introduce the notion of self-efficacy. Albert Bandura uses this term to describe the conviction or belief a person has that he can successfully execute the behavior required to reach an outcome (Bandura, 1977). Self-efficacy differs from locus of control in that the locus of control refers to the belief that a behavior will lead to an outcome, whereas self-efficacy refers to whether or not you feel you can perform the behavior. If you think writing will make you rich and famous, that is locus of control. But if you think you can write, that's self-efficacy. We will talk about both locus of control and self-efficacy

90

because they both relate to trying. However, locus of control is usually a generalized expectancy while self-efficacy is situationally specific.

SELF-EFFICACY: The belief that you can successfully perform the behavior required to attain a desired outcome.

*12. Define self-efficacy.

*13. How does it differ from locus of control? How is it the same?

Another concept related to locus of control is learned helplessness(Seligiman, 1975). There has been a good deal of research on this notion recently. Essentially, the research has shown that creatures (animals and humans) will exhibit patterns of behavior characterized by not trying, listlessness, and lack of interest in the immediate environment when they have been exposed to experiences in which there has been no connection between what they do and what happens to them. For example, if a dog is placed in an experimental cage and given small amounts of unpleasant electrical current, he will engage in attempts to escape. If, however, escape is made impossible, the dog will eventually give up and will then exhibit the behaviors of learned helplessness. You should be able to see the similarity of the learned helplessness concept to the concept of external locus of control. In both cases a lack of trying occurs because of being exposed to events over which there is no personal control. Research on learned helplessness is important because it has resulted in specifying the precise effects of the role of different environments on the class of behaviors involved in locus of control, self-efficacy, and learned helplessness. Much of what is being discussed in this chapter is based on that research.

LEARNED HELPLESSNESS: The tendency to behave in a "helplessness" manner (not trying, listlessness, etc.) that results from being exposed to an environment in which there is little connection between effort and outcome.

A final area of research related to locus of control is attribution theory (Weiner, 1978). In this model the

91

goal is to understand why people attribute the causes of
their behavior to certain people or things in their environments. For example, if a person attributes success in a
task to their own high ability rather than to the ease of
the task, there will be greater pride. Or failure attributed to a lack of effort causes greater shame than does failure
attributed to bad luck (Weiner, 1978). This idea of
"causal attributions" is related to locus of control in
that internal people attribute the causes of their behavior
to themselves and people with external loci of control attribute the causes of their behavior to things outside of
themselves. Research in the area has shown that four factors
are most responsible for perceived success or failure: ability, effort, task difficulty, and luck. The research done
in the area of causal attributions is very helpful in understanding how and why perceived control is learned.

CAUSAL ATTRIBUTIONS: The perceived causes of success or
failure. These are influenced by
four factors: ability, effort, task
difficulty, and luck

MEASURING LOCUS OF CONTROL

In 1966 Rotter introduced a personality scale that
purported to measure the dimension of internal-external
locus of control. It was called the internal-external or
I-E scale. This device has been used in literally hundreds
of experiments, and it is generally accepted as the means
by which locus of control is assessed. It is a self-report
questionnaire in which the person chooses one of two alternatives that he considers more applicable to himself. A
few items are contained in Table 5-1.

TABLE 5-1

ITEMS FROM THE I-E SCALE (ROTTER, 1966)

6. A. Without the right breaks one cannot be an effective
leader.
    B. Capable people who fail to become leaders have not
taken advantage of their opportunities.

15. A. In my case getting what I want has little to do with
luck.
    B. Many times we might as well decide what to do by flip-
ping a coin.

20. A. It is hard to know whether or not a person really
       likes you.
    B. How many friends you have depends upon how nice a
       person you are.

Rotter makes the point that the I-E scale measures what
a person believes to be true about himself, not what he wants
to be true. Thus, the scale measures perceived locus of
control rather than desired locus of control. While there
are many other scales that measure the dimension of locus
of control (even some for children; e.g., Nowicki & Strickland, 1973), the I-E scale is the most popular. Some researchers have factor analyzed the I-E scale and found that
the scale measures more than just internality-externality.
One such study, for example, found that the I-E scale reflects two separate beliefs: the first is that hard work
will or will not determine personally relevant outcomes.
The second is that a citizen can or cannot influence the flow
of events in government (Mirels, 1970). Dr. Herb Lefcourt
of the University of Waterloo has done considerable work in
the area of locus of control. He suggests that these two
dimensions should be labeled "personal" and "ideological"
beliefs (1972). Lefcourt has also recently stated that
measurement in locus of control should become situationally
specific (1978). A person may believe she can effect change
in her job but feel powerless at home with her family. Or
someone may have developed a generalized expectancy of
reinforcement when dealing with children but be bumfuzzled
when interacting with adults. Measurement of these specific
generalized expectancies will greatly enhance our understanding of locus of control.

*14. Describe the I-E scale.

*15. Why is the measurement of locus of control better when
     it is situationally specific?

    For example, Levenson (1973) has devised a scale that
measures locus of control but breaks down the external dimension into two factors: the fact that a person believes
luck or chance governs his life or the belief that powerful
others control what will happen to him. In addition to this,
Bandura introduces questionnaires for self-efficacy measurement that are specific to one particular response class
(Bandura and Adams, 1977). The person is given a list of

performance tasks included in the response class and asked to rate the certainty with which they can perform each behavior on a scale from 10 (completely uncertain) to 100 (completely certain). Table 5-2 contains some sample items from a similar questionnaire developed by Jaremko and Walker (1978) for measuring self-efficacy in a public speaking situation.

TABLE 5-2

SELECTED ITEMS FROM "SPEECH SKILLS
SURVEY" (JAREMKO AND WALKER, 1978)

10	20	30	40	50	60	70	80	90	100
Great Uncertainty			Moderately Uncertain					Completely Certain	

1. Choosing an appropriate topic.

4. Practicing the speech with a friend.

9. Delivering the speech for a grade.

10. Receiving criticism from the class for your speech.

****

*16. List two of the factors of the external dimension of locus of control (Levenson, 1973).

*17. Describe a self-efficacy measuring scale.

Self-Monitoring

The move to assessment of specific self-efficacy expectations is an important step in measuring locus of control. It offers a more precise way to measure this dimension. However, the format is still self-report. Sometimes, as we have seen, people don't always do what they say they are going to do. While having all good intentions and trying to be as open and honest as possible, people still have the tendency to give themsleves more credit than is due.

94

You might say that you are going to start jogging as soon as the midterm test in biology is passed. You talk it up and commit yourself verbally to others, but on the day after the test you don't run. You may even say that you will wait until the weekend is over. But it gets delayed again and again and again...

It's not hard to see why your words are "cheap." The reinforcers and punishers maintaining the verbal behavior are quite different from those maintaining the real behavior. Other people provide rich reinforcement for the verbal behavior of saying your're going to run. The negative effects of such talk are slight in terms of energy expended. But running itself is a different ballgame: legs hurt, chest aches, and you are exhausted for the rest of the night. These minor setbacks dissipate after keeping at it for a week or so. But the setbacks can sure keep you procrastinating. A discrepancy between verbal behavior and real behavior is often present. When using self-report measures, the discrepancy can lead to inaccuracies in assessment. One solution used by many clinical psychologists is to teach the person self-monitoring of specific behavior. Let's see how this procedure would work.

*18. Explain why there is often a discrepancy between verbal behavior and what a person actually does.

*19. How does this discrepancy affect self-report measures of personality?

****

"Well, Bill, this is the third week in a row that you told me you were going to ask someone for a date. But still no date. What's the problem?" The counselor was a bit exasperated with his wayward client.

"I really try, Dr. Reynolds, but get no results. I talk to girls more now--since I've come to see you. But it's not working. I still can't get up the nerve to ask one of them out. What else can I do? You said that if I talked with girls more, I'd get to the point where I could ask them out. It's just not working." Bill looked somewhat dejected.

"I see your point. Let me ask you this: how do you really know you talk to girls more?"

95

"I can tell. I feel it. I see more of them, and I just talk to them more. What have you got in mind?"

Reynolds stroked his beard. "Bill, I think you may be kidding yourself about the increased contact. I'd like to try an experiment with you. Are you willing to try it?"

"Doc, I'll try anything to get a date. What is it?"

"Well, you see this little device" It's a wrist counter. I want you to put it on and press the button everytime you talk to a girl." Reynolds continued. "Now 'talking to a girl' is defined as saying more than 'Hi' or "how are you?'-- Let's say you have to say more than five words..."

Next week...

"Hey, Doc, I came by to tell you that this counter really works. I wasn't really saying much to girls, but the counter made me realize that. So I started talking more--12 times this week. I even went to the dining hall with a girl last night, and I have a date set for ..."

Reynolds stroked his beard and smiled.

****

Self-monitoring is a procedure whereby the person is taught to define as precisely as possible a behavior (or usually a response class) and then to count instances of when he does that behavior. It is not totally accurate, but it can be more accurate than self-report measures. In locus of control, we would want to measure the numbers of times a person attempts something. "Attempts" could be de-fined as behavior which is designed to meet a prearranged goal. It is a very wide and encompassing response class. In order to make the response class more specific one might choose to narrow it to "attempting to talk with women" as Bill did. The internal person will show a greater number of "attempts." (He tries harder than the external person.) Such self-monitoring may be an accurate measure of locus of control. Moreover, self-monitoring is more specific to the individual person since the measurements take place in day-to-day life in this way, this approach holds promise as a valid way to measure locus of control.

SELF-MONITORING: A measurement procedure in which the per-

son defines a behavior and counts
the number of times he or she performs that behavior.

*20. Define self-monitoring and give an example.

*21. What are two advantages of this approach?

THE DEVELOPMENT OF LOCUS OF CONTROL

Since the locus of control is a behavior--an "expectation" held by someone--you can imagine that the same principles that operate to develop and control any other behavior
do so with expectancies of reinforcement. History of
experience once again becomes the key. In general, if your
behavior has made no difference in terms of yielding reinforcement, externality will develop. On the other hand, if
reinforcement has been contingent-on your behavior--that is,
dependent on it--you will have developed an expectation
of controlling things, namely internality. In like manner,
the words and labels about what you "expect" from yourself
for which the verbal community reinforces you are important
in the development of internality. Counselors are not in-
frequently involved with clients who in fact have quite
effective skills and who do many things but have words that
say they can't do things. These negative self-evaluations
can be seen as a verbal community differentially reinforcing
bad talk. Parents who call their children clumsy, stupid,
etc., are pitiful examples. One might even be able to make
a case that the socially-sanctioned "game" of "one-up-manship"
in which people put each other down contributes to a discrepancy between what the person can do and what the person
thinks he can do.

*22. What kind of history is associated with internality?
      Externality?

*23. Describe the place of the verbal community in the
      development of locus of control.

By now you can guess that differential reinforcement
and the verbal community are important notions in the development of locus of control. But that is speaking in
general terms. It may help us to understand the development
of locus of control by being more specific. Indeed, if locus
of control is better conceived of as specific generalized expectancies as many of psychologists have suggested, then un-

97

derstanding the development of internality or externality within a single response class is a more fruitful approach. This is the approach Dr. Albert Bandura takes in an article on self-efficacy (1977). Bandura traces four of the influences in the development of self-efficacy. This section will present and discuss these influences.

Performance Accomplishments

Bandura thinks the development of self-efficacy proceeds along the lines of information processing. We get information from our environment and use that information to form expectancies. In many ways Bandura is talking about consequences when he uses the term "information." When we are positively consequated for some behavior, we are "receiving information" about that behavior, that is, continuing the behavior will be profitable. There is no doubt that we sometimes do "use information", but other times we are merely exposed to the consequences of our behavior and the conscious processing of information does not enter into awareness. The information processing model of behavior, therefore includes instances of being aware of the information value of environmental experience and not being aware of it. Bandura's self-efficacy model states that there are four sources of self-efficacy information: performance accomplishments, vicarious experience, verbal persuasion, and emotional arousal. Each source is more powerful than the next with performance accomplishments contributing the most to the development of self-efficacy and emotional arousal contributing the least.

*24. What is "information processing?"

*25. What are the four sources of self-efficacy information?

Performance accomplishemnts refer to the successes a person has had. If you want to be a good, self-confident speaker, the best way to go about it is to be successful at giving speeches. Accomplishing a performance provides much self-efficacy and makes it more likely that you will do the act again. In fact, you will probably do it better. Nothing succeeds like success, as they say. It may be that other sources of self-efficacy information get you to initially try a behavior, but once you've done it successfully you're on your way to confidence, self-efficacy and internality. As support for the superiority of this source of

information in enhancing self-efficacy, Bandura cites psychotherapy treatment studies that show that performance-based
treatments are more effective than imaginal or symbolic treatments. For instance, it is generally more effective to
treat a person who has a fear of riding elevators by actually
getting him to ride one while relaxed rather than by having
him imagine he is riding one while relaxed.

On the negative side of this source of efficacy information is the fact that to avoid doing something that fright-
ens you or repulses you will only serve to make it harder
to do the next time. A client I once knew found it very difficult to go to parties where "eligible men" were to be
present. She consequently stayed home, lacked confidence
about herself, and felt lonely. The more she avoided opportunities to "party," the greater her fear became. The
greater her fear became, the less likely she was to venture
out. Such avoidance behavior is insidious because not going
to the party (avoiding it) was negatively reinforcing since
she avoided the unpleasant feelings of being anxious. In
the future she would then be less likely to go, only making
matters worse. She had to start out by going to a non-
threatening social affair in order to have a "fear-free"
time, and work up from there. Her psychological treatment
arranged such a plan, and she gained self-efficacy along
the way. She now has an active social life. The importance of "doing" in developing an expectation of internal
locus of control should be obvious.

*26. What are performance accomplishments?

*27. Why is the avoidance of doing something bad for self-
 ·efficacy?

Vicarious Experiences

When one of us is a winner, in a sense we are all winners.
When we see a friend graduate, see a couple raise a darling
child, observe the promotion of a fellow worker, or watch an
athletic team win a championship, we experience vicariously
the fruits of their performance accomplishments. The word
vicarious is defined as experiencing something through another person's experiences. The fact that others can do
something successfully provides information that we can also
do it. However, sometimes jealousy or envy is elicited when
we observe another's success, but aside from those instances
we can derive information that it is possible to do certain

things. Many of us started careers by emulating the feats
of others who came before us. "When I grow up," we said,
"I wanna' be just like her (or him)." This source of information is not as powerful as the first because it is
symbolic rather than real. But as we stated before, it
may be the spark that gets the fire roaring which leads
to performance accomplishments. Observing someone else
accomplish a success may lead a person to trying the feat on
his or her own. If success is then forthcoming, self-efficacy will be strengthened.

*28. Why do vicarious experiences lead to self-efficacy?

Bandura has spent a long and illustrious research career demonstrating the power of vicarious learning. He
maintains that we learn more in this manner than by direct
experience. He is probably correct, but we must remember
that vicarious experience gets potency in the first place
from direct experiences (see Chapter 2). Nonetheless, if a
person is exposed to self-efficacious models, she will be
more likely to be self-efficacious. However, if one is
exposed to listless and self-doubting models, the opposite
could result; that is, externality and a low rate of attempting behavior.

Verbal Persuasion

A third source of information for self-efficacy, according to Bandura, is verbal persuasion. This source refers to
the words and encouragement from others that we can accomplish something. Imagine that you're "down in the mouth."
You have an entire class lecture/discussion to give in senior
seminar next week. Your roomie says, "You'll do fine. You're
so good in that class." That's information that will boost
your confidence, make you feel better. Depending upon whom
those words came from, they can be as powerful as any source
of self-efficacy information. I remember one time, a particular model of mine called me aside and told me that I was
good at asking questions in class. I've been asking questions and making comments in groups ever since! On the other
hand, you might not get as much of a lift out of your mother's
encouragement because you may believe that she is obligated
to give it since she is your mother. The point is that
verbal support from others can prove self-efficacy enhancing.
Most "verbal" psychotherpaies in which the counselor urges
her clients upward and onward are examples of this source of
self-efficacy information. If that's the only source of in-

formation, however, the client won't make it far. Eventually, those words need to be backed up by successes.

*29. What is verbal persuasion and how can it be a powerful source of self-efficacy information?

Emotional Arousal

The final source of information cited by Bandura comes from within our bodies. As we perform a fearful feat, we can be aware of internal physiological response (we called this behavior "feeling" in Chapter 4). If our "innards" are calm, that can be information that we are less fearful and will increase self-efficacy in that situation. In like manner, many verbal attempts to persuade a client that he is no longer afraid of something have ended in failure because the person's emotional reaction (i.e., physiological reaction) gave information to the contrary, that he was, in fact, nervous and aroused. As the least powerful source of efficacy information, emotional arousal may be relegated to a confirming role; that is, it confirms (or disconfirms) other sources of information. But we should be aware that we can derive self-efficacy when we observe our own bodies.

The four sources of self-efficacy information are constantly changing and updating our beliefs about our own skills. The analysis provided by Bandura is a good one because it shows the "originating" role of the person in the development of behavior. It is also good because it is specific and affords precise investigation. Using this analysis we can understand how locus of control develops and, perhaps even more imporant, how it is changed.

CHANGING LOCUS OF CONTROL

One of the more persistent lines of research in the locus of control area is one in which a correlation between internality and good psychological adjustment is sought. Rotter (1966) has suggested that being extremely internal or external is bad, but that, in general, internals are better adjusted than externals. Lefcourt (1972) notes that the goal of psychotherapy may be conceived of as helping the person to be more internal. The correlation, however, between psychopathology and locus of control has not been consistently shown. Some researchers have found a correlation between externality and psychotic (extremely distrubed) behavior.

Other researchres have found correlations between externality and depression. But other correlational evidence has not been consistently found. Further work is needed to specify the exact relationship of locus of control to psychological disturbance. However, if it is assumed that internality is a desirable state, how do we help someone to change from having external to internal expectancies of reinforcement? This section will present information relevant to this question.

*31. How is internality related to positive mental health?

Successful Experiences

The most effective way to change self-efficacy or locus of control is by increasing the rate of successful experiences that the person has. For example, a very helpless-acting, external middle-aged housewife will develop an internal locus of control if successful experiences in new "ventures" can be arranged. Learning to be assertive with her husband, taking a class and doing well in it, finding a worthwhile job or taking better care of her children are all successes that enhance a woman's self-efficacy. One of the major tasks of the clinical psychologist is to help the client rearrange his environment so that successful experiences are more likely to result. Group therapy is often a successful experience for some clients who lack confidence in interpersonal situations. Being in a situation in which intimate self-disclosure occurs between group members is a very gratifying experience for some people. The purpose of a group leader shoud be to make sure that these attempts at self-disclosure are successful. When the group environment is "safe," the self-efficacy enhancement effect is greater(Rogers, 1970).

*32. List three examples of how successful experiences can change a person's self-efficacy.

The place of successful or unsuccessful experiences in changing a person's locus of control has been shown in a number of laboratory experiments. Being successful at a task will increase internaltiy (Phares, 1957; Eisenman, 1972) and failure will increase externaltiy (MacArthur, 1970). The effect is also present in real life situations. Nowicki and Barnes (1973) found that inner-city children changed I-E scores to a more internal direction when they were exposed to a structured summer camp experience. In another real-life experiment, it was found that the I-E scores of young men who drew low draft numbers in a recent military draft lottery became more external. Bandura (1977) shows that the successful experiences of fearful subjects in dealing with the feared object reduces the fear. It is clear, then, that the most powerful means of changing locus of control is to arrange success experiences for external individuals in which they demonstrate mastery or competence in areas in which they have previously failed.

*33. Give some research support for the idea that successful experiences can change locus of control.

Anytime, however, that an experience increases internality, the question of generalization is raised. Will one success make it likely that the person will expect reinforcement in other situations? This question is addressed by counselors who try to get clients to have as many successes in as many different situations as possible. The problem, however, of being limited by changes in locus of control that are peculiar to only one situation should be accounted for. A concerted effort to get people to experience mastery or control of outcomes in a variety of settings is the most fruitful way to make lasting changes in locus of control.

*34. What is the best way to make generalized changes in locus of control?

Other Clinical Techniques

Most other techniques to help a person become more self-confident are in some way derived from having mastery or control over outcomes--there is no substitute for it. Sooner or later, people must master or control outcomes for themselves if they wish to feel competent. However, in cases where the person is in fact competent but does not feel confident, a "cognitive restructuring" procedure can help bring self-efficacy back in line with the real successes the person has. A procedure, introduced by Todd (1972) and Mahoney (1971), involves getting the person to talk to himself in a more realistic way. By having the person list aspects of himself that are accurate descriptions of good qualities (e.g., "I am sensitive to others.") on small index cards, a way to remind him of his effectiveness is established. Everytime the person does something that occurs frequently (e.g., smoke a cigarette or go to the bathroom), he is required to read one of the positive self-statements. Since this reading

103

happens several times each day and in a number of different
situations, the person reminds himself of the more positive
attributes he possesses. This has the effect of bringing
his self evaluation in line with his real effectiveness.
His self-efficacy is thereby increased because he now sees
himself as more worthwhile. However, such a procedure will
be doomed to failure if the person has no successful experiences to talk to himself about.

*35. Describe a cognitive restructuring technique for chang-
     ing locus of control.

     Changing locus of control is a very vital although
sometimes difficult thing to attempt. Sometimes one minor
failure can destroy the effect of many other successes.
Effecting change in those who don't think they can do anything is not as easy as it has been made to sound here. It
is a long process that requires patience if solid and lasting
expectancies of reinforcement are to be established. However,
it is a noble enterprise because, as we shall now see, locus of control is a very important human characteristic in
terms of survival.

LOCUS OF CONTROL AND SURVIVIAL

     Behaviorally, locus of control most clearly relates
to people trying things. It is in this response class of
attempting that locus of control finds its usefulness in
terms of survival. It's hard to imagine a world in which
people didn't try. This is, without doubt, one of the basic
human characteristics. Locus of control is the psychological process that underlies attempting things. Without
the expectation that what we do is related to reinforcement,
the rate of trying things would be greatly reduced, perhaps
even nonexistent. In this section we will specify some of
the ways in which locus of control as a dimension of personality is related to survival of the individual, culture, and
the species.

Psychopathology

     We have briefly mentioned the role of locus of control
in human adjustment. Basically, there is a hypothetical
relatioship; empirical support is only beginning to be found.
Arnkoff and Mahoney (1978) provided a conceptual model for
investigating the role of perceived control in psychopatho-

logy. The possible contact points at which externality
(or the belief that what you do doesn't matter) interfaces
with maladjustment are many. For example, the depressed
person may be despondent because he perceives that what he
does is useless, and he, therfore, doesn't try to accomplish
things anymore. Or the person with a phobia may have an
acute sense of lack of control when in the presence of
the fear object. The more severe types of psychopathology also might relate to a lack of perceived control.
The paranoid person who believes others are out to get him
does not believe that he is in full control. Or the near-
psychotic person who is deathly afraid of losing control
is another example.

In clinical situations, therefore, the relationship
between locus of control and behavior problems is still
somewhat speculative. Much more research is required, but
the ideas make sense. In the area of self-health care,
however, locus of control has been shown to have a strong
influence. Strickland (1978) cites data that support the
notion that people who are internal take better care of
their bodies than do externals. For instance, people who
are internal and have high blood pressure are more likely
to medicate themsleves and eat correctly to control their
condition than are externals. However, sometimes internality
is maladaptive because these people don't do what their physician prescribes for them but carry their own prescriptions.
In either case the relationship between locus of control
and medical or behavioral adjustment is important.

*36. Give three examples of externality interfacing with
       maladjustment.

*37. How is internality good for health care? How is it
       bad?

Social Activism

Concern with world affairs and controlling political
situations has been related to locus of control. For
instance, Abramowitz (1973) found that people who indicate
a high level of political activism are also internals on the
I-E scale. Gore and Rotter (1963) found that black students
who were internal were more likely to attend a political
rally. To the extent that political activism and govern-
mental action are considered desirable, locus of control is

an important issue in the survival of a cultural way of life. Those who have been reinforced for political action will develop expectations that something can be done about conditions, and will consequently solve important problems. It might be interesting to note that political scientists are also beginning to investigate locus of control as a variable important in understanding political behavior (e.g. Renshon, 1978)

*38. How might locus of control relate to political activism?

Personal Adjustment and Curiosity

De Charms (1978) has discussed the person who feels like a "pawn." He has differentiated this type of person from one who feels in control, who tries things, who attempts to tackle difficult problems, who seems to become stronger in the face of a challenge. In everyday life the expectation that what happens to you is under your control may not have life or death implications. Many people go through life "following" and wanting nothing more. To force these people to be in control more would take away the security they find reinforcing. It may not be possible to be free and secure simultaneously. However, one may be able to argue that the quality of life of the internal person is greater in a very important way than that of the external person.

When an internal person tries more, she is also more likely to get more reinforcement. Among other things, reinforcement "feels" good. Thus those who have a lot of reinforcement usually report "feeling happier." They also are, therefore, more likely to try other things and to receive more reinforcement. In this way, a never-ending cycle is started in which some members of the human race strive for answers. They strive for answers because they believe they can find them. They are people with internal loci of control who have been reinforced in thier past for finding answers and therefore, hold the belief that answers can be found.

Such is the way in which human curiosity works. One of the things humans do well is to ask questions. Internal people are probably more likely to ask questions than are external people. Satisfying curiosity not only results in personal reinforcement, but it further results in information

106

that is valuable to the survival of the species and its members. A vaccine for polio, an electric light, a more efficient means of air travel, and many other technological advances are born of attempts by people with internal loci of control. When these people make an attempt to ask questions and find answers, we all benefit from their belief in controlability. "Being human" may essentially amount to asking questions and looking for answers. To the extent perceived locus of control relates to curiosity, it is an important dimension of personality in terms of continued survival for the human race.

LOCUS OF CONTROL: EPILOGUE

We have seen the role of perceived control in human behavior, how it is measured, how it develops, how it is changed, and how it relates to survival. It is indeed a significant fact about the human that he or she does or does not develop a sense of being in control. The implications of such a belief are important for the individual, the culture, and the species. Developing ways to enhance a feeling of control in people is a highly worthwhile cause This chapter attempted to explicate the characteristics of the locus of control dimension in order to increase the probability that such ways can be developed.

*39. Why does internality lead to a better way of life?

*40. How is locus of control related to survival?

*41. In what two ways does curiosity help survival?

CHAPTER 6

INTERPERSONAL RELATIONSHIPS AND EXTROVERSION

Perhaps one of the most important things humans do is
to interact with other human beings. Our relationships with
other people constitute the bulk of our experiences. Much
of our sorrow, joy, anger, and other emotional behavior is
generated by or around others. It is not unusual to spend
a lifetime looking for satisfying interpersonal relationships.
Such a pervasive influence on human behavior should be considered in a book about personality. This chapter will
describe a model of how and why humans interact with each
other. The personality is greatly influenced by interpersonal relationships. For this reason, it is important to
have some understanding of the psychology of interpersonal
relating.

Our task in this chapter will be to review some of the
experimental literature on the initiation and development
of relationships, how people perceive each other, and how
communication processes work. The focus will be on dyadic
relationships. Often we will discuss the dyad in terms of
cross-sex relationships in which a man relates to a woman
(or vice-versa). When the number of people interacting
increases beyond two, other social influences sometimes take
over. Some of these principles of group dynamics will be
touched on here but we will still concentrate on dyads.

ATTRACTION

First of all in order to be engaged in an interpersonal
relationship, two people must be around each other. In social psychology, considerable research has been directed to
attraction. The basic question is: Why is person A attracted to person B? The importance of attraction in terms of
two people spending time with each other should be obvious.
When people are attracted to each other, they spend time
together. This allows the other processes of interpersonal
relating to operate. Conversely two people not attracted
to each other will probably not spend time with each other.
In this section, four factors that influence attraction will
be presented.

Chance

Did you ever wonder how much of your life is determined

by fate or chance? In the chapter on locus of control we saw that some people form generalized expectancies that what happens to them is controlled by chance. People external in locus of control may believe that chance controls what happens to them. In locus of control it doesn't matter what the real facts are, it only matters what the person believes to be true. The question before us now is concerned with whether chance really does influence a situation. How much of what happens to us is truly the result of random chance factors? In interpersonal attraction fate or chance is really an important determinant. Consider the roommate who may be one of your special friends. It may have been a random room assignment that thrust you two together. If you had not been roommates, your relationship may not have developed as much as it did. Chance had an influence.

No doubt, other factors need to be present for you and your roommate to become fast friends. The start of it, however, was dependent on chance. This is what is meant when we look at the influence of luck, chance, or fate in interpersonal relationships. Being in the right place at the right time may result in a torrid love affair that greatly influences other personality dimensions. Perhaps the first meeting between you and your spouse was a chance occurrence. Further, you may have had the experience of wondering what might have been had you done one thing rather than another. The plain fact stares us in the face. One of the most important aspects of our lives is significantly influenced by chance ,over which we may have little control. There are other influences on attraction that are under our control, but it may be wise to remember the place of chance in human relationships.

Empirical support for these ideas come from a number of sources. Mainly, however, research demonstrates that people who are closer together are more likely to develop relationships. For example, students who share classes, dormitories, or are otherwise close to each other develop more friendships (Bryne, 1961). Workers develop closer relationships with people who work physically close to them (Zander and Havelin, 1960). Caucasians who experience increased contact with blacks become less prejudiced as a consequence of the contact (Deutsch & Collins, 1955). Likewise people who are close to each other are more likely to marry (Katz and Hill, 1958). The point that proximity, which is often influenced by chance, influences attraction is well supported.

*1. Why is attraction an important aspect of interpersonal relationships?

*2. Give two examples of how chance influences attraction.

*3. Cite empirical support for proximity being related to the development of relationships.

Physical Attraction

A number of social psychologists have contended that most people think "beautiful" is good. This statement is based on the research that supports the idea that people are more attracted to physically pleasing people. In fact, it is not uncommon for physically pleasing individuals to be judged smarter, more diligent, and happier than less attractive people (Dion, Berscheid, and Walster, 1972). Furthermore, physical attractiveness has been shown to be the main variable that influences attraction at the start of a relationship. Social skills, intelligence, and personality do not seem to be very good predictors of attraction; but physical appearance does (Walster, Aronson, Abrahams, & Rottman, 1966).

Physical features seem to be most important in terms of the initiation of an interpersonal relationship. Physically attractive people have many more relationship options than less attractive people. As a relationship develops, however, other determinants become important in maintaining the interaction. But at the start, beauty (like chance) has a strong effect. In addition, it should be noted that men are more influenced by physical features than are women (Middlebrook, 1974).

*4. How does beauty influence attraction? Support your answer with research findings.

Similarity

Dr. Donn Bryne of Purdue University has studied the notion that we are attracted to people who hold the same attitudes that we do. You are more likely to be attracted to a person who agrees with you about political, religious, or moral attitudes. For example, it is quite probable that your firends hold similar attitudes to you. In fact,

110

Bryne & Nelson (1965) found that the more your attitudes agree with someone else's attitudes, the more you are attracted to that person.

We are also attracted to people who are similar to us in ways other than attitudes. People who hold similar personality characteristics tend to be attracted to each other. Bryne, Grifitt, & Stefaniak (1967) found, for example, that people who coped with things by ignoring them (repressors) were attracted to other repressors more than to people who cope with things by being vigilant (sensitizers.) Likewise, sensitizers were more attracted to other sensitizers. London (1967) found that people with similar abilities are also attracted to each other. And finally those who are economically similar are attracted to each other (Bryne, Clore, & Worchel, 1966). It appears then that a major part of attraction has to do with similarity of attitude, personality characteristics, abilities, and economic status.

*5. Attraction is enhanced by attitude _____.

*6. Give an example of similar personality characteristics enhancing attraction.

*7. What two other types of similarity enhance attraction?

Personal Evaluations

We are also very attracted to people who are attracted to us or who tell us good things about ourselves. Such positive evalutions from others have been shown to be about three times more powerful in determining attraction than is attitude similarity (Bryne and Thamey, 1965). It should be fairly obvious that positive feedback is a major source of attraction. Since social reinforcement is a very powerful aspect of human life, and positive evaluation is a form of social reinforcement, we respond readily to positive evaluations. We also respond just as negatively to unfavorable evaluations. Lack of attraction (or even repulsion) is, of course influenced by negative feedback. The implications of the data that show that attraction is influenced by personal evaluation are quite important. If you want others to like you, you can encourage them by giving positive feedback to them. If others are not attracted to you, it may be that you are, in some way, giving them negative feedback

(or at least not giving them positive feedback). The place
of mutual positive interchange in healthy interpersonal
relationships is well documented (e.g., Rogers, 1968).

*8. How does positive feedback influence attraction?

Reinforcement, the Key to Attraction

The four sources of attraction we have covered so far
(chance, physical appearance, similarity, and evaluations)
have in common that they all involve reinforcement. In
summary, we can say that we are attracted to those who
provide us with reinforcement. For example, we are attracted to physically pleasing people because of aesthetic
and sexual reinforcement as well as the social prestige
gained by being with someone physically appealing. Likewise,
attitudes have been shown to function as reinforcers (Golightly and Bryne, 1964) and, therefore, those who hold
attitudes similar to our own are providing reinforcement.
The same process seems to hold true in similarity of personality characteristics (self-esteem reinforcement),
abilities, and economic status. Walster and Prestholdt
(1966) have shown that attraction is enhanced for people
for whom we provide help. Since people we help are likely
to provide us reinforcement, the increase in attraction is
understandable. Further, Bersheid and Walster (1969) review
literature that shows that we tend to like people who
negatively reinforce us by anxiety reduction, loneliness
reduction, or insecurity reduction. The place of reinforcement in enhancing attraction is, therefore, a well-
documented point. However, there are some exceptions
to the effectiveness of reinforcement in enhancing attraction. We briefly present these exceptions now.

*9. Explain how reinforcement influences who we are
     attracted to.

Exceptions

There are three exceptions to the potency of reinforcement in enhancing attraction: reward imbalance, ingratiation, and satiation. Reward imbalance refers to the notion
that a person concludes that he is giving more reinforcement
to another than he is receiving from that person. Under
these conditions, the person is likely to devalue what
reinforcement is given and not be as attracted to the other

person. Suppose, for example, that you were very attracted to a woman in your psychology class. You provide reinforcement for her in the form of dates and social attention. A relationship develops and as time passes you begin to feel cheated and taken for granted. At first, the complaints are vague, but eventually you put your finger on it. She isn't putting as much into the relationship as you are. Under these conditions of reward imbalance, you will tend to become less attracted to this person.

REWARD IMBALANCE: A situation in which another person provides less rewards to you than you provide to that person. Or conversely, a situation in which another person likes you more than you like him/her. In both cases, attraction tends to be reduced.

*10. What is reward imbalance? Give an example.

Another exception to the attraction effect of reinforcement is ingratiation. In this situation, the person providing reinforcement has something to gain by doing so. If students can get better grades by buttering up the professor, he/she will receive many compliments. Ingratiation arouses suspicion and reduces the effect of the reinforcement. (Dichoff, 1961). In some cases we can discriminate ingratiation very easily. When a person compliments us in a way that is too discrepant with our own self-evaluation, we are likely to suspect insincerity (Berscheid & Walster, 1969). You probably can't tell Herbert Homely, the ugliest guy on campus, that you think he's cute, without arousing some suspicion. Such ingratiation may result in reduced potency of the reinforcement.

INGRATIATION: Reinforcement provided by another person who has motives other than sincere attraction to the object of his reinforcement.

*11. Give an example of ingratiation.

The final exception to the potency of reinforcement in interpersonal attraction is satiation. Satiation is the tendency for a reinforcement to become less effective the more that it is provided. You get filled up on food rein-

forcers after Thanksgiving dinner. You get fed up with the
social reinforcers of roommates at times. Or you get satiated on social attention from members of the opposite sex.
In attraction research, strangers have been shown to be
more effective sources of social reinforcement than familiar
people (Harvey, 1962), thus exemplifying some truth in the
statement that "the grass is greener on the other side of
the fence."

SATIATION: A reduction in the power of a reinforcer due to
its being provided too much.

*12. What is satiation? How does it reduce the potency
of reinforcement?

Attraction, then, is a complex and multi-determined behavior. Mainly, however, we are attracted to those who
provide reinforcement. While there are some exceptions to
the effect of social reinforcement in enhancing attraction,
it is a good bet that those you like are providing reinforcement to you in some way.

*13. Review: List four determinants of attraction.

*14. Review: List three exceptions to the power of rein-
forcement in influencing attraction.

INITIAL COMMUNICATION DEVELOPMENT

Once people get together due to attraction, what happens next? Where does a relationship go after initial contact? The answer has to do with communication. People
begin to communicate with each other. A shaping process
can begin that either maintains or reverses the attraction
or repulsion of the first contact. In this section we will
discuss how communication develops from "small talk" to
intimate interchange.

It might be helpful to understand the process in this
phase of interpersonal relationships by thinking back to
occasions in which you were just starting to interact with
another. Imagine yourself having just met a person. What
do you talk about? Who says what? How do you feel? Let's
look at a fictitious initial interaction to jostle your
memory...

"Do you work with all these people?" Sam Suave asked of Mary Merry while they both waited for another drink at the office spring party.

"I just started last month and still feel like an outsider a little bit. What section do you work in?" Mary took her third gin and tonic from the bartender.

"I came with a friend. I don't work at Consolidated. I'm actually an insurance salesman. Shall we have a seat at that empty table? Where did you work before here?"

I didn't work. Went to school. This is a nice setup for a party. I really think the pool is beautiful," commented Mary as she sat down.

"Don't be surprised if someone is thrown into it before the evening's over. Peter has invited me to this party for the last three years and things tend to get a little out of hand. Better watch out for who's behind you."

They both looked around the patio in silence for a few seconds that seemed like hours. Sam noticed the provocative way Mary's eyebrow arched. He wanted to say something about it but felt it might be too forward at this point. Mary shifted her crossed legs and thought about the man sitting to her left. While he seemed nice enough, he was probably like the rest. She wanted to be direct and ask him why he was talking with her, and even more, why he had been looking at her all night. No, that might be too risky. Better see what he does. Sam spoke next.

"What did you study in school?" he said, thinking more about that eyebrow than about school.

"Computer science. Where did you go to school?" Mary felt the tedium of this small talk. She wanted some real conversation.

"Wichita Southern. My first wife and I were born in Wichita." Sam risked a self-disclosure.

"Oh, your first wife! How many times have you been married?" Her interest perked up.

"Just once. Three years ago for two years."

"I am just in the process of separating from my husband. It's not very easy after six years." A distant look came in her eyes.

"Yeah, I bet it must be lonely for you at times." Sam felt involved and wanted to know more about Mary. "Did you have children?"

"One. Mikey is living with his grandmother now. I should get him back in a few months." Mary thought he might not be like the rest. He seemed interested.

"Well, I've got a little one myself. Rita has her. I get to see her on second and fourth weekends. Do you get out much, Mary? You know, you have a nice way of cocking your eyebrow..."

"Now that's more like it," Mary thought.

                    ****

In that little vignette there are a number of important processes operating. The conversation begins with small talk. Essentially non-risky, small talk is a safe way of becoming acquainted with another person. At times it is tedious and even uncomfortable, but it has a definite place in communication--it breaks the ice. If we were too forward or intimate at the start of a relationship, it might offend or scare the other person. Small talk has the feature that it is safe because it is not substantive; that is, it has relatively little value to it in terms of interest level for the conversationalists.

SMALL TALK: Non-risky, non substantive conversation usually engaged in at the start of interpersonal relationships.

Eventually, however, small talk ceases to be reinforcing. It has mildly reinforcing qualities at first because of the novelty of the new person. But as people get more comfortable with one another the samll talk loses its reinforcing potential. It is then that risks may begin to be taken. Sam reveals he has been married--a slightly risky disclosure. Mary responds favorably to it, and Sam is reinforced. Sam, then, takes a bigger risk and points out the eyebrow. The more he gets reinforced for risking non-small talk conversation, the more intimate will the interchange become. In essence, risk taking is shaped during the initial stages of communication development. This shaping occurs because of the differential reinforcement that comes from successful risks.

If I disclose something to you that I consider risky and you guffaw, I am less likely to take such a risk with you again. On the other hand, if you respond favorably, my risk is successful, and I will probably do it again. Successful risks lead to trust, the belief that another person will treat you with care and respect and intimacy. Trust is a major part of good communication. Trust is born out of the differential reinforcement of risk taking in conversations.

RISK TAKING IN CONVERSATION: The communication of a relatively intimate topic whose acceptance by the other person is uncertain.

The above process shows that good communication, like any other behavior, becomes differentiated through reinforcement. Beginning with safe small-talk, risk-taking is differentially reinforced by the acceptance from the other person, trust is thereby established, and the channels of communication are opened for further interchange. We will talk about communication but the point to remember now is that communication is initially developed by way of the differential reinforcement of risk taking. We now turn our attention to the process of social perception.

*15. What is the function of small talk?

*16. In an initial communication, how do people get more comfortable with each other?

*17. What is the role of risk taking in conversation?

*18. Explain how trust develops because of differential reinforcement.

117

SOCIAL PERCEPTION

In this section we are concerned with how you come to
form impressions of other people. What is perceived in
other people is a complex process that is dependent on
previous experiences. We will see how your perceptual processes influence what you think of another person and thereby how you act toward that person. This process of interpersonal (or social) perception is learned in the early
years but continues to be formed and modified throughout
one's life.

Signal Detection Theory

Perception refers to the behavior of discriminating
something from other things. When you"perceive" the presence of a friend, what you are doing is making a discrimination between presence and non-presence. Such discrimination behavior is controlled by its consequences. Discriminating the presence of your friend when she is not there will
result in no meaningful consequence. However, if you perceive her when she is there you will be reinforced for that
discrimination(she will say "Hi" in return). As such,
perception is a special case of discrimination in which an
object or event sets the occasion for a response (perceiving)
to be reinforced.

PERCEPTION: Discrimination behavior in which an object
controls the behavior of perceiving it.

Perception is a branch of study in psychology separate
from personality or social psychology. However, the concept of perception has been applied to the discrimination
of social events as well. "Social" perception involves the
discrimination of or "perception" of the behavior of other
people. More basically it involves the discrimination of
the existence of another person. We can understand social
perception by looking at it as a response class that is controlled by the contingencies of reinforcement that have been
present in its development. Dr. Isreal Golddiamond of
Chicago University has applied one branch of the area of
perception, signal detection, to clinical psychology (Golddiamond, 1962). Dr. Don Whaley of North Texas State University has expanded and elaborated on the place of signal detection in understanding social perception (Whaley, 1978).
The section that follows is based on the ideas of these two

psychologists.

*19. What is perception? Give an example.

*20. What is social perception?

Signal detection can be another way of looking at
perception behavior. It involves two basic notions. The
first is that perception is a behavior like walking or talking, etc. The second notion is that whether an object or
event is <u>detected</u> (that is, discriminated) depends on how
important or consequential such detection has been in the
person's past. Essentially we tend to detect or notice
those things that are important to us. If you and I sat in
my living room, you probably wouldn't hear my daughter cry,
but I would. I have been reinforced for noticing the crys
of my daughter in my past, so I am more likely to notice
them in the future. Another example is the experience you
may have had when you **bought** a new car and suddenly noticed
how many other cars of that make and model were on the road.
Did a rush of purchases on that model occur? No, detection
of that car model is more likely for you now because you
have invested a significant sum of money in the car. Signal
detection is the process of specifying the likelihood of a
detection response by analyzing the consequences of such
detection.

SIGNAL DETECTION: Specification of the likelihood of wheth-
                     er or not an object or event will be
                     detected based on how important or con-
                     sequential detection is.

*21. What are the two basic notions of signal detection
     theory?

*22. Give two examples of how important consequences in-
     fluence signal detection.

*23. Define signal detection.

The social signals that are noticed also depend on how
important or consequential such notice is. We will specify
some of the many classes of social signals that are detected
and that contribute to the formation of an impression about
another person. But first let's look at some empirical support for the fact that perception is modified through reinforce-

ment.

Stone (1967) performed an experiment in which reinforcement for perceiving autokinetic movement (the apparent movement of a point of light against an otherwise dark back-
ground) greatly increased reports of having perceived the
movement. Subjects not reinforced reported no change in
perception and subjects who were given negative feedback
for perceiving the effect reported less detection of it.
James and Lott (1964) reinforced children by giving them
nickels for interacting with some children but not others.
Results showed that target children who were associated with
reinforcement were perceived as more likeable. And
finally Mausner (1954) showed that subjects who were not
reinforced for estimating the length of a line (that is,
were told their estimates were incorrect) were more likely
to be influenced in subsequent line judging tasks by the
judgments made by a group of people. On the other hand
subjects who were told that their estimations were correct
were less influenced by the group. These and other studies
show that what is perceived is determined, at least in
part, by reinforcement.

*24. Cite research that supports the notion that perception
      is influenced by reinforcement.

Signal detection, then, is the study of whether or not
an evenet or object (signal) in a person's world will be
detected. Such detection is determined by the consequences
it has. You can see the importance of the contingencies of
reinforcement analysis in understanding signal detection.
An object (cue) sets the occasion for detection (response)
to be reinforced (consequence). Of course, it is obvious
that what you detect in a person will influence what you
think about her. If you detect the physical beauty of someone, you form a different impression of that person than if
you detect the person's loyalty. The major point of signal
detection is that what the perceiver detects is dependent on his/
her past experience as much as (if not more than) it is dependent on the characteristics of the perceptual object. We now
now discuss signal detection by enumerating the social signals tha
that are detected in interpersonal relationships.

*25. How does isgnal detection apply to the contingencies
      of reinforcement?

*26. What is the major point of signal detection?

Social Signals

As you make contact with or are interacting with a person, the signal detection process is operating. The signals you as a perceiver detect are in large measure part of your "personality." Unique past histories of reinforcement cause some people to pick up on one class of signals, whereas other people pick up on another class of signals. Regardless of what the characteristics of the object or event (potential signals) are, what is detected depends on the perceiver's history of reinforcement. Signal detection, therefore, refers to the perceiver's behaviors, not the perceived's signals.

*27. Signal detection refers to the _____ _____, not the perceived object.

The range of potential social signals is almost infinite and only a sample will be treated here. The major point to remember is that social reality to one person differs from the social reality of another person. This difference is due to the difference in the past histories of reinforcement for detecting some signals as opposed to others. For example, the client who is called paranoid has a history of being reinforced for detecting persecutory signals; that is, comments and acts that he interprets as persecuting him. The real intent of the "persecutory" comments is immaterial. The paranoid's history causes him to detect them as such and that is his reality. In a sense, then, social perception is somewhat arbitrary. We construct our own reality. Fortunately, however, most of us are fairly accurate in what we detect and how we interpret it is the way it really is. The potential, however, for perceptual distortion is inherent in the perceptual process. Let us now look at some of the signals we detect while interacting with others.

*28. Why is the social reality of two people bound to be different? Give an example.

We talked about physical characteristics when discussing attraction. There are some specific classes of physical appearance signals that influence how we relate to others. Clothing is a class of signals that can be detected. It may be, for example, that men are more likely to detect dresses with low necklines than pant suits. The past history of reinforcement of males is the key in understanding

why this would occur. It is important to note that certain
styles of attire will lead to the formation of certain impressions. The elderly man who wears faded blue jeans and
jacket with a bright red polka-dot shirt will elicit a
certain impression. The same goes for someone wearing cow-
boy boots and a western hat, a grey pin-striped three-piece
suit, or someone wearing no bra. The signals we detect
provide information which we use to form impressions.

Makeup is another class of signals. Modern society
encourages the usage of facial makeup and the extent of
such makeup influences impression formation. What do you
think, for example, of a person with a half-inch of powder
on the face, or long eyelashes, or rouge on the cheeks?
Names are another set of signals of importance. "Herbert"
may strap a young man with a difficult stereotype to overcome. Body odor also influences impressions. In a crowded
elevator, what   you think of a person who smells like an
over-ripe rutabaga is influenced by the signal of odor.
The cologne of a previous lover is one of the easiet signals
to detect for many people.

Eye contact is an especially important set of signals.
The person who avoids eye contact may be thought of as shy
(or perhaps crooked). People who make too much eye contact
may be viewed as pushy,but someone who has the skills of
appropriate eye contact can be ascribed with other characteristics such as confidence. The class of signals called
body language is a popularly known set of social signals.
Such things as distance, touch, posture, and facial expression are often taken to mean things and thereby influence
impressions. Hall (1966) has reviewed some of the possible
signals in this class. Voice qualities are another set of
signals. For example, we can attribute obnoxiousness to a
person with a loud voice or fear to a person with a quaver-
ing voice.

*29. Certain sets of signals lead to certain _____.

*30. Describe several sets of social signals that are
      detected. Give examples of impressions they lead to.

Words are a final set of signals we detect. These may
be the most pervasive class of social signals because words
can be symbolic for so many things. Words are, probably, more
precise than some of the other signals mentioned, but can

be sometimes still possessing arbitrariness. "I love you"
means different things to different people. Similarly,
"loaded" words have been associated with significant consequences in the past and could be presently easily detected by a person with the right history. Calling someone
"stupid" who has suffered educational humiliation by being
placed in a slow learnersclass may stimulate sensitive
areas in that person. In any case, what is said to you is
as much a set of social signals as the other classes already discussed. These signals are detected immediately in
the context of interpersonal relating. They then lead to
the formation of impressions about what the person is like.
That impression in turn influences other aspects of the
relationship. We will now propose a scheme for the process of interpersonal relationships that encompasses all
the processes discussed so far.

*31. Why are words a class of social signals that is more
    precise than other signals but still can be somewhat
    arbitrary?

A SCHEME FOR INTERPERSONAL RELATING

The scheme described here contains five stages and
is depicted in Figure 6-1. It is not meant to be an exact
representation of what happens in interpersonal relationships. Such schemes are never totally exact; they are
merely ways of organizing what we already know about something. Since we don't really know everything yet, the
scheme is incomplete. However, it will organize already
known facts and aid in understanding of what happens in relationships.

SIGNALS DETECTED (PAST HISTORY)	GENERAL IMPRESSION FORMED	EXPECTATIONS FOR ACTION	ACTION	GOOD OR BAD COMMUNI- CATION

Figure 6-1: A scheme of interpersonal relationships

123

At first you are around a person. We discussed the influence of chance and attraction in determining whom you will be around . Being around another allows you to get information about that person. You detect the signals that you have been reinforced for detecting in the past. An impression is then formed on the basis of the information about the person that you have filtered through your biases, etc. We haven't talked a great deal about this impression except to provide some examples when discussing signal detection. Essentially, this is a general impression expressed in attitudinal or emotional judgements. A classmate or a roommate is strong-willed and you like that. A new co-worker is judged (on the basis of signals detected) to be antisocial and you don't like that. A professor is perceived by you to be conceited and that gives you mixed feelings. There is an entire area of theory and research in social psychology involved in understanding impression formation (e.g., Warr and Knapper, 1968). A treatment of these findings is beyond the scope of this book. We are most interested in the fact that an impression is formed on the basis of signals detected.

The impression that is formed has the effect of causing expectations for action, the third step in the scheme. You expect a person whom you perceive to be gentle to act in a certain way (not use four-letter words, smile, touch, etc.). When your impression of someone holds that he is competitive, you might expect him to work hard at doing better than you. If your impression of a handsome man is that he is "stuck up," you may not expect him to bother you. These expectations for actions come from the cultural and personal stereotypes (impressions) of what a particular kind of person will do. You may be quite conscious of the expectations or they may be automatic and non-verbal. In the latter case, you usually know you have an expectation after it is confirmed or disconfirmed. You might, for example, only realize that you expected blond women to be unintelligent after you came across one who was bright, articulate, and interested.

*32. How and why do impressions lead to expectations for action?

*33. Under what condition will expectations be made known to you only after they are disconfirmed?

Expectations are a double-edged sword, both good and bad. They result in predictability, a feature of the world by which humans are reinforced. In a single day, the amount of information that is assimilated by a person is very great. In order to take it all in, we organize things into impressions and expectations. Such organization helps us predict what will happen in our worlds. The ability to predict can make us feel better (since we perceive we have some control), and it may make us more effective in dealing with the environment. Everytime you get in an automobile, for example, you are predicting the brakes will work. It's a good thing we can predict and that we expect things to be a certain way.

On the other hand, expectations are bad because they put people in pigeon holes. A husband is expected to remember his wife's birthday and when he doesn't feelings are hurt. Many times the hurt feelings are unnecessary. The birthday really didn't matter, but what's bad is that the expectation was not confirmed. Sometimes we create unrealistic expectations and it is difficult for others to meet them. We shall see shortly that expectations can be a major source of relationship problems. This is especially true when the expectations are not articulated. If you expect your girlfriend to write letters to you but you never tell her your desires, she probably won't write which in turn may hurt your feelings. If you expect your roommate to turn out the overhead light at 11:30 but don't tell her that you shouldn't expect her to turn out the light. The point that expectations are bad because they are often broken and cause us to feel bad is a crucial idea in interpersonal relating.

*34. The good thing about expectations is that they
      provide _____.

*35. Why are expectations bad?

The next stage of the scheme is action. Something is done. Based on what is expected from the other person, you behave in a certain way around that person. You might, for example, introduce yourself to someone whom you expect will be attracted to you. You might avoid someone you expect doesn't like you. The action part of the relationship is maintained by the consequences of the action. If you ask a woman out whom you expect will accept, and she doesn't,

125

you probably won't ask her out again. If you expect a professor to be a very friendly person, you might go to her office and try to get to know her. However, if she more or less ignores you, the rate of "getting to know her" would decrease.

Action often implies some form of communication when it involves interpersonal relationships. Our communication with someone can be good or bad. Communication is the last step in the scheme. Good communication implies that both parties are saying what they want to and hearing what the other is saying. Bad communication is usually character- ized by imbalance. One isn't getting the message across. The two people don't know exactly where they stand with each other. Since communication is a very vital aspect of rela- tionships we will devote the next section to the presen- tation of some of the principles of good and faulty com- munication.

*38. The action part of interpersonal relating is often

_____.

*39. Review: Describe a scheme of interpersonal relation- ships.

COMMUNICATION

Communication is defined by a dictionary of psycholo- gical terms (Chaplin, 1975) as the process of transmitting or receiving signals or messages. In the last two decades, psychologists have become very interested in this process, because human communication is central to the experience of being human. It is doubtful that anything you do takes up more of your time and attention than trying to get your ideas across to someone else or trying to receive what someone else is communicating. The style of communication in western culture is changing. Carl Rogers (1968) has noted that people are becoming more and more open in what they disclose about themselves and what they want to hear disclosed from other people. There is no doubt that com- munication is a very complex activity influenced by a variety of variables. In this section, some instances of faulty communication and effective communication will be explored.

Faulty Communication

We will discuss five separate mistakes in communication here. The common factor in all of them is that what someone says (or doesn't say) results in misunderstanding or negative emotions. The goal of communication is to express what you feel and/or want. In the cases presented below such expression is not obtained.

Assuming without checking out is a problem in effective interchange. In this instance, one party assumes that the other feels or thinks a certain way. But the assumption is never verified. We touched on this problem when considering the attitude of scientific empiricism. Suppose your husband comes home from work very fatigued and relaxes by reading the paper and watching TV. You take this behavior to mean that he finds you boring. By laboring under this assumption for some period of time, you begin to get angry at your husband, which causes him to become angry with you. The basic assumption was never checked out; the marital problem results because you didn't ask him if his behavior was due to boredom.

Take another example. A worker feels that his boss is displeased with his work because the boss never gives compliments or praise. In point of fact, the boss simply doesn't give praise directly to any employees. But the worker's assumption affects him just the same. His work rate goes down and the boss has to "call the worker on the carpet." This confirms the worker's assumption that the boss is displeased with him. The incorrect assumption could have been checked out by saying to the boss, "I get the impression from you that you think I'm not doing a good job". Ineffective communication can be avoided by checking out assumptions.

ASSUMING WITHOUT CHECKING OUT: Having the impression that a person feels or thinks a certain way without asking the person to verify the assumption.

*40. What is the common factor involved in faulty communication?

*41. What is "assuming without checking out?" Give an example.

Expectations have been discussed as both good things and bad things. Here expectations are considered faulty because they often lead to undesirable outcomes. A parent expects an offspring to go to college. When the offspring doesn't, bad feelings result. A teacher expects a student to take a certain class. When the student doesn't, the teacher lowers his opinions of the student. A man expects his girlfriend to be attracted only to him. When she displays attraction for others, he feels cheated. The problem with expectations is that they are our own ideas about how someone else should act. Obviously our ideas don't make a difference in determing how a person acts. Other variables (consequences, that person'a goals, etc.) are more important. Nonetheless the negative emotions still result when our expectations are broken.

A solution to this is to try not to hold any expectations about what the other person should do. This is a very difficult thing to achieve but it is possible to reduce our expectations and then to inform the other person of what we expect of him/her. This latter strategy is important. It gives the other person the ability to tell you that something is an unrealistic expectation and it should not be held. Hard feelings can often be short-circuited in this manner. An open and respectful interchange is developed between the two people when they let each other know what their expectations are. Otherwise expectations have a high probability of not being met. People don't always act the way we wish them to; they act in ways determined by other variables.

EXPECTATIONS: Anticipating that a person will behave in a certain manner. These often lead to negative feelings when they are not met.

*42. What is the problem with expectations?

*43. What can be done to avoid broken expectations?

Passive aggression is another instance of faulty communication. It involves the indirect expression of anger. Once in a while people experience anger. Much of that anger is interpersonal. You're mad at your roommate because he snores at night. A boss is angry with one of her workers because the worker arrived late for the third day in a row. Passive aggression is occurring when anger is ex pressed in a passive, indirect way. Fred Fan wants to go to the baseball game. He informs his wife he is going. She gets angry because he's going out again. Rather than tell Fred, however, she pouts. She slams the dishes down in front of Fred at dinner. Not a word is spoken while they eat. Fred ventures an inquiry, "What's the trouble, Myrtle?"

"Nothing!" she snaps back, gritting her teeth. Fred decides not to go to the game. Myrtle smiles begrudingly.

Most of us have received the "silent treatment" before. Being treated in a passive-aggressive manner is a hard thing to take. Usually it generates a feeling of guilt in the person who is its target. The problem with passive aggression is that, oftentimes, the indirectness makes it ineffective. The target person doesn't know what she is being made to feel guilty for. It is usually much better to be direct in the expression of angry feelings. Such assertive behavior will be discussed shortly.

PASSIVE AGGRESSION: The indirect expression of anger by way of forced silence, pouting, and/or displaced hostility.

*44. What is passive aggression? Give an example.

*45. What feeling does it lead to? Why doesn't it work?

A fourth instance of faulty communication is reward imbalance. This notion, already discussed, is when one person gives a certain amount of reward to the other, but the other gives either much more reward or much less. Reward imbalance can lead to a state of discontent. A common example of reward imbalance is when one person takes another for granted. A husband works all day and when he comes home he makes no comments on the mowed lawn, the new curtains, the clean house, and the seven-course meal. He isn't providing enough reinforcement for the things his wife has done. Eventually her behavior will undergo extinction and along the way there will be emotional outbursts of anger and discontent. Everyone needs to be appreciated and reward imbalance is a state of affairs that prevents mutual appreciation.

Not listening is the final communication problem presented here. Sometimes we have other things on our mind and we just don't listen to what someone is telling us. We often assume we know what another will say <u>before</u> he/ she says it. At some later time when the information from the message we didn't listen to becomes imporant, we aren't able to function efficiently. A wife may tell her husband in a number of ways that their sexual relationship is un-fulfilling. Sex isn't important to him so he doesn't lis-ten. Anger and resentment build up and the two may separate. Life can become easier if attempts are made to take the time to understand where others are trying to communicate.

<u>NOT LISTENING</u>: Not paying attention to the exact message being sent by another person.

These instances of faulty communication are all cases of incomplete messages not given clearly and directly enough or not received completely. Accurate communication is hard work. To understand what another person is communicating requires diligence and effort. In the principles of ef-fective communication we can see the extent to which atten-tion to detail is important.

*46. What is a common example of reward imbalance in inter-personal relationships? Give an example.

*47. What is "not listening?" Give an example.

*48. What do all instances of faulty communication exem-plify?

<u>Effective Communication</u>

We will present five notions that are integral to get-ting your ideas across to other people. Basic to all of these is the notion of reciprocity or mutuality. Masters and Johnson (1974), sex therapists, have discussed how im-portant mutuality is in adequate sexual functioning. Like-wise, many other writers have noted its importance in inter-personal communication (e.g., Strayhorn , 1977). Essentially, reciprocity refers to the fact that both people hold the belief that they are understanding each other. For example, a girl feels her boyfriend knows what she needs to be happy in terms of the amount of time they spend together. She also knows that he knows she feels that way. He, in turn, feels the same way (that she knows what he needs) and that she knows he feels that way. Such mutuality comes about through effort at positive communication. We will now turn to the ways to achieve reciprocity.

RECIPROCITY: Mutually held beliefs that one understands another person and is being understood by the other person.

*49. What is reciptocity? Why is it important to effective communication?

Self-disclosure is the first consideration in effective communication. You have to tell others how and what you feel and think in order for them to understand you. Rubin (1973) has researched disclosure extensively. One of the things he has found is that a moderate amount of self-disclosure causes better reactions in others than does a low amount or a high amount. Of course, in an intimate relationship disclosure is likely to be greater than in a less intimate one. Some psychologists feel that extensive disclosure is warranted (e.f., Stevens, 1975). Others feel that what you tell about yourself should be discriminatory. The latter position may be closer to the truth since most people probably don't share everything they think and feel. But when it comes to communicating, some disclosure, especially when it concerns feelings or thoughts important to the other person, is necessary.

SELF -DISCLOSURE: Revealing feelings and thoughts you hold.

*50. Define self-disclosure. Discuss whether it should be done a great deal or not very much.

Honesty or sincerity is the next ingredient in effective communication. While it may be possible to disclose too much about yourself, it is never possible to be too honest about what you say. There are, however, those that advocate "controlled dishonesty" as long as it doesn't hurt anyone else (e.g., Heinlein, 1973). However, dishonesty and lying may lead to an erosion of trust. Such a breakdown in trust occurs when someone is caught in the act of dishonesty. When trust breaks down, communication takes a totally different direction. Intimate disclosure decreases and small talk increases. Consideration of the possible consequences of dishonesty, then, may tempt one to opt for being honest.

Additionally, the perception of sincerity of others'

131

disclosures is a well-researched process. People can detect dishonesty or insincerity fairly easily (Middlebrook, 1974). Four processes have been shown to be important in the detection of sincerity. First is whether or not the person's message is consistent with what we already know about the person. Next is whether or not we receive confirmation about the person's sincerity from other people. Third is whether or not the person has any external pressure to influence the other in a specified way. The professor who receives compliments on his teaching during final exams is an example. Finally is the presence of a prior expectancy or stereotype as in the case of "all old people are honest." Since honesty is a crucial aspect of communication, it is well to learn how to be that way.

*51.   What is a likely result of being dishonest in interpersonal communication?

*52.   What are the four processes involved in detecting sincerity?

   Another aspect of effective communication is asserting negative feelings. As a remedy for passive aggression, assertion is an important part of effective interchange. By learning how to assert your negative feelings (anger, fear, resentment, etc.), you let people know where you stand. Others then know better what to do and how to act around you. Usually the thing that holds people back from being assertive about negative feelings is the belief that it will hurt other people's feelings. In most cases this doesn't happen. Other people respect those who can be assertive (e.f., Alberti & Emmons, 1975). An additional positive outcome that results from assertion is that problems and conflicts come to the forefront and are more likely to get worked out.

ASSERTING NEGATIVE FEELINGS: The disclosure of negative thoughts and feelings to other people.

   Positive assertion is just as important. Positive assertion is an antidote for reward imbalance and involves the sharing of one's positive feelings about other people and their actions. It is a skill to be able to tell a husband or wife that you love him or her and appreciate all he or she has done for you. When communication is at its most efficient peak, positive assertion is operating at a

132

high rate. This aspect of communication is only beginning to be investigated. We can expect it to become more and more important in our understanding of good relationships.

POSITIVE ASSERTION: Sharing positive thoughts, feelings, and feedback with others.

*53. What is asserting negative feelings? What usually holds one back from being this way?

*54. _____ _____ is an antidote for reward imbalance.

*55. Why is positive assertion so important to interpersonal relationships?

A final feature of effective communication is active listening. By taking certain steps it is possible to make sure that you let the other person know you have received his message. The steps involved are simple but sometimes require constant prompting until they become automatic. The steps presented here are derived from Worrel and Nelson (1974) but there are many other sources (e.g., Gorden, 1970) that describe active listening. In order to show others that you have heard what they have said, you should stop doing other things, focus on the other person, let the person finish his/her message, and repeat back to the person what you thought you heard. This will set up a dialogue that will enable the message to be communicated. This process reduces the rate of not listening and improves communication.

*56. List the steps in active listening.

We have briefly explored some of the aspects of good and bad communication. There is much more but space constraints prevent an in-depth analysis. The point to be derived here is that interpersonal relationships begin and end with some kind of communication. This brief treatise on communication will help us to understand how relationships work.

EXTROVERSION/INTROVERSION

So far we have discussed a scheme for observing interpersonal relationships. We have seen that such relationships are motivated and maintained by a wide variety of reinforcers, such as social attention, sex, and so on. However, one of the most active areas of theory and research in personality has been the topic of extroversion/introversion (Eysenck, 1973) and the dimension of personality can be viewed as a motivating force in interpersonal relationships. In this section we will briefly review some of the theory and research pertinent to extroversion. Extroversion is relevant to interpersonal relationships since many people think of social interaction when referring to extroversion. In common usage, extroversion refers to how "outgoing" or gregarious a person is. On the other end of the dimension, introversion, reference is made to a shy and retiring type of person. While we have chosen to use the majority of this chapter to focus on a scheme for understanding inter-personal relationships, a brief treatment of extroversion is in order since it has spawned considerable research.

What is Extroversion/Introversion?

The following quote, from Eysenck and Eysenck (1964), is a good description of the two poles of the extroversion dimension:

> The typical extrovert is sociable, likes parties, has many friends, needs to have people to talk to, and does not like reading or stydying by himself. He craves excitement, takes chances, often sticks his neck out, acts on the spur of the moment, and is generally an impulsive individual. He is fond of practical jokes, always has a ready answer, and gen-erally likes change; he is carefree, easygoing, optimistic, and likes to "laugh and be merry." He prefers to keep moving and doing things, tends to be aggressive and loses his temper quickly; alto-gether his feelings are not kept under tight con-trol, and he is not always a reliable person.

> The typical introvert is a quiet, retiring sort of person, introspective, fond of books rather than people; he is reserved and distant except to in-timate friends. He tends to plan ahead, "looks before he leaps," and distrusts the impulse of the moment. He does not like excitement, takes matters of everyday life with proper seriousness, and likes a well-ordered mode of life. He keeps his feelings under close control, seldom behaves in an aggres-sive manner, and does not lose his temper easily.

He is reliable, somewhat pessimistic and places
great value on ethical standards.

We can see that the extroverted person has a higher
rate of interpersonal interaction than does the introvert.
It may even be that the extrovert and introvert differ with
regard to the nature of their interpersonal relationships.
For example, the extrovert may be more likely to have relationships in which manipulation of the other person is a
key motivating force. Introverts, on the other hand, may
have relationships characterized by mutual influence. Research concerning differences between extroverts and introverts has addressed such questions. Wilson (1978) has
reviewed a great deal of research on the differences between
extroverts and introverts. Among other things extroverts
are not as sensitive to stimulation, they are not as good
at vigilant tasks, are more prone to try to please others,
respond better to social situations, are more practical,
learn better in informal learning situations, have better
"social poise," choose "people-oriented"professions, are
more suggestible, take more risks, are more likely to break
laws, and do better at social forms of psychotherapy. It
is apparent, then, that extroverts spend considerably more
time engaging in actions that bring stimulation and excit-
ment. Introverts are more content to engage in less
stimulating and/or social activities.

Measurement

The most common personality inventory measure of extroversion is the Eysenck Personality Inventory (Eysenck & Eysenck, 1964). This is a fifty item true/false questionnaire.
Sample items include: Do you often long for excitement?
Do you do things on the spur of the moment? Do other people
think of you as being very lively? The questionnaire is a
well researched one and possesses the necessary qualities
of a good paper and pencil measure (that is, it has reliability and validity, is difficult to fake, and so forth).
However, as with all self-report measures, the Eysenck
Personality Inventory is limited. Other measures such as
rates of behavior in social situations, social skills, and
so forth are also useful ways to measure extroversion/intro-
version. Another aspect of the measurement of extroversion
is the idea that some people may want to interact more but
can't because they don't have the necessary social skills
or because they are afraid of social rejection. It is

important, then to measure the person's intention to interaction as well as the person's interaction level.

The Development of Extroversion

Eysenck (1967) proposed the idea that differences in
extroversion are determined by differences in the arousal
level of the cerebal cortex of the brain. This theory
states that introverts are more highly aroused in the cortex
of the brain than are extroverts. The introvert, therefore,
has to exercise more control over his/her social environment
in order to keep the arousal level at an acceptable one.
In other words intense social excitement would create greater arousal in the cortex of the introvert. This state of
affairs would tend to be unpleasant. Therefore, the introvert tends to shy away from exciting activity. The extrovert, on the other hand, would be reinforced by exciting
activity because this person has less cortex arousal to
begin with and increasing the arousal level would be reinforcing. Therefore, social excitement is more reinforcing.

Eysenck and others have tried to show that the behavior
of introverts and extroverts fit the above theory. For
exmaple, it has been found that introverts tolerate sensory deprivation better, have lower sensory thresholds,
are more susceptible to pain, and are better at vigilance
tasks than extroverts (Geen, 1976). All of these differences
can be accounted for by the idea that introverts have higher
levels of arousal in the cortex than extroverts. However,
this physiological theory may not be the total picture.

The behavioral history of the person is also an influence on extroversion. Whether one has been reinforced
or pusnished for outgoing behavior helps determine the rate
of behavior in that response class. (McGinnis & Ferster,
1971). Whether one has had the opportunity to learn the
skills of social interaction will influence rate and nature
of interaction (Curran, 1977). Obviously, a person will be
less likely to interact if he/she doesn't know what to do
or say. And finally, whether or not a person has learned
to be afraid of social rejection will affect the rate of
extroversion (Jaremko, 1980). If someone is afraid of
interaction, then there will be less of a chance to behave
that way. It is apparent, therefore, that extroversion/in-
troversion is a class of behaviors that are developed by
an interaction between the person's physiological character-

istics and behavioral history.

Changing Extroverted Behavior

If the assumption is made that some forms of introverted behavior are not healthy for the person, then it
stands to reason that there should be some methods for
changing such behavior. It may be that some introverted
people are in need of change since they may experience loneliness and isolation as a result of being less than socially
active (Shaver, 1979). On the other hand, some extroverted
people may be in need of change because they are abusive to
others or they are doing things detrimental to themselves
(transient relationships and the like). The topic of assertiveness training will be presented in the context of
changing extroversion/introversion behavior. Assertiveness
training is a way to learn social skills that will allow a
person to express him/herslef more accurately and completely
without violating the rights of others. (Lange & Jakubowski,
1977). It is a way to enhance human communication and foster
openness and sharing.

Assertiveness training consists of teaching,through
instruction, example, and practice,the most effective way
to get one's ideas and/or feelings across. Butler (1976)
suggested four areas in which people need to be assertive:
expressing positive feelings, expressing negative feelings,
setting limits, and standing up for oneself. The training
involves learning how and when to be assertive in these four
areas. The assertive response has four elements: stating
what you think or feel, stating what made you think or feel
that way, stating what you want from another person, and
stating how you think the other person is affected by your
assertive response. An example of an assertive response in
the expressing positive feelings category would be: "You
make me feel very useful when you ask for my advice. I hope
you continue to seek me out because I think you enjoy making
me feel good." The bulk of assertion training is devoted
to learning and practicing specific instances of assertiveness like the above. It is important to learn when to be
assertive and when not to be assertive. The training attempts
to achieve that also. Assertion training can be an effective
way to change the behavior of someone who is overly introverted or overly extroverted. There is no doubt that interpersonal relationships would be more healty if more inter-
changes were assertive ones.

INTERPERSONAL RELATIONSHIP: EPILOGUE

We have seen the process that is involved when two people interact with each other. The influences of attraction, initial communication development, social percpetion, expectations, and effective or ineffective communication have been explored. The contention has been held that there is no single more important influence on our behavior than interpersonal relating. An understanding of these relationships will help us greatly to appreicate human personality. We also looked at the role of extroversion in motivating interpersonal communication. The person who is highly extroverted may have the kind of central nervous system that encourages a high rate of interaction.

CHAPTER 7

ANXIETY

Everyone of us has experienced the feelings of apprehension and dread that is often characterized by the term anxiety. In an interesting review about the history of the conceptions of anxiety, McReynolds (1975) points out that anxiety has been a major concern to man since the earliest days of civilization. As man became more and more individualistic, McReynolds contends, anxiety became a more common condition. Human beings experience the feeling of anxiety, in part, because of self-preoccupation. We fear rejection, humiliation, evaluation, abandonment, and personal harm. All of these subjective feelings can be seen as stemming from a well developed self-system. In this chapter we will explore anxiety by asking what it is, how it is measured, how it is developed, and how it may be changed.

Individuals differ with regard to how much anxiety they experience. While all people feel anxious at one time or another, some people are more prone to this experience than are others. In this sense, anxiety is a personality dimension along which people differ. However, it is also a response to a situational threat. We will touch on both varieties of anxiety in this chapter. Since the notion of anxiety has attracted a great deal of research activity, we have a good understanding of what it is, how it feels, and what can be done about it. Many of these ideas will be addressed in this chapter.

*1. Anxiety is both a _____ _____ and a response to situational _____.

WHAT IS ANXIETY?

While many people are all too familiar with what anxiety is and what it feels like, others are not aware of when they are anxious. Systematic investigation in attempting to describe anxiety has been done and has been helpful in understanding the idea. In this section, we will describe four somewhat overlapping models of the nature of anxiety.

Three Channel Model

Dr. Stanley Rachman of the Maudsley Hospital in England

discussed the nature of anxiety in a recent article (Rachman, 1976). He contended that anxiety is best conceived of as having three components: self-report, behavioral, and physiological. For the last ten or fifteen years research on the nature and treatment of anxiety has followed this model (Lang, 1970). The three channels of anxiety refer to the way in which the emotion is manifested. Each of the channels is presumed to be independent so that anxiety may be experienced in self-report but not in behavior or psychophysiology. Or it may be manifested in behavior but not the other two. While the independence of the three channels has been questioned by some researchers, in certain cases there is evidence that anxiety is experienced in only one or two of the channels, but not the others.

*2. What are the three channels of anxiety?

*3. What is meant that the channels are independent?

Self-report refers to the conscious cognitive experience of anxiety. It is the cognitive or verbal aspect of anxiety. When you are going out on a date with, the self-report aspect of anxiety manifests itself in comments to yourself about how anxious you feel. You might say, "I hope she enjoys my company," or "What if she doesn't like me?" These negative self-statements might be very explicit (i.e., you actually say the words to yourself) or they may be "conceptual" or intuitive (i.e., you think them without being aware of it, they are automatic (Langer, 1978)).

Behaviorally, anxiety is the avoidance of doing something. If you have a fear of riding elevators and don't do it, your anxiety is in part expressed behaviorally. We shall see the importance of behavioral avoidance in the development of anxiety in a later section. The psychophysiological channel of anxiety is composed of the autonomic nervous system activity that occurs when one is anxious: butterflies, sweaty palms, rapid heartbeat, and statements about certain physical changes going on in the body. The psychophysiological channel of anxiety is the physical changes occurring that are often commented on during the anxiety experience (the self-report component). As you approach the front of the room to give your speech in speech class, you may notice the fact that your heart is beating fast. The "noticing it" is the self-report component and the beating of the heart is the psychophysiological aspect.

Anxiety can be conceived, therefore, as having three channels of experience that can operate independently. Consider, for example, the person who is really upset by air travel but flies anyway. In this case the self-report and psychophysiological channels are operative, but the behavioral channel is not. Rachman's model, however, doesn't tell us how the three channels interact and influence each other. Another model, stress inoculation, provides a specific way in which to view the interaction of the three channels of anxiety.

THREE CHANNEL THEORY OF ANXIETY: A model of anxiety that holds that anxiety is experienced in three independent ways: self-report, behavioral, and psychophysiological.

*4. Describe each of the three channels of anxiety.

*5. Give an example of how the three channels of anxiety show independnece.

Stress Inoculation

Dr. Donald Meichenbaum of Waterloo University in Canada has designed a set of treatment procedures for helping people deal with stress (Meichenbaum, 1977). The package is called stress inoculation and has been shown to be effective in overcoming a wide range of anxiety responses (Meichenbaum & Jaremko, 1980). Part of the treatment involves teaching the person what anxiety is and how it works. This "educational model" is the aspect of stress inoculation with which we are interested here. The education model for stress inoculation was developed by Jaremko(1979) and is partly based on a theory of emotion developed by Stanley Schachter (1966). The model has by no means been unequivocally verified, but it does provide an idea of how the three channels of anxiety work together.

The model, depicted in Figure 7-1, is based on a cycle of anxious thoughts, feelings, and physical reactions. The cycle has the tendency to perpetuate itself unless something is done to break it. As seen in Figure 7-1, a stressor leads to some physical arousal (butterflies, etc.) The arousal leads to an appraisal or interpretation of the situation (stressor) as anxiety-provoking. This appraisal in turn leads to negative self-statements which generate more physical arousal starting the cycle again. When a person gets into the stress cycle, the only way to stop it is to avoid the stressor (behavioral channel) or control the physical and cognitive aspects of the anxiety. The stress inoculation treatment package attempts the latter.

From this model we can see that the three channels of anxiety all influence each other in such a way that often makes it appear that there is no anxiety in one of the channels. However, on closer inspection we can see that there may be activity in a particular component that is "automatic" and, therefore, not detectable. Such is the case when the appraisal of the situation is automatic. The person may not explicitly say to him/herslef that a particular situation is anxiety provoking; but, if asked, would no doubt report the presence of upset. Likewise, with the physical component, the physical change may happen so fast that the person doesn't "know" it. In the stress model, however, all three channels are present, no matter how concealed or automatic.

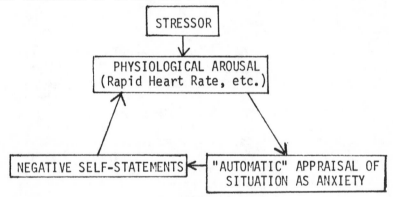

Figure 7-1: A Stress Inoculation Model of Anxiety
(From Jaremko, 1979).

*6. Describe the stress inoculation model.

*7. How can the stress cycle be stopped (two ways)?

As an example of how this model works let's consider public speaking anxiety. The prospect of giving a speech is a stressor. It makes your autonomic nervous system kick into action. Right before your speech, these physical symptoms are appraised as anxiety. You might say, "Boy, I'm nervous." The next step in the cycle for the anxious person is negative self-statements. These come in all forms: "What will the audience think of me?" "I'm going to forget my thoughts." "I'm not a good speaker." All of which have the effect of maintaining the physical arousal and the cycle. Usually if you go on with the speech, things calm down and you stop making the negative statements as you concentrate on what you are doing, i.e., speaking. Occasionally, however, the person panics, blows the speech, and stops the cycle by escaping the stressful situation. As we will see later this only makes it worse later; that is, the cycle will be even more likely to occur.

*8.   Explain the stress inoculation cycle by way of an
      original example.

It is important to remember that the model is presented here in a step-by-step way merely to show the processes involved. In fact, when anxiety is experienced, the processes seem to occur automatically with little conscious awareness. Additionally it is sometimes an anxious thought that sets off the physical arousal (Lazarus and Averill, 1972) which then goes into the rest of the cycle. The specificity of the model is helpful, however, in slowing the anxiety experience down enought to determine how the components interact.

STRESS INOCULATION MODEL OF ANXIETY: A model that views anxiety as a self-perpetuating cycle of physical arousal, anxious appraisal, and negative self-statements.

*9.   Thought Question: How might an anxious thought set
      off the stress cycle? (rather than physical arousal)

For most people one of the main reasons the stress cycle is broken is that the person becomes involved in the task demands of what he/she is doing. In the speech

143

example, the cycle may stop because the person becomes involved in the speech. Anxiety as a response interference phenomenon is another model to be dealt with here. I. G. Sarason has done considerable work with this idea (1972). We will now explore this model.

Response Interference

Dr. Sarason has investigated the notion of test anxiety during the last fifteen years. Test anxiety is the nervousness and tension that is experienced when one's work or one's self is being evaluated by others. In most research the test anxiety has been what college students feel when they are taking course exams and tests. Sarason has found that some people are more test anxious than others. He has investigated the cognitive, physiological and behavioral components of test anxiety.

*10. What is test anxiety?

What happens in test anxiety is that the person's anxious self-preoccupation interferes with what he needs to do on the test. If you are taking an important exam and begin thinking about what grade you will receive (negative self-statements), your concentration on the questions is diluted and your performance suffers. Sarason has repeatedly found this response interference in test anxious people. They report more negative self-statements when taking an exam, are more physiologically aroused, and do more poorly on the test than non-test anxious students. (Sarason, 1978). But, as important, is the fact that test anxious people experience internal events that interfer with what they are supposed to be doing. Test anxiety cause response interference.

*11. Test anxiety causes _____ _____.

The reason test anxiety causes response interference is that the person's attention is directed away from the task. Instead of paying attention to task relevant things, the person thinks about task irrelevancies. In a complex task, such misdirected attention will impair performance. Sarason and other researchers (e.g., Wine, 1971) have demonstrated the performance impairment caused by task irrelevant cognitions. Houston (1977) had discovered some of the content of task irrelevant cognitions in research

144

he did with college students. It was found that students
who worry about the results of their performance, who
compare themselves to others, and who deny the existence
of stress have more test anxiety and poorer performance.
Test anxiety, then, is the response interference caused
by task irrelevant cognitions that generate physiological
arousal and direct attention away from the task. It shall
also be pointed out that many situations other than exams
can cause test anxiety. Being evaluated in any way can
be a stressor that leads to test anxiety. Being on a
date, being watched, and giving a speech are only a few
examples of some stressors that can lead to response
interference.

RESPONSE INTERFERENCE: Attention directed away from a task
                        because of task irrelevant cogni-
                        tion. It occurs when an evaluation
                        situation causes test anxiety.

*12. Why does test anxiety cause response interference?

*13. What is the content of some of the task irrelevant
      cognitions discovered by Houston?

Types of Stressors

So far we have talked about what happens when a stressor affects a person. A list of common stressors will be
helpful in understanding the nature of anxiety. It should
be remembered that stressors, in general, will lead to the
same kind of anxiety responses. Those response patterns
include the interaction of the three channels of anxiety
(the stress inoculation model) and the task irrelevant
cognitions that cause response interference.

A stressor can be defined as anything that causes
physical tissue damage or "psychological" damage (Malott
& Whaley, 1976). Put another way, a stressor is anything
that causes "stress" (Selye, 1974). According to Dr.
Hans Selye, stress is the reactions of the body to stressors.
These reactions are common across situations and constitute
the definition of stress. Anything that causes them is
called a stressor. An ulcer is an example of tissue damage
reaction caused by a stressor. Response interference and
negative self-statements are examples of psychological
damage caused by stressors. Much research has been done

in determining what stressors are (Holmes & Raye, 1967)
and how people cope with them. A review of this research
is not necessary here, but you should know that many
factors have been identified that temper a person's response to stressors. Having control over the stressor, having choice between two stressors, whether the stress is
signaled or unsignaled, delayed or immediate, predictable
or unpredictable, all influence the potency of a stressor
(Glass & Singer, 1972). Two excellent reviews of these
data are provided by Lazarus (1966) and Geen (1976)
These authors show that stress is a complex process influenced by many variables.

*14.   What is a stressor? Give an example of physical
       damage and psychological damange caused by a stressor.

*15.   What are some of the variables that influence a stres-
       sor's effect?

    In this section we will merely list some of the common
stressors in modern life. Loneliness can often be stressful, as can conflict with a boyfriend or girlfriend
(husband or wife). Work pressures produce a great deal of
stress and strain. Values conflicts with parents or others
will cause stress. The area of social acceptance can be
seen as a stressor. Occupational choice might prove
stressful as well as job competition. Stressors like
financial problems, marital discord, social isolation are
commonplace. Sexual difficulties constitute a large class
of stressors. Religious questions, existential uncertainty,
and cultural paranoia have produced stress in today's life.
It should be apparent that stress is a common accompaniment
of our daily lives. Some behavioral scientists have seen
this preponderence of stress and seen the need to study
stress and how to cope with it. A multi-volume publication
edited by psychologists Charles D. Spielberger and I.G.
Sarason, Stress and Anxiety, is an example of such scientific effort (Spielberger & Sarason, 1975). Since stress
is such a pervasive influence, ways of understanding it
are important issues for modern society.

*16. List some common stressors.

State-Trait Anxiety

    A final model of anxiety to be covered here is an important idea in regarding anxiety as a dimension of personality . Dr. Charles Spielberger (1966) conceptualized two types of anxiety. State anxiety is a transitory emotional state that occurs in response to immediate situational influences. Trait anxiety refers to a relatively enduring individual differences in anxiety proneness. At one time or another all people will experience state anxiety in response to the stressors of life. However, individuals high in trait anxiety will respond to these stressors with more state anxiety than those low in trait anxiety. Spielberger's notions of state and trait anxiety are quite useful in drawing the distinction between anxiety as a specific response to a specific situation and anxiety as a dimension of personality. The state-trait notion assumes that there is an interaction between the situational specificity and individual differences of anxiety.

MEASURING ANXIETY

Accuracy in the measurement of anxiety may be as advanced as measurement in any other aspect of psychology. While there are still problems, procedural refinements have led to effective measures of anxiety. This section will present the general classes of anxiety measurement: self-report, cognitive measurement, and psychophysiological measurement.

Self-Report Measures

Earlier it was mentioned that anxiety is a dimension of personality as well as a response to situational stress. Speilberger developed a self-report measure of anxiety that measures both trait anxiety and state anxiety. The State-Trait Anxiety Inventory (STAI) (Speilberger, Gorsuch, & Lushene, 1970) is a widely used measure of anxiety. The flexibility as a measure of both trait and state conditions has contributed to its popularity.

The respondent is asked to indicate whether certain statements apply to him/her. Twenty such statements are used to describe how the person generally feels (trait anxiety) and twenty statements are used to describe how the person feels right now. As you would expect, under certain conditions all people will report state anxiety (e.g., taking a final exam). However, people differ in the extent of trait anxiety they report. Spielberger, et al (1970) describe many specific response tendencies that

147

have been measured by the STAI. For example, high trait people report more state anxiety during stress conditions than do low trait anxious people. While the STAI is a good self report measure we should remember the problems with self-report measures such as social desirability and lack of specific discriminatory ability.

*17. The STAI measures both _____ and _____.

*18. Describe the STAI.

Other self-report measures of anxiety are also available. Some measure trait anxiety such as the Taylor Manifest Anxiety Scale (Taylor, 1953) and others measure state anxiety such as the Multiple Affect Adjective Checklist (Zuckerman and Lubin, 1966). Mandler and Sarason (1952) devised the Test Anxiety Scale (TAS) as a measure of test anxiety. It is a 37 item true-false questionnaire that asks the respondent to indicate whether certain statements are true about him/her. It is frequently used in I.G. Sarason's work on test anxiety and has been shown to discriminate people high in test anxiety from those low in it. Examples of statements found in the TAS are given in table 7-1.

Table 7-1. Items from the Test Anxiety Scale

(T) If I were to take an intelligence test, I would worry a great deal before taking it.

(T) I sometimes feel my heart beating very fast during important tests.

(F) I really don't see why some people get so upset about tests.

(T) Even when I'm well prepared for a test, I feel very anxious about it.

*19. Describe the TAS.

Cognitive Measurement

An anxiety measurement approach that appears to hold promise is the specification of cognitions while a person is anxious (Kendal & Korgeski, 1979). Houston (1977) for example, asked students what they were thinking of while taking a final exam in a class. The statements given by the students were grouped into "cognitive categories" (worry, denial, social comparison, active mastery, and so forth). It was found that students who were high in test anxiety were more likely to be thinking interfering or task irrelevant thoughts. Thus, the presence of task irrelevant cognitions can be detected and these cognitions may be considered indications of anxiety.

*20. How can cognitions during anxiety be measured? Why is this a promising measure of anxiety?

Distline, Shanahan, & Jaremko (1977) extended Houston's approach by composing a multiple choice cognitive questionnaire. Students were to choose one or two classes of thoughts that were most similar to the thoughts they were having when taking a test. There were a total of nine classes of cognitions. Some classes indicated task relevancy, some indicated task irrelevancy. Results showed that highly test anxious students were more likely to choose the task irrelevant classes of cognition (worry and social comparison). In this way a quick and efficient way of measuring cognitive behavior in testing situations was developed. Another measure of cognitive activity in stressful situation that was evaluated by Jaremko, Hadfield & Lindsey (1979) makes use of videotaped vignettes. A series of eight scenes are shown to respondents who are asked to assume the role of one or more of the actors and actresses. They are asked what they would think, feel, and do if they found themselves in a situation like that depicted on the videotape. The scenes include strained conversation (small talk), jealousy, sexual conflict, social rejection, and other socially awkward scenes. Preliminary results with this approach has shown that people differ with regard to the content of their cognitions and that anxious people have cognitions that are different from non-anxious people. People can be screened on the basis of the content of their cognitive activity in stressful social situations. The importance of cognitive activity in the treatment of anxiety will be explored shortly.

149

*21. Describe two measures of cognitive activity during
       anxiety.

Psychophysiological Measurement

   The final area of anxiety measurement considered here
is physiological responding. Sophisticated equipment aids
the measurement of bodily functions that are related to
anxiety. There are several possible channels of psychophysiological recording that have been related to anxiety.
Most of these channels are energized by the sympathetic
branch of the autonomic nervous system. When a person is
anxious, the sympathetic nervous system is operative.

   Sympathetic nervous system response is characterized
by any or all of the following tendencies. Heart rate
monitors reveal an increase in beats per minute during
anxiety. Blood pressure also increases and is manifested
by a rise in standard units of pressure within the cir-
culatory system. Skin temperature decreases with anxiety
because blood vessels constrict and reduce blood flow thereby reducing the friction that warms the skin. Muscle
tension can be measured by an electromyograph (EMG) and increases in millivolts when anxiety is present. Rate of
breathing can also be measured since it has been shown to increase during anxiety. Skin conductance is a widely used
measure of anxiety. The surface of the skin becomes more
likely to conduct electrical charges when the person is
anxious. This change can be detected by two electrodes
positioned on the skin surface.

*22. The psychophysiological channels of anxiety are
       energized by the _____.

*23. Describe the channels measured in psychophysio-
       logical recording.

   Eventhough technology used to measure these psychophysical channesl is fairly advanced,measurement is sometimes difficult. Since people tend to react more strongly
in some channels than others (autonomic response specificity),
multi-channel measurement is best. However, having sensors,
electrodes and straps fastened to the body often interferes
with other activity and even makes the person somewhat
more responsive simply because he/she is being measured
(measurement reactivity), and sometimes, what is measured

is merely the person's external movement rather than sympathetic activity (movement artifact). There are, therefore, a number of difficulties in psychophysiological measurement. However, as the measurement technology advances, solutions to these problems may be found. In the meantime, psychophysical measreument is quite important to anxiety measurement.

*24. Why is multi-channel psychophysiological measurement better?

*25. Name three problems with psychophysiological measurement.

THE DEVELOPMENT OF ANXIETY

Where does anxiety come from? Is it present at birth or does it develop during the course of a person's life? In this section we will see that anxiety develops from both biological and environmental influences. There is a built-in behavioral potential for the human being to experience anxiety. However, anxiety also becomes associated with environmental cues throughout the person's life. Three separate mechanisms by which anxiety is learned will be explored in this section. Understanding how anxiety is learned or developed is the next step in controlling it.

Classical Conditioning

We have mentioned the sympathetic branch of the auto-nomic nervous system. This is the part of the physical system that takes over under conditions of stress. The organism's body becomes ready for fight or flight. Several specific physiological changes occur when the sympathetic system is operating. Digestion, elimination, and sexual activity stop. Heart rate speeds up and blood vessels constrict which raises blood pressure. Hormones are released into the blood stream. The person's body becomes ready for action.

Under certain circumstances these changes aid the survival of the creature. In a fight, decreased blood flow will result in less blood loss if injury occurs. The fact that the blood is closer to internal organs provides more energy to the brain and muscles which support vigorous activity. Hormones in the blood stimulate white blood cell counts and therby aid in fights against infection. The

151

entire sympathetic nervous system makes the creature ready for action. It is also the physical substrata of anxiety.

*26. Describe the physical changes brought about by the sympathetic nervous system.

*27. How do these changes aid survival?

Since the sympathetic nervous system has been developed over millions of years of evolution, the tendency for it to be activated is innate or automatic. There are certain events that energize this system. John Watson, an early behavioral psychologist performed an experiment with a human infant that demonstrated the effect of the system. Even more important, Watson showed how the reaction of the sympathetic nervous system could be conditioned, that is, attached to cues in the environment that were originally neutral.

In 1920 Watson (and a colleague, Raynor) energized the sympathetic nervous system of an infant by clapping two pieces of wood together near the infant's ear (Watson & Raynor, 1920). The noise startled (that is, the sympathetic nervous system was set off) the baby. This loud noise was paired with a rabbit with which the child was playing. Eventually, after enough pairings of the loud noise and the rabbit, the rabbit came to energize the sympathetic nervous system. In other words, the fear (sympathetic response) had been conditioned to the rabbit. This process is called classical conditioning (Pavlov, 1927).

*28. The responses of the sympathetic nervous system are _____ or _____.

*29. Describe Watson and Raynor's experiment with the infant.

*30. Why is this experiment important? What two points does it demonstrate?

In some ways anxiety is learned through classical conditioning. Traumas occur; a fall off a horse, being locked in a closet, being burned in a fire. These traumas, which induce sympathetic arousal, occur in the present of previously neutral cues in the world (horse, enclosed space, fire). The sympathetic activity gets conditioned to those cues and fear is learned.

The sympathetic activity from these conditioned cues can then generalize to other previously neutral cues (the fear of a horse generalized to the cues of being outdoors). However, this process of classical conditioning and its generalization only describes the physiological component of anxiety. The behavioral component is learned through avoidance conditioning. Sympathetic activity is unpleasant, whatever reduces it will be negatively reinforced. Avoiding the feared cue (outdoors) reduces the fear and the behavioral component of anxiety is thereby learned. The cognitive component comes about by way of the verbal community which gives words by which you describe the feared object and your response to it.

Some psychologists feel that the classical conditioning of a trauma will not occur unless a threat to the self-esteem of the person has taken place (e.g., Bonney, 1970). When a person's self-system is threatened, the sympathetic system is activated. This learning usually occurs somewhat later in a person'a life (after the self is well developed) but does represent an important class of traumas. Consider as an example the child who is placed in a slow learners' class in shcool. If this is a threat to his self-system he may develop school phobia. Anytime we are "bruised in the ego", the potential for the development of fear and anxiety is possible.

*31. How does classical conditioning work to condition fear? Give an example.

*32. Classical conditioning only explains the _____ component of anxiety. _____ _____ explains the behavioral component.

*33. What is a very important class of traumas that lead to fear and anxiety conditioning?

Avoidance Learning and Signal Detection

As we have mentioned, much anxiety is learned and maintained through the negative reinforcement of avoidance learning. Here's how it works: John Jock is made anxious by public humiliation (most of us are). He is chewed out by the football coach just about every day. Practice

becomes a very unpleasant experience. One day he complains
of a hip injury and misses practice. He avoids the usual
humiliation. A week later he avoids practice by complain-
ing of dizziness. A couple more instances of avoidance
result in John being highly reinforced (negatively) for
being injured. The negative reinforcer is that he gets
out of practice and therby avoids the humiliation. The
avoidance of practice also did something else for John
that is much worse than being injured.

The avoidance also reinforced the detection of the
feared object and the anxiety it generates. Next time,
in some other situation John Jock will be more likely to
detect that he is being humiliated. Since he has been
reinforced for avoiding, it is likely that the new humiliation he detects will also lead to avoidance. This will
in turn make it more likely that he will detect anxiety
sooner the next times.

After being dropped from the football team because
of injury, John is in Poli Sci class and gets into a discussion with his professor in which they disagree on
some point. He detects the public humiliation and feels
very anxious. The next time class comes up, he sleeps
through it and gets reinforced again for avoiding anxiety.
The avoidance only results in the anxiety becoming stronger.
Most probably never once did John Jock think that he was
"copping out." The verbal behavior of awareness usually
comes later. The avoidance learning of copping out and
increasing the detection of humiliation cues come first.

This is probably the major way in which people
learn anxiety. An event leads to the unpleasant response
of the sympathetic nervous system which is then avoided.
The avoidance behavior is negatively reinforced by escape
from the unpleasant-physical feelings and the detection
threshold of anxiety is decreased so that the next time
it takes less of the original event to set off the cycle.
Generalization quickly occurs becasue of the misperceived
anxiety-provoking events occur frequently. Anxiety is
learned and spread by avoiding it (Krasner & Ullman, 1973).

*34.   Explain how avoidance learning leads to the earlier
       detection of anxiety. Give an example.

*35. How does avoidance learning cause anxiety to be
      generalized?

      Even though avoidance learning and signal detection
are very useful in explaining the development of the physical and behavioral components of anxiety, the cognitive
component has yet to be explained. In order to explain
how this channel is learned we will discuss the role of
modeling in learning anxiety.

Modeling

      In Chapter 3 modeling was described as a process of
learning by observation. An event becomes a discriminative
stimulus for behavior that is topographically similar
to it. The point was also made that modeling is a major
way in which the verbal community influences our behavior.
We see others in our verbal community engaging in certain
behavior and model that behaivor. The example used was
self-reinforcement. We are imitating others reinforcing
us when we reinforce ourselves. This, we said, occurs
through generalized imitation. It's just another way
(besides differential reinforcement and the two questions)
that the verbal community influences us. The learning of
the cognitive component of anxiety can also be seen to
progress along the mechanisms of modeling.

      Not only do we observe others reinforcing themselves,
we also observe others putting themselves down. Part of
the "putting the self down" response class is the negative
self-statements often present in anxiety. These negative
self-statements,along with verbal appraisals of anxious
situations,constitute the cognitive component of anxiety.
We simple see others engaging in these behaviors when certain stimuli are present and imitate them when we are under
the same conditions. We imitate these cognitive behaviors
for two reasons. The first is generalized imitation--we
imitate almost anything. The second is that we have been
reinforced for describing our world. We, therefore, see
oursleves in a situation in which a stressor is inducing the
anxiety cycle and describe the process to ourselves (and
sometimes to others as well).

      An example will clarify this important process. Imagine

a youngster observing his mother and father engage in a
domestic quarrel. Tears flow, voices are raised, frowns
exchanged. The mother says that she is very upset due
to the husband's negligence. The child observes the situation and mother's behavior. He sees her cry, shake, talk,
and describe. This provides information that the child
will use later on to describe his/her own upset or anxiety
when he/she is presented with anxiety provoking situations.
Thus, it can be seen that the verbal component of anxiety
can come from the verbal community influence of modeling.

*36. Review: How does modeling work as a major mechanism
               of the verbal community?

*37. Review: What are the other two mechanism by which
               the verbal community influences us?

*38. Explain how the cognitive component of anxiety is
      learned through modeling. Give an example.

*39. Give two reasons we imitate the cognitive component
      anxiety in others.

    Modeling is, of course, not the only mechanism by
which the verbal community operates. But it is quite
important as an information source. The interaction of
the person with his/her verbal community also influences
the verbal component of anxiety. When the child (or adult)
describes the anxiety process to someone else, it is
likely that he/she will receive reinforcement in the form
of social attention, sympathy, and so forth. This makes
the description of the anxiety more likely to occur in
the future. In some cases where the verbal community ir-
responsibly reinforces such "bad talk," people can get down
on themselves so badly that other important functions are
interfered with. Perhaps you've had a friend who has been
influenced so much by the sympathy of the verbal community
when he/she described his/her anxiety that he/she discon-
tinued studying. The process often gets that extreme or
worse.

*40. How does interaction (differential reinforcement)
      with the verbal community also lead to the cognitive
      component of anxiety?

    In recapitulation, we have seen how the innate tendency

to respond with sympathetic activity can be classically conditioned or learned through avoidance learning and signal detection. This explains the physical and behavioral components of anxiety. The cognitive component is learned through the verbal community influences of modeling and differential reinforcement for anxious self-description. Thus, having an idea of how anxiety develops, we can now turn to the prospect of changing this emotional process.

*41. Review: Explain how the three channels of anxiety are developed.

CHANGING ANXIETY

It would be safe to say that more clinical research has dealt with changing anxiety than any other emotional problem. This is probably true because almost everyone who sees a mental health professional is in some way engaging in anxious behavior. There are, fortunately, a number of well tested ways to control anxiety. In this section we will briefly explore the most widely used methods.

Relaxation

Since anxiety starts with the sympathetic nervous system, it follows that by reversing those sympathetic processes, anxiety will be reduced. Various forms of physical relaxation and aids to relaxation have been shown to be very helpful in reducing anxiety (Goldfried and Merbaum, 1973). For example, muscle relaxation techniques are most commonly used and can inhibit anxiety. By learning to tense and relax muscle tension in specific muscle groups, a person can control anxiety. Deep breathing can also inhibit anxiety. Meditation and yoga are also effective relaxation techniques. Some drugs have been shown to induce relaxation and thereby reduce anxiety. Biofeedback is a way in which the person can be made aware of how relaxed he/she is. The feedback from specific bodily processes can greatly enhance the learning of relaxation.

*42. List the types of relaxation procedures that can reduce anxiety.

Cognitive Restructuring

In order to reduce or change the cognitive component of anxiety, a series of techniques that attempt to change the negative self-statement part of anxiety have been developed. Dr. Marvin Goldfried of the State University of New York at Stoney Brook has been a major researcher in this area (Goldfried & Goldfried, 1975). Cognitive restructuring is a way to replace negative, maladaptive thoughts with positive coping thoughts. The procedure involves identifying the specific negative thought and the situations in which is occurs. A substitute verbal statement is then devised. This replacement self-statement should be a positive coping statement. Everytime the person has the negative thought,that negative thought becomes a cue for the positive replacement thought. The negative thought becomes a cue for the positive one because the person is asked to imagine this sequence of anxiety-negative thought-positive thought many times while he/she is in the therapist's office. The repetition of the sequence causes the association to be made.

A person who is afraid of asking women out for dates has a negative thought: "She won't like me; I'm too young." This happen everytime he is about to ask someone for a date. The therapist determines that an appropriate coping statement is "If she doesn't go out with me, I can ask others." The therapist has the person imagine the sequence of asking for a date; "She won't like me.", "I can ask others." thirty or forty times while in the therapy sessions. When the client actually goes to ask for a date, he is more likely to emit the positive thought and is, therefore, more likely to ask for a date. Anxiety can be controlled by replacing the negative self-statements that are in the anxiety cycle.

*43.　Describe cognitive restructuring by giving an example of it. Why does it reduce anxiety?

Precluding Escape

Another way to decrease anxiety is to preclude or deny escape (Emmelkamp, Kuipers, & Efferaat, 1978). Remember it is the avoidance of the feared object that maintains the fear. By making the person confront the feared object, the fear will extinguish as the person becomes more confident in dealing with the situation. An example of this approach is the work of Dr. Albert Bandura who reduced the fear of snakes in people by having them gradually handle a live snake in the therapy sessions. This treatment is called participant modeling. In it the person watches the therapist touch the snake, then does so himself. This continues until the person's fear is extinguished. Bandura and others (e.g., Bandura and Adams, 1978) have shown that precluding avoidance is the most powerful way to reduce anxiety. This makes sense if you accept the idea that the major way anxiety is learned is through avoidance learning.

*44.   Describe participant modeling and tell why it works.

Treatment Packages

A number of treatment packages combine two or more of the anxiety reduction techniques. Systematic desensitization is a procedure in which the person imagines the feared object while he is physically relaxed (Wolpe, 1973). This combines imagined exposure to the fear object and relaxation. Therefore two of the three ways to reduce anxiety that we have discussed are used in this procedure: relaxation and precluding escape. Some forms of desensitization are "in vivo," that is, the person actually interacts with the feared object while he tries to maintain relaxation. As might be expected in vivo desensitization is very effecteive as well.

*45.   Systematic desensitization combines what two ways of reducing fear?

A package that inclues all three approaches we have presented is stress inoculation (Meichenbaum and Cameron, 1973). In Figure 7-1, you see the educational rationale for stress inoculation. A person using this package will learn that model of anxiety. Then he/she will learn relaxation skills to control physical arousal and cognitive restructuring techniqes to reappraise the situation and replace negative self-statements while he is actually interacting with the feared object. This treatment package is successful with a number of anxiety objects (Jaremko, 1979). It's comprehensiveness is powerful since it deals with all three channels of anxiety and uses all the available methods for anxiety reduction.

159

*46. Describe the stress inoculation treatment package.

    Coping with stress and anxiety are things that we
all have to do daily. An effective arsenal of techniques
exist for these purposes. There is no reason why most
people cannot learn to control anxiety. By applying
the same techniques in preventive ways, it may also be
possible to even prevent the learning of fear and anxiety
(Jarenko, 1978). However, as we will see now, the complete absence of anxiety is not a favorable state of
affairs since this emotion performs some of the valuable
functions in human life.

ANXIETY AND SURVIVAL

    While anxiety is often troublesome to people, it is
also very helpful to them at times. By learning how
to cope with stress and anxiety, some people gain feelings
of self-efficacy (Chapter 5). Anxiety can thus be seen as
the grist for the mill of personal struggle. Without
it we might not be able to achieve as many things as
we have. It is possible that this emotion has driven
some humans to the limits of their capability and endurance.
And it is often at those limits that the great things of
humanity are achieved.

    Anxiety is a motivator. Without the fear of failure,
rejection,humiliation, etc., many of us would be content
to lie back and do little with our talents. The experience of anxiety helps to keep us striving. Admittedly
such ambition often becomes frenzied and overbearing. But
for the most part, it is what human beings will choose if
given the choice between sedentary living and achievement
orientation. When rewards of life are handed to you "on
a platter" (non-contingent reinforcement), the reinforcers
don't make you feel as good as when you work for them (contingent reinforcement). Work implies anxiety and uncertain-
ty--motivators that keep us striving.

*47. Explain and substantiate how anxiety as a motivator
      is helpful to survival.

    Another way in which anxiety is useful is that it
serves to keep us away from real dangers. If we didn't
experience fear of speed, we might all drive too fast and
kill each other more than we already do. Like people who
have lost pain sensitivity due to nerve damage who might

160

bleed to death because they feel no pain; lack of anxiety would deprive us of a vitally important signal mechanism that tells us to be careful. So anxiety is, like the other dimensions of personality, not good and not bad. It simply is. Whether it contributes to survival is determined more by how extremely it is expressed and how timely its expression is.

*48. How is anxiety an important signal mechnism?

ANXIETY: AN EPILOGUE

In this chapter some of the current models of anxiety have been described. We have seen anxiety as a cycle of three behavioral channels: physical, behavioral, and cognitive. It is measured by self-report questionnaire, cognitive assessment devices, and psychophysiological reocrding. The development of anxiety proceeds along the lines of trauma conditioning, modeling, and avoidance learning. It can readily be changed by a number of effective techniques. And finally we saw that anxiety has a positive survival function as well as a negative function.

CHAPTER 8

SENSATION SEEKING BEHAVIOR

The weekend was coming up and Scott was becoming more and more depressed. This was the one weekend he dreaded--going home for fall break. Sure, he wanted to see his mom and dad; he hadn't seen them since the first of September. But how could he tolerate two days in Victoria--population 182? He had been happy to come to school. No more boring nights looking for action. At school, there was always something to do--movies, plays, basketball games, frat parties--never a dull moment. But Victoria was a different story.

"Hey, Scott, you going home for the break?" Scott's roommate had just come in from class.

"Yeah, I'm afraid so. It's going to be a long weekend."

****

Dr. Marvin Zuckerman is a psychologist at the University of Delaware who has spent a considerable amount of time investigating the subject of this chapter, <u>sensation seeking</u>. According to Zuckerman, sensation seeking refers to the extent that people seek out varied, novel, or complex experiences. Some people look for novel experiences a good deal of the time. These people don't seem to be content unless there is a high rate of activity going on around them. Others do best in routine environments. They are easilty overloaded by outside stimulation. They like the same people and the same experiences occurring in their daily lives. There can be no doubt that the dimension of sensation seeking will have a profound influence on behavior. It is the purpose of this chapter to investigate sensation seeking within the context of our dimensional questions and the rules of a science of behavior.

<u>SENSATION SEEKING:</u> The tendency to seek out novel, varied or complex experiences.

WHAT IS SENSATION SEEKING?

For years it has been recognized that people differ

in the extent to which stimulation can be tolerated. Generally, it is felt that small degrees of novel stimulation
are pleasant, but that too much novelty becomes unpleasant.
For example, if you have been studying for a couple of hours
and someone comes into the room to share a few minutes of
time, the break will probably be welcome. Imagine, however,
that you are in your office working on a paper due two days
ago. Three people come in, all wanting something right now.
You will probably find this a frustrating situation -- too
much going on. You will find it hard to concentrate, become
emotionally upset, easily angered, and insensitive to others
around you. You will be overloaded In the first instance,
however, you will become similarly distracted, fidgety and
irritable if you don't take a break. Very similar patterns
of behavior ensue when you deviate from an optimal level of
stimulation, that is, the level of stimulation above which
more stimulation is punishing and below which more stimulation is reinforcing. Each person has an optimal level of
stimulation (OLS), which operates on a homeostatic principle. When deviation from the OLS occurs, those behaviors
that bring the level of stimulation back to the person's OLS
will be reinforced. This is the conceptual basis for what
Zuckerman calls the "sensation seeking motive".

HOMEOSTASIS: The tendency of a person to maintain a state
              of constancy or equilibrium on some dimemsion.

OPTIMAL LEVEL OF STIMULATION (OLS): That level of external
                                     or internal stimula-
                                     tion for each person
                                     above which more stim-
                                     ulation is punishing
                                     and below which more
                                     stimulation is reward-
                                     ing.

        Dr. Zuckerman feels that the OLS differs from person
to person. Since people differ on this aspect of susceptibility to an important environmental dimension (stimulus
change), their behavioral tendencies will be very different.
As always, the behavioral differences among people on the
dimension are the most important consideration.
        Since some behavioral scientists do not care to use
unobservable notions like the OLS, it may be alternately
stated that there are some people for whom stimulation change

163

is a reward and some for whom it is not. Rather than looking inside the person   (OLS) for an explanation of why this
is so, it may be better to look outside the person. In the
section on the development of sensation seeking, attention
will be given to deprivation schedules and activity levels
in life (external environmental occurances) which could contribute to making sensation seeking a powerful reward. We
will also look at the OLS idea, but remain aware that such
a model can be seen as mentalistic.

To demonstrate how the OLS operates to control the
consequences in a person's life, another example may be useful. During the middle of the week,your biology professor
is likely to be at his/her busiest -- grading papers, conducting research, attending committee and department meetings,
keeping appointments. You probably should not ask him/her
for an extension on a term paper at that time. An extension is a hard decision for a professor to make and he/she
has enough ongoing activity. To add more stimulation would
be punishing or unpleasant, thereby decreasing the likelihood of a favorable response. Alternatively, a good time
to approach one of your professors with a project proposal
would be when he or she has relatively little going on.

*1. Define sensation seeking.

*2. What is homeostasis?

*3. Describe how the optimal level of stimulation works.

Sensation seeking behavior

Those considered high in sensation seeking can be
seen as engaging in at least one (perhaps more) of four
classes of sensation seeking behavior (called "factors" by
Zuckerman); namely, thrill and adventure seeking, experience
seeking, disinhibition, and boredom susceptibility. There
is some overlap among these classes, but each represents
enough of a separate response class to warrant analysis of
its own.

Thrill and adventure seeking behavior, characterized by risky activities of a physical nature, is exemplified
in fast driving, hang-gliding, mountain climbing, sailing,
contact sports, and so on. The crucial aspect that differ-
entiates thrill and adventure seekers from others is that
the risky behavior is reinforcing. I once knew a man (we'll

164

call him Mike) who was this kind of person. He rode motorcycles, raced cars, and kept on the go with some physical
activity all the time. Mike derived a lot of pleasure from
these activities and they served as incentives for him to
do other, less appealing tasks--such as work. He was an
interesting person because his restlessness and boredom
would always become evident when he was unable to do something physical. Thrill and adventure seeking is a class
of behavior that goes beyond the normal love of the outdoors
that many of us have. The elements of risk and uncertainty
play a large part in the reinforcing properties of these
activities. People who demonstrate high rates of such behavior are thrill and adventure seekers.

THRILL AND ADVENTURE SEEKING BEHAVIOR: A class of sensation
seeking behavior characterized by participation in risky
physical activities.

    Experience seeking refers to seeking new experiences
through the mind and the senses, and through new and unconventional forms of behavior. It may be traveling to
a remote and inaccessible place, wearing flashy clothes,
taking drugs, meeting new and perhaps unusual people, or
engaging in spontaneous activites. The social critic who
unabashedly says outrageous things comes to mind. A professor I once had was a classic example. He almost seemed
to enjoy saying shocking things just to see the effect.
Goading his students into a radical defense of a particular
intellectual position was his delight. New experiences can
come in many forms; therefore, this factor is a broad one.
Novelty and unconventionality seem to be the common denomina-
tor of these behaviors. Durg use or abuse, cigarette smoking
and sexual activity are also included in this class.

EXPERIENCE SEEKING BEHAVIOR: A class of sensation seeking
                             behavior in which the person
                             is reinforced by non-conven-
                             tional, unusual, or novel
                             thoughts or acts.

    You probably know a person who engages in a great deal
of behavior from the disinhibition class. Drinking, wild
parties, and exciting sexual partners are reinforcing to people who constitue this group. Alcohol usage, a variety of
sexual partners, party-going, and social disinhibition are
the behaviors in this classificaiton. It appears that these
people are reinforced bythe arousal that is produced by these

165

behaviors. Hedonistic social activity characterizes this
factor of sensation seeking. One of the men in my social
fraternity was high in the disinhibition factor. J. R. was
always having a party. The parties he had were loud and long.
He spared no expense to make his guests happy. Drinks, drugs,
music games, and movies were common accouterments at these
affairs. Unfortunately for J. R., he flunked out of school
after three semesters. It was hard for him to yield to his
disinhibition tendencies and keep up with school. We sure
missed his parties, however.

DISINHIBITION: A class of sensation seeking behavior
                characterized by hedonistic social activity.

Boredom susceptibility is the final class of behavior in
sensation seeking. This refers to a distaste for repetitive
experiences, routine work, boring people--and the presence
of restlessness in the face of monotony. These people are
very sensitive to boring activity and when bored, they get
very restless. People who frequently feel that the "grass
is greener on the other side of the fence" are probably
susceptible to boredom.

BOREDOM SUSCEPTIBILITY: A class of sensation seeking behavior
                         referring to a tendency to easily
                         reach a state of being bored.

In summary then, Zuckerman would say that the person
who is high in sensation seeking has a high OLS. Many
activities are reinforcing because he or she is often below
the OLS. These people, therfore, are susceptible to boredom, find drinking and varied sexual behavior highly en-
joyable, are very reinforced by novel or unconventional
things, and enjoy risky physical activity. Novelty wears
off quickly. Many of their behaviors are mischievious and
sensationalistic. They live life in the fast lane, so to
speak. It's not uncommon to hear a person like this describe themselves as restless, excitable, easily bored, and,
very often, discontented. As we shall see later, the culture has a lot to do with these behaviors and the feelings
that accompany them. The culture often communicates standards of happiness and excitement that impel some individuals
to engage in sensation seeking behavior.

But what of the person who can take it easy, one who
is satisfied to live a life of predictability, who favors

conventionality and routine? What about those to whom excitement is punishing or unpleasant and any activity disruptive of routine or overloading is undesirable? There are people who are sedate like this and are punished by having too much going on. They have low optimal levels of stimulation. Many new things are unpleasant because they are often above the OLS. Sameness and low rates are reinforcing to such people. They may be content to spend time on the weekend reading a book. (Although sometimes reading a book is a form of sensation seeking). They shun the wild parties, preferring more intimate social interaction, if any at all. When we call a person an introvert, we often think of fear of interaction. The truth is that interaction is just not reinforcing for some people.

With this picture of a person low in sensation seeking, the dimension of sensation seeking is set -- high sensation seekers are on one end and low sensation seekers on the other. Our interest in this important dimension of personality is that all of us are influenced by the reinforcers and/or punishers of stimulus change at one time or another, and some of us are extremely affected by these consequences. Let's now look at ways to measure this dimension.

*4. List the behavioral charcteristics of thrill and adventure seeking?

*5. Experience seeking?

*6. Boredom susceptibility?

*7. Disinhibition?

*8. What is a non-mentalistic alternative to Zuckerman's model of sensation seeking?

MEASUREMENT

The sensation seeking scale (SSS) developed by Zuckerman is the most commonly used way to assess the extent to which someone is reinforced by stimulation change. This scale is a 72 item forced-choice questionnaire which requires the respondent to choose between two alternatives for each item. Each one of the pairs of alternatives represents either a sensation seeking response or a non-sensation seek-

167

ing response. The items are classified into the four classes of behavior described above. Table 1 presents a few sample items from each scale. On the basis of a person's responses, a score for each scale, plus a "general score" is
obtained. In this way, it can be determined whether a person is high, medium, or low in sensation seeking behavior,
as well as what type (or types) of sensation seeking is most
reinforcing to him/her.

Zuckerman (1974, 1978) presents much data supporting
the reliability and validity of the SSS. Reliability, remember, measures how consistent a personality inventory is,
how well it yields the same score from testing to testing.
Unless someone's behavior changes greatly and consistently
("personality change"?), the SSS score remains about the
same for most people. The validity data for the SSS has
been procured by correlating the scale with a number of other
scales that try to measure the same construct (concurrent
validity) and by correlating the scale with tendencies toward different action patterns (construct validity). Many of
these correlational tendencies were presented in the first
section of the chapter. In summary, however, the SSS (or
one of the subscales), has been shown to be related to sexual behavior, drug use, alcohol comsumption, cigarette smoking,
food preference, hallucinatory behavior, daydreaming, and in-
volvement in risky sports. Evidently, this personality inventory is successful in describing sensation seeking behavior
and designating who engages in such behavior.

TABLE 1

Sample Items from the Subscales at the Sensation Seeking Scale

A. Thrill and Adventure Seeking

    10. a. I often wish I could be a mountain climber.
          b. I can't understand people who risk their necks
            climbing mountains.

    21. a. A sensible person avoids activities that are
            dangerous.
          b. I sometimes like to do things that are a little
            frightening.

31. a. I would like to try surfboard riding.
    b. I would not like to try surfboard riding.

B. Experience Seeking

3. a. I would like to hitchhike across the country.
   b. Hitchhiking is too dangerous a way to travel.

13. a. I like to dress in unusual styles.
    b. I tend to dress conservatively.

50. a. I often enjoy flouting irrational authority.
    b. I am generally respectful of lawful authority.

C. Disinhibition

6. a. I like "wild" uninhibited parties.
   b. I prefer quiet parties with good conversation.

23. a. I find that stimulants make me uncomfortable.
    b. I often like to get high (drinking liquor or smoking marijuana).

30. a. Most adultery happens because of sheer boredom.
    b. Adultery is almost always the sign of a sick marriage.

D. Boredom Susceptibility

9. a. I find a certain pleasure in routine kinds of work.
   b. Although it is sometimes necessary, I usually dislike routine kinds of work.

24. a. A person should change jobs from time to time simply to avoid getting into a rut.
    b. A person should find a job which is fairly satisfying to him and stick with it.

70. a. I have no patience with dull or boring persons.
    b. I find something interesting in almost every person I meet.

*9. Describe the Sensation Seeking Scale.

Other measures of sensation seeking

Is the SSS the only way to measure this class of behavior? No, there are other ways; but Dr. Zuckerman has
been very productive and thorough in his work with the SSS
and it is probably the most widely used. We know, however,
that there are problems with personality inventories. Sometimes such questionnaires don't always measure exactly the
behavior in which a single individual engages, and such un-
measured behavior may well be sensation seeking (that is,
maintained by its stimulation change properties). We might
be able to say, for instance, that the rate of divorce in a
culture is a measure of sensation seeking. Certainly, not
everyone gets divorced because of boredom susceptibility or
some other sensation seeking motive; nevertheless, from talking with many people who divorce, we do find that a significant percentage are motivated by such reasons. The point is
that the divorce rate may in some respects be a measure of
sensation seeking. It is a crude one, but it is a measure
nonetheless.

The same logic might be applied to other behaviors in
the culture on which actuarial statistics are tabulated.
People are called " work-a-holics" when they engage in excessive rates of work behavior. Perhaps such behavior is
reinforced by the changes it brings in their otherwise dull
lives. A so-called sexual revolution can also be seen to
have sensation seeking properties. Such measures are not
precise and do not have utility for the individual. However,
they do have sociological ramifications for a culture. The
culture having mambers with high rates of behavior maintained by sensation seeking reinforcers will produce peculiar
effects that may have survival implications for the members
of that culture. Such a line of thought will be returned to
shortly.

*10. What are two alternative ways to measure sensation
      seeking?

*11. How are sociological statistics measures of sensation
      seeking?

In summary then, the SSS is the major way sensation
seeking is now measured. It is an excellent device and has
many features that speak well of it. There are, however,
other aspects of sensation seeking that can and should be

measured such as the cultural effects of sensation seeking
-- divorce rates, heart disease rates, and so forth. You
can expect that future developments in measuring sensation
seeking will take these into account.

THE DEVELOPMENT OF SENSATION SEEKING BEHAVIOR

Before beginning this section on the development of
sensation seeking, it might be well to elaborate on a non-
mentalistic view of sensation seeking. By no means is such
a view extensively accepted in the scientific community.
Coverage of these points, however, may be helpful in understanding further the nature of sensation seeking. While
sensation seeking implies a purpose in the person's behavior,
the actual maintaining factors of the behavior are the stimulus change results of the behavior. A person does not behave in order to seek sensation. He/she does things that
have led to stimulation increase or change in the past. For
example, the sexually promiscuous person can be unaware of
sensation seeking motives controlling his/her behavior. In
this way, he/she is not seeking thrills. However, a person
can be aware of being bored by such sensation seeking and
often is. When such self-produced verbal cues (awareness)
occur, the setting for sensation seeking behavior is present.
This represents a change in the contingency controlling the
behavior. In this way the person appears to be seeking sensation but the initial origin of the behavioral sequence
(external setting, self produced verbal cues, sensation-seeking behavior) is in the person's environmental history. With
that view of sensation seeking covered, let us turn to some
possible influences on the development of this dimension.

There are three major factors important in the development of sensation seeking. Biological variables contribute
to individual differences among people. Such differences,
which are thought to be determined by genetic endowment, are
manifested in many things -- one of these things is the poss-
ibility of an hyperactive nervous system. Some personality
psychologists, Zuckerman among them, feel that such an under-
lying biological difference could be very important in determining sensation seeking. The role of the immediate environment of the developing child could be instrumental in
enhancing and maintaining sensation seeking behavior. For
example, children exposed to environments of very high activity may habituate to that activity level and become sus-

171

ceptible to sensation seeking reinforcers. The cultural factors involved are very important in determining the form of sensation seeking behavior. A culture that has much leisure time and which also values "happiness" may be likely to produce sensation seeking reinforcers. We will deal with each of these factors separately. Much of what follows is based on experimental evidence; while some of it is inferred from such data.

Biological bases of sensation seeking

The main idea behind attempts to find physical or biological causes of sensation seeking is the belief that people have differences in their physical constitutions. These differences involve the reactivity and satiability of the central and autonomic nervous systems. In others words, some people have nervous systems that are more excitable (in the sense of more quickly conducting chemo-electrical charges) and less able to be satiated; that is, overloaded -- or filled up. If there are differences in nervous systems, then people will repsond differently to different levels of stimulation. High levels of stimulation will overload some and not come near the tolerance level of others. In like manner, novel stimulation will generate stronger and quicker electrochemical reactions in some nervous systems, and a less pronounced effect in others. All this can be related to sensation seeking behavior because those high in sensation seeking may have very reactive nervous systems and/or very insatiable nervous systems. Such a state of affairs would explain some of the reasons why sensation seekers are paid off by high levels of stimulation and low sensation seekers are not.

Since it is not possible to go around dissecting and experimenting with the central and autonomic nervous systems of human beings, personality psychologists have worked backward. They have studied people who are high on the SSS and sought to determine if constitutional differences exist in such people. Some interesting facts have been discovered by this course of action. First, you might expect that constitutional differences in people might be passed along to their offspring. Indeed it has been found that identical twins (monozygotic -- from the same egg and therefore possessing the same genes) have higher correlations of SSS scores than do fraternal twins (dizygotic -- from the same mother but from two eggs). This result means that there is something more than environment responsible for the correlations be-

172

tween the twins' SSS scores. This is true since most twins will be reared together (in similar environments). The similarity of genes would therefore, be the only significant difference between monozygotic and dizygotic twins. Such a result suggests that there is a biological component to sensation seeking. Other data also support this notion.

When a loud noise is made, a cat will perk up its ears. You would probably look up from your book if someone entered the room while you were reading. These are examples of the "orienting reflex", or OR. For years, psychologists have used the OR and habituation to it (that is, the subject is allowed to become accustomed to a particular stimulus) as a measure of the reactivity of the central nervous system. It has been shown that high sensation seekers have stronger initial OR's than low sensation seekers. The strength of the OR in high and low sensation seekers, however, becomes equal the second time the stimulus is presented. These results happen with both complex and simple stimuli. The conclusion reached is that high sensation seekers are more aroused by novel stimuli than lows, but there is no difference between them in response to non-novel stimuli. Results like these are taken by Zuckerman and others as evidence that there are differences in constitutional factors; and that such differences are important in sensation seeking behavior. Indeed, the nature of the data collected on this topic is very complex. We have only dealt with a very small part of it. More is known, but more needs to be known to make sound conclusions and predictions. It is an emerging area of investigation and one that is quite exciting.

That there are biological differences among people and that such differences lead to personality behavior differences is an intuitively understandable idea. It is important to remember, however, that we do not yet know for sure the specifics of such biological considerations. Research efforts should continue in this area, but other areas of research may also be fruitful in terms of investigating the origins of sensation seeking behavior. In fact, some psychologists feel that we now know enough from an environmental view about understanding and controlling behavior that we need not worry about the genetic factors. While such a position may be risky since it tends to ignore important research, it does emphasize the importance of the environment. We will turn now to the role of the environment.

*12. How are constitutional factors related to sensation
      seeking behavior?

*13. How do studies with twins support this position?

*14. What is the orienting reflex and how does it relate
      to sensation seeking behavior?

The role of the environment

     We have learned throughout this book that the conse-
quences of a person's acts are very important in determining
behavior. The contingencies of reinforcement control many
of our behaviors. In order to understand behavior, we must
describe the contingencies of which it is a function. We
have seen how such contingencies are not often very obvious
and how we sometimes attribute the cause of behavior to
"inner" man. Such mentalism offers an incomplete picture of
behavior. Enough is known about the effects of the environment to explain much behavior. In those areas in which we
do not yet have knowledge, we can learn by assuming a scientific analysis of the role of the environment. Such an environmental analysis can be applied to sensation seeking.

     Suppose you know someone who has a high rate of sensa-
tion seeking behavior. Let's say that a young man of your
acquaintance likes to ride motorcycles, party a lot, say
shocking things, and has a hard time sitting still for more
than thirty seconds. It is possible that you attribute his
behavior to an "active" personality. Since this would be a
reification, you would be incomplete in your analysis. You
have created something to explain his behavior. Such a
thing as "personality" does not exist. If pressed, you might
"specify" by saying that he is that way because he likes to
party, etc. This explanation can also be seen as incomplete
because liking something may be best viewed as an emotional
by-product. "Liking" doesn't cause behavior. At best, it is
a concommitant behavior (occurs only with something else).
We still have to explain why the "liking" behavior has occurred. Perhaps after being thoroughly befuddled, you might
say that your active friend did all those things because he
had a need to be active and alive. This last explanation can
also be seen as inadequate since a need in some way refers to
a history of experiences in the past.

Each attempt at explanation was inadequate because of the tendency to explain the behavior by something that was happening (or exists) in the present with the behavior. The history of the person is not obvious and is, therefore, over-looked. But the origins of a behavior do begin (are caused by) in the past. In order to understand your friend's sensation seeking behavior, we have to look at his past history of experience in termsof the contingencies of reinforcement.

The contingency of reinforcement refers to the interaction between three variables: the setting in which the behavior occurs, the behavior itself, and the results of the behavior. We analyze the environment when we analyze the contingencies under which a behavior is developed. Sensation seeking behavior is controlled by the contingencies in the past. The stimulus setting in which it occurred during formative years influences the development of sensation seeking. The sensation seeking behavior itself; its form, its speed, the effort required to produce it -- all influence its recurrence and maintenance. Finally, the consequences of the sensation seeking behavior contribute to the developing behavioral process.

With regard to the setting variable, we look at such aspects of the environment as the people who were present: perhaps emulating others who were high in sensation seeking behavior influenced your friend's sensation seeking. Maybe he was reinforced for engaging in high activity behavior only at night and he is now not a "morning person" but a "night person". It could have been that your friend grew up in a household with ten other people and there was always something going on. Such highly active environments might make reductions in activity level a punishing event. That past setting could influence present sensation seeking behavior. The possible combinations and permeations for just one aspect of the contingency are great and provide a rich source of research hypotheses and theory.

The topography of the behavior also influences the sensation seeker's development. Consider the effort required to behave in a non-sensation-seeking way. For some people more energy and effort is required to consistently plod along and stick to an activity or project. Some people have not been rewarded enough for perserverence because the amount of effort required was greater than the reward they received.

Consequently, they engage in a number of smaller, less ef-fortful behaviors that take the form of sensation seeking. The point that the form, speed and effort of a behavior in-fluences its development and maintenance is also to be con-sidered in an environmental analysis of sensation seeking.

Finally, the results of a behavior influence its course of development. Results can be divided into two ma-jor areas: natural and social. Suppose the natural results of the sensation seeking behavior of your friend were that he accomplished a great deal of work that resulted in his promotion. Such is often the case with the "work-a-holic". He has not worked hard to get promoted. He has merely work-ed hard and then received a favorable result. The result is to strengthen your friend's tendency to behave actively. He has been reinforced into becoming a sensation seeker. A significant dimension of his "personality" has thus been learned. Similarly, a person who parties a great deal and has been generously rewarded by the esteem of others in the form of being "popular" has been socially rewarded for a class of sensation seeking behavior. Many of these social rewards are derived from the values of some subgroups of the culture (e.g., the sanction of the fraternity to "raise hell").

By considering the many varied and complex contingen-cies of reinforcement that prevail in a person's life from birth on, we can determine the course of the development of any behavior, including sensation seeking. A few examples have been provided here, but it must be remembered that the analysis is extensive and complex. The role of the environ-ment, described by analyzing the contingencies of reinforce-ment of which sensation seeking is a function, contributes heavily to the causation of this class of behavior.

*15. List three pseudo-causes of sensation seeking behavior.

*16. Review: what is a contingency of reinforcement?

*17. Describe how the contingencies of reinforcement influ-ence the development of sensation seeking behavior.

Cultural values

"The pursuit of happiness" is a cultural value for west-ern man. As you know, a value is a label used for a class of

rewards or reinforcers. Therefore, the pursuit of happiness
is a reward which maintains the behavior of the people in a
culture. In other words, much behavior, expecially sensation
seeking behavior, in western culture can be seen as being
maintained by "happiness" rewards. The question then becomes "what are 'happiness' rewards?" and that is why the
"pursuit of happiness" value is considered in a chapter on
sensation seeking. These rewards are often the ones that
maintain sensation seeking behavior.

What does it take to be "happy"? If we really knew
the answer, the world might be a better place. There are
many influences that convince us that things such as youth,
exciting people, exotic places, fast cars, good looking
clothes, and other such rewards will make us happy. The persuasion is effective because we "feel good" when we receive
these rewards and they often maintain our behavior. Much of
that behavior is exactly what we have called sensation seeking behavior. The point is that features of our environment
(commercial television, advertising campaigns, romantic literature and music, etc.) serve to reinforce sensation seeking behavior.

What are the things that will excite most people? Parties, travel, interaction with others; and in general, keeping up high rates of behavior. The third class of causes of
sensation seeking behavior, therefore, is the value a culture
places on the results of sensation seeking. Such value would
make them reinforcers and serve to maintain the sensation
seeking behavior. But there is also another cultural factor
in sensation seeking: leisure time.

What do the people in a culture do when they have taken
care of all of their basic physical needs and then have time
to spare? Non-human creatures go to sleep. While man also
does this, it is often only for a short while. Leisure time
may still exist. One commercial advertisement reminds us that
"weekends were made for recreation"; or perhaps they were
"made for Michelob." It seems to be true that when there is
a great deal of leisure time, reinforcers that are not as
powerful in times of less reinforcement become powerful.
(Skinner, 1969) In the case of sensation seeking behavior,
rewards that are very powerful, such as food and shelter,
have maintained basic needs. Weaker rewards then have a
chance to take over; drugs, sexual behavior over and above
that required to perpetuate the species, gambling and other

games (both as a participant and spectator), and some forms of non-serious social rewards (parties) are examples. It is probable that sensation seeking rates go down when the needs of food and shelter are not yet taken care of.

Therefore, a culture in which there is much leisure time and a set of values involving excitement and activity, will have many members who have high rates of sensation seeking behavior. Such a state of affairs is both good and bad. We will next consider the results of sensation seeking behavior in terms of survival.

*18. Explain: Happiness is a value which explains much sensation seeking behavior.

*19. What is "happiness"?

*20. What effect does leisure time have on reinforcers?

*21. How does leisure time lead to more sensation seeking

The development of sensation seeking - summary

We have considered three main causes of sensation seeking ing behavior. First, constitutional factors such as differences in reactivity and satiability in central and autonomic nervous systems. Second, we found that the role of the environment requires precise analysis along the lines of determining the effects of the contingencies of reinforcement to which a person is exposed. Finally, we considered the effect of a culture valuing excitement, youth, travel, and which affords a great amuunt of leisure time. In such a state of affairs, the contingencies of reinforcement are arranged so that weaker rewards control behavior. We saw how the weaker rewards of drugs, gambling, sports, and excessive sex can maintain sensation seeking behavior. As such, this behavioral dimension is an integral part of the description of personality and has dramatic effects with regard to cultural and species survival.

THE EFFECTS OF SENSATION SEEKING

Ted and Mary were seniors and, as soon as they graduated and found jobs, they planned to marry. They came to the counseling center because they knew marriage was hard work. They wanted to try to learn how to avoid many of the pitfalls of "connubial bliss". I was more than happy to work with them, as a preventive approach to personal problems has long been an ideal of mine.

The first task was to find out how compatible Ted and Mary were. We quickly discovered that the two had basic differences in sensation seeking. He enjoyed taking a day to do absolutely nothing. She always wanted to be doing something. For Mary, it was no fun just to sit around and have conversation. If they had a few free hours, she wanted to go to the lake, drive to the mountains, go to a game, have a picnic. Ted, on the other hand, felt that none of those activities were worth the initial effort required -- especially when you could stay at home and enjoy a good book. This difference in sensation seeking between Ted and Mary had been a sore spot for most of their relationship. They managed to "negotiate" differences at times, but more often than not, Ted got his way because Mary wasn't overly assertive. It soon became apparant that this sensation seeking difference could have a very important effect on their marriage. They seemed to be compatible in every other way save sensation seeking. We will return to Ted and Mary's story when discussing how to change sensation seeking behavior. The story is brought up at this point to demonstrate how the dimension of sensation seeking may affect a person's life.

Individuals and Societies

Sensation seeking effects both the individual and the society. This personality dimension can be an influential part of each person's life. If you are high in this behavior, the way you live your life can be totally affected. If you are low on this dimension, your behavior and the way others see you is accordingly influenced. At the same time, a culture which contains much sensation seeking behavior will have to consider the results of such sensation seeking at some point. As an example, one may be able to point to the ancient Roman culture in which sensation seeking behavior (decadence and so forth) flourished. It is argued that this decadence in some ways led to the fall of the Roman culture.

The dual effect of sensation seeking on the individual and society creates important implications for personal and cultural survival. The society which makes the pursuit of

179

happiness a high value will reap some benefits and suffer some consequences. Although there are many effects of sensation seeking, we will deal here with a specific listing of five such effects and their implications.

In search of the Golden Ring of Happiness

Probably the most obvious effect of sensation seeking behavior is the way so many people live their lives with the idea in mind of finding "happiness". Being married and "living happily ever after"; being divorced to try it again; buying a new television set; taking a trip to the Carribean; taking a new job in another locale; or having a baby, are only some of the things people do to "be happy".

Happiness seems to be an elusive and mysterious quality. Whoever discusses it has their own idea of what it is. Some even say that you "know" when you have found it. Unfortunately, many either do not know they have found it or can't find it. Such people may spend a great deal of time searching for the golden ring of happiness and either fall short, or drop the ring after they reach it. This pursuit is sometimes expensive. These people often begin to ask existential questions, "what's it all about?", "why an I here?". Sometimes the answers people give to these questions are depressing ones, answers that cause them to give up, to become "burned out", or to stop caring. A person who becomes burned out is not only unhappy but may be a drain on the culture.

EXISTENTIAL QUESTIONING: A form of verbal behavior which questions prevailing conditions and whether or not there is meaning to life.

Until recently, a number of modern-day housewives were good examples of this precess. She probably got married with the idea that she could and would be happy forever. In many cases the dream didn't come true. A "wife" is exposed to a lot of work with very low wages (no reinforcement). It can be said that she suffers a form of extinction in which she reaches for a golden ring that has tarnished too easily. Her children fail to commend her for her hard work, her husband is preoccupied with his own duties and does not properly reward or encourage her. Her work may be unexciting and unchallenging.

In many cases, existential questioning accompanies this extinction process. In other cases she simply becomes burned out without wondering why. Fortunately, recent cultural change has helped women realize that there can be more to happiness than taking care of home and family; consequently, fewer women now fall into this extinction trap.

Some factions of a culture receive advantageous results when people are engaged in the constant pursuit of happiness and well-being. Goods and services are manufactured and consumed. Jobs and economies flourish. Even individuals receive the benefits of hard work and the reinforcement that often goes with it. This pursuit of happiness, however, is a double-edged sword. The good result is the high rate of behavior and economic activity -- the bad is when people begin to believe that happiness is a result. Disappointment follows when it is discovered that happiness is not an end product. When it is realized that one is not made happy by accomplishment, people often begin existential questioning.

Happiness may be a by-product of a process that occurs when people are working hard for much reinforcement. If this reinforcement is contingent (that is, dependent upon what the person does) then happiness can result. An occasionally non-contingent reward might even make us "happier" when such a process in ongoing. To think that some thing or some state leads to happiness is a dangersously narrow view. When the object is achieved or reached, the happiness often dissipates. The problem, then is not that happiness is unobtainable, but that the culture can lead its members to believe that happiness is an end-product. When cultures are so arranged, much disillusionment and unhappiness can result. Happiness may be better viewed as that emotional by-product that occurs when people are in the process of working and receiving contingent rewards.

*22. What two main entities doessensation seeking affect?

*23. What is existential questioning?

*24. Describe how a person could come to engage in existential questioning.

*25. What is happiness?

Drug use

We have already mentioned drug use as one of the behaviors of sensation seeking. The stimulation change value of drug-taking is obvious. When a normal state of mind is transformed into a different than normal state of mind, that transformation can be exciting, novel, or "euphoric". The tendency is to repeat whatever created the change. In most cases, the behavior of taking a drug created the change that resulted in euphoria or "getting high". Consequently, a person will drink, ingest, snort, smoke, inject, and otherwise introduce into his physical system the chemical substance responsibie for the change.

Further, in many cases, the complex interaction of three things will lead a person to take massive amounts of a drug: the person's past history of taking drugs (as well as the past history of being reinforced in general), the other sources of reinforcement or punishment currently operating in the person's life, and the lack of inhibitory factors, such as guilt and "desperation." Such people are called alcoholics, addicts, "dopeheads", and so forth. Taking massive amounts of some drugs have physiological effects that cause tolerance to build up and a dependency or addiction is established. In these cases, the person becomes extremely sensitive to the substance as a reinforcer. He or she will spend more and more time taking the drug and attempting to procure the drug. The cycle is commonly known to most of us as drug dependency or addiction.

When a significant portion of the members of a culture are addicts, the cost to the culture in terms of energy and time, for maintenance and/or rehabilitation is great. Even in those who are not addicted, drug usage for recreational purposes leads to ill effects at times, as in alcohol-related automobile accidents. The point is that a culture producing much leisure time will often use the leisure time for drug use and abuse. Such sensation seeking behavior has effects that may not be conducive to the survival of the individual or the culture.

*26. Why are drugs sensation seeking reinforcers?

*27. How do "addicts" develop?

Sex

Another way in which the stimulation in a person'e environment can be increased or otherwise changed is through increased sexual activity. Many extra-marital affairs are motivated by the boredom that ensues from sex with the same partner. When a state of sexual deprivation is present, the reinforcing value of sexual activity is greatly increased. Such an increase makes sex a very powerful reward, and, consequently, sexual activity occurs at a high rate among people high in sensation seeking. A number of things can contribute to a high rate of sexual activity: the boredom mentioned above, the physical pleasure of sexual contact, the reinforcing properties of having "scored another sexual conquest", and the newly-found sexual freedom in the culture.

The effects of such a state of affairs for the individual can be both good and bad. The diversionary aspects of sex can increase productivity in other areas. For example, it is not uncommon for a sexually promiscuous individual to be highly successful in business. The effects of sexual promiscuity, however, can also be disillusionment and bitterness due to the temporary nature of the interpersonal relationship. Suppose, for example, a woman who engages in sexual behavior with many men develops, each time, an expectation of a permanent relationship. These unfulfilled expectations can be psychologically costly, leading to anger or apathy. To engage in sexual activity as a sensation seeking behavior, therefore, may be harmful.

*28. How can sexual promiscuity be both good and bad?

Aggression

One of man's primary genetic sensitivities seems to be reinforcement for aggressive behavior. There is obvious survival value for a creature which aggresses under conditions of harm or pain from the enviornment, as the aggression may remove or reduce the source of danger. Such a genetic endowment may have lost its utility, however, in a world where physical needs and dangers are satisfied and leisure time is abundant, nonetheless, the tendency to aggress when pain is present makes aggressive behavior a very prevalent component of our daily lives.

Consider how much of a person's leisure time is spent doing or watching some form of aggressive behaior. Many sports activities are aggressive -- football, hockey, or boxing. A person is said to be an aggressive bridge player and thereby enjoys the game. Movies and television are replete with aggressive content. Producers tell us that "it sells" -- people watch it. The point is that many of the sensation seeking behaviors in which we engage are aggressive. This search can reach an extreme in a situation such as a gang of youths "looking for some action" on a dull Saturday night.

There are several effects of this sensitivity to aggressive rewards. Physical aggression often leads to violent crimes like rape and murder. Verbal aggression causes personal misery in the daily lives of many a family member. Children learn to model such aggressive behaviors and the tendency to aggress is perpetuated. Aggressive behavior can become a way of life for some cultural subgroups, as in street gangs. Anthony Burgess describes such a condition in the futuristic Clockwork Orange (Burgess, 1962).

On the other hand, sensation seeking aggressive behavior in the form of "aggressive business" is condoned and encouraged by the culture. Males are encouraged to be "tough" and not allow themselves to be pushed around. (Females are also beginning to be told this.) The culture allowing such "legitimate" aggressive behavior will probably also have the unauthorized variety unless special steps are taken to prevent it.

There can be no doubt that aggression is one of the major forms of sensation seeking and that its effects are pervasive.

*29. List some of the aggressive aspects of our daily lives.

Sublimation

Sublimation is the redirection of an unacceptable impulse toward one that is more culturally approved. (Freud, 1959; Malott & Whaley, 1976). For example, a young person might create beautiful poetry or art because of an inability to deal directly with sexual feelings. Sublimation is a special kind of displacement where action is motivated for a reason other than its result.

Displaced aggression is one example. If you are angry
with your father, you probably will not hit him -- instead,
you become the president of the student government becuase
you are reinforced by importance in your father's estimation.

SUBLIMATION: Displaced acts that produce culturally approved
results.

DISPLACEMENT: Acts that transfer or "displace" an emotion
from its original object to a more acceptable
substitute.

Sublimation is important to sensation seeking because
many actions understandable in terms of sublimation may be
motivated by sensation seeking rewards. For example, what
about your friend's father who works eithteen hours a day?
It may be that boredom during leisure time has increased the
potency of sensation seeking rewards and that these rewards
maintain excessive working. The productivity of these so-
called "work-a holics" is culturally worthwhile, but it is
maintained by sensation seeking motives. It is possible that
many people who are high in sensation seeking behavior engage
in sublimated behavior.

*30. What is displacement?

*31. What is sublimation? Give an example.

*32. How does sublimation relate to sensation seeking?

Effects of sensation seeking: summary

We have looked at five different effects of sensation
seeking: the search for happiness, drug use, sex, aggression,
and sublimation. Each of these classes of behavior has good
and bad effects. Often, high rates of productivity result
from this activity; however, the negative by-products in terms
of individual suffering and cultural problems are less desirable. It should be remembered, however, that sensation seeking
is not good or bad in itself. It merely exists. In fact,
some psychologists look upon sensation seeking as a basic
force in human behavior that is directly responsible for many
of the human's most positive qualities, for example curosity
and creativity (Kish, 1966). Our discussion of the effects
of sensation seeking has enumerated individual and cultural

results related to these qualities.

CHANGING SENSATION SEEKING BEHAVIOR

Remember Ted and Mary? Whatever happened to them?
How did they solve the problem of incompatibility? Theirs
is a rather complex solution and is only briefly described
here, but it does show the major ways in which sensation
seeking behavior can be changed on an individual level.
Four strategies for change are presented here: resignation,
reversal of affect, careful planning and hope programming.
While it is doubtful that any one of these could change
behavior on this dimension, we see in the case of Ted and
Mary that all four provide a workable solution

Resignation

You may remember how someone famous once said that the
only thing we have to fear is fear itself. One of the things
one learns in counseling is that, many times, much of the
client's problem is the fact that he/she is upset over being
upset. In such a case, the need is to help the person calm
down about the secondary upset. So it was with Ted and Mary
(escecially Mary -- who felt she was "high strung"). They
were very concerned that this sensation seeking incompatibility would ruin their marriage and that they would disrupt
each other's lives. The actual problem (or upset) was that
he was low in sensation seeking and she was high. An additional problem was that they were very upset by this upset.
Resignation is a cognitive strategy for reducing the stress
of the secondary upset (Houston, 1977). Resignation works
by getting the person to admit that this is how he or she is,
that it is not likely to change and that the best thing to do
about it is learn to cope with it. In a word, the person
resigns himself to his/her condition. Such patient endurance of a situation had been shown in research to be quite
effective in reducing anxiety about a problem. It is not,
however, effective in solving the problem.

RESIGNATION: A cognitive stretegy or way of thinking characterized by patiently enduring an upsetting
situation.

I was able to convince Ted and Mary that resignation was a good strategy to help control their incompatibility by discussion with them the source of their sensation seeking tendencies, how long it took such a pervasive behavior to develop, and how influential it is in their daily lives. In this way, they were able to see that this was a dimension of personality upon which they differed and that the situation could not be changed overnight, but would require much clear and careful thought. Adopting the resignation strategy slowed them down enough to get them more prepared to engage in other problem solving. More preparation, however, was still needed.

Reversal of affect

Reversal of affect is another cognitive coping strategy that has been shown to be effective in reducing stress (Jaremko and Lindsey 1979). In addition, this strategy can be helpful in solving the problem. Ted and Mary were not yet ready to change because they still saw the dimensional difference between them as a bad thing. Reversal of affect entails looking on the bright side of a bad situation. By being positive about a harsh reality one may be in a better position to see the right things to do in order to solve the problem. One may also be better able to determine realistically the results of problem solving attempts. Reversal of affect helps a person to be more task-relevant; that is, to give more attention to the problem with a solution in mind (Sarason, 1972).

Using this reversal of affect strategy was helpful with Ted and Mary because they were able to look upon a solution of their difference as a challenge and as a way in which they could grow closer. In the discussion to convince them to use this strategy, we talked about the fact that sensation seeking was the way rewards affected a person and that their approach to solving the problem of incompatibility could be to rearrange these rewards so that both Ted and Mary were more satisfied. Since rearranging rewards is somewhat like spending money, Ted and Mary were quickly able to see the bright side of their "problem".

REVERSAL OF AFFECT: A cognitive strategy characterized by looking at the positive aspects of an unpleasant situation.

Careful planning

When Ted and Mary were ready to apply some solutions to their incompatibility, careful planning was the first one suggested. This solution is specifically designed for the sensation seeker. It involves planning activities for an extended period of time. For example, Ted and Mary planned one weekend trip per month, they agreed to go to dinner and a show once every two weeks, have friends over at least once a week and go to as many of the school's basketball games as their schedules allowed. In this way, each knew what to expect and Mary, the high sensation seeker, had many things to "look forward to". Such careful planning also kept the terms of Ted and Mary's contract clear. Each knew what the other could expect. This solution worked very well for Ted and Mary, as they both reported six months after I first saw them that they were happier than ever. While no controlled experimentation is available on the usefulness of careful planning; its applicability to the sensation seeker is promising.

CAREFUL PLANNING: A strategy utilizing thorough planning of activities so the sensation seeker always has an event to anticipate.

Hope programming

Dr. Donald Whaley describes "hope" as the continuation of activity due to positive reinforcement (Whaley, 1979). By supporting each other with words of encouragement, we can give each other hope to continue difficult tasks. Ted and Mary needed such hope. They were trying to solve a problem that had long-term consequences that were favorable to them. They therefore, each needed to feel rewarded for their attempts. To this end, they agreed to institute a self-management program between themselves with a goal that each would reach a certain rate of positive verbalization toward the other each week. This high rate of positive encouragement prevented them from taking each other for granted, and both felt hopeful for their marriage and their lives.

*33. List and describe four ways to change sensation seeking.

Cultural design and changing sensation seeking

Although it is always more difficult to change a culture
than it is to change an individual, it is possible to modify
sensation seeking by means of cultural change. Cultural design, however, is a matter of concern to more and more people.
Those who are against cultural design fear that it will eventually lead to an Orwellian, 1984-like world in which people
are slaves to the worst tyrant of all -- the system. On the
other side are those who say that if we don't design our future, the problems will overwhelm us and eventually end in
our extinction. They say we are controlled by the system
anyway, so why not make the system better. Regardless of the
position you take, the need exists for those who espouse cultural change to describe such change. B.F. Skinner is a pro-
ponent of cultural design. Some of his ideas follow.

A first approach is to try to arrange things so that
man is less sensitive to the sensation seeking reinforcers
that cause bad by-products. One way to do this is to prevent
discovery of the reinforcing effects of some substance or activity. For example, a heroin addict first experiences the
positive effects of the drug which later controls many forms
of his sensation seeking behavior. Preventing discovery of
the rewarding effects may serve to stop the later maintenance
of behavior. In a similar manner, sensation seeking behavior
is usually arranged in behavioral chains in which much behavior is maintained by a single reinforcer. Such a chain occurs in gambling, for example. By changing the schedules of
reinforcement for such behavior, the troublesome behavior can
be changed. Encouraging only so much gambling per month may
achieve such a result.

At the same time, contingencies can be arranged in the
culture so that more useful forms of sensation seeking behavior are generated. Such attempts have been made in the past
to generate long chains of behavior with small amounts of reward. Soldiers who fought in wars for the promise of plunder
are an example. In the same way, we could make problem solving behaviors like the ones described in Ted and Mary's story
contingent upon other sensation seeking reinforcers. We could
arrange contingencies so that "content" verbal behavior is
paid off and thereby maintained. The development of such a
"positive verbal community" has been successfully tried in
smaller groups (Whaley, 1979). By designing a culture that

differentially reinforces only porductive sensation seeking behavior, we may elemenate some of the bad by-products
of this dimension.

There can be no doubt that cultural design has never
been worked out very well. Systematic attempts have been
only rudimentary and sporadic. A plan to give tax money
back to those who consume less fuel is an example. Some
communes may be other examples. But these attempts are
rare, and the urgency of the problems we face because of
our sensation seeking behavior is immediate. Some writers
think we have not yet used the most powerful sources to
control human behavior (Skinner, 1971). With our present
state of knowledge about human behavior, we may be able to
make more attempts to design a culture in which sensation
seeking tendencies are used for us but no against us.

*34. What are two positions on cultural design?

*35. Describe some suggestions for designing a culture in
     which sensation seeking is adaptive.

Changing sensation seeking: Summary

Two basic approaches to changing sensation seeking are
to change an individual or to change a culture. The methods
of cognitive coping by resignation and reversal of affect can
prepare the person for applying problem solving to the difficulties encountered in sensation seeking. The solutions of
careful planning and hope programming can then be powerful
in helping a person deal with his/her position on this dimension. On a cultural level, the contingencies that maintain
long chains of unproductive sensation seeking behavior can
be developed by arranging the sensation seeking reinforcers
so that productive behavior is paid off more than behavior
that is less desirable. A practical solution is a long
way off, but attempts can still be made.

SENSATION SEEKING: AN EPILOGUE

Sensation seeking is one of the most pervasive classes
of human behavior. Modern man has developed ways to deal
with most problems in the physical enviornment, thus leaving a
large amount of leisure time. We have seen how sensation

190

seeking behavior often takes up this leisure time, what forms it takes, how it is measured, and how it is developed. We presented some of its effects and ways to change them. It could be said that sensation seeking refers to one of the basic dimensions of human personality. It affects many of the other dimensions and forms a great part of each person's uniqueness.

CHAPTER NINE

SEX AND AGGRESSION

It is the purpose of this chapter to discuss two additional dimensions of personality that have received attention in the literature. The two topics to be covered are sexuality and aggression. Space limitations require only brief treatment of these dimensions. They are included in this book because they represent important influences in human behavior

SEXUALITY

One of the most basic biological facts about the human being is that he/she possesses a sex-type. This sex-type is a complex concept probably best conceived as part of the person's self-system. This section will briefly discuss the nature, origin, functions, and consequences of the sex-type aspect of the self-system.

Sex-typing

While sex-typing is not exactly a dimension of personality since it is usually conceived as a dichotomy (that is, a person is either masculine or feminine), there are some recent developments in this area that have shown that sex-type is not an either or issue (Bem, 1974). Recently, the idea of psychological androgyny has been proposed. Androgyny refers to the idea that a person, regardless of biological sex, can possess certain personality charcteristics that have been previously considered only a male trait or only a female trait. For instance, it has been a long-standing cultural expectation that men were not supposed to cry, be tender, or show emotion. Androgyny, however, is the idea that under certain conditions, it is acceptable for a male to behave in such "feminine" ways. Crying or being tender is a part of being human, not just being female. Research on sex-typing has tried to uncover the characteristics of masculinity, femininity, and androgyny. As such, this research can be considered a dimension along which people differ. Let's look at the aspects of these different sex-types.

The masculine characteristics that have been developed by cultural stereotypes include assertiveness, interest in things rather than people, being analytical, manipulation, good leadership, strength, unexpressiveness, and the general myth of machismo (Forisha, 1978). Women, on the other hand, are stereotyped to possess the following characteristics, interdependence, interest in others, skill in interpersonal relating, nurturing, tender, receptive, empathetic, submissive, unable to do math, irrational, emotional, and intuitive (Forisha, 1978). The androgynous person, however, can possess any of the above characteristics depending on his/her beliefs, needs, desires, and upbringing. Androgyny is, in essence, the attempt to break away from the confining sex-role stereotypes that have been accepted for a number of years (Bem, 1975). The rationale for this breaking down of sex-role stereotypes is based on individual freedom.

If a man or a woman is exposed to strong expectations that he/she can only feel, think, or act in certain ways, the potential is present for preventing that person from expression of his/her potential. The "women's movement" has been a sociological reaction to this restriction of freedoms. In many ways women (as well as other minorities) have been unfairly blocked from certain opportunities because it was assumed or expected that they could not perform the tasks of a job. For example, while women represent more than half of the population in the United States, there are less than two percent women in the Congress of that country. Furthermore, when women did get the opportunity for a traditionally male job, their compensation was less than a man's doing the same job. On the other hand, men have been discouraged from being dancers, nurses, or secretaries on account of the stereotypes. The point is that people should be free to pursue what they want or what they are potentially effective at. While the freedoms technically exist, the encouragement and social reinforcement that motivates people to do such tasks is often lacking. A major idea of the women's movement is that the culture should be changed so that this encouragement for androgyny is present.

All of this doesn't mean that there are no differences between males and females. Besides obvious anatomical differences, there appear to be some emotional, physiological, and cognitive differences that are based on the biology of the gender, not the culture of the sex-role (Mischel, 1976, Maccaby, 1966). For instance, males are more active

193

at birth, females develop language sooner, and males are less dependent on parents at earlier ages. However, the implications of such differences have not been determined. It may well be that cultural influences override basic biological sex differences. It is safe to say, however, that traditional sex-roles are many times less than useful.

The measurement of sex-roles

Sex-roles have been measured by a device called the Bem Sex-Role Inventory (Bem, 1974). The sex-role inventory is a set of sixty adjectives to which the respondent indicates the degree each adjective is an accurate description of him/herself. Adjectives such as self-reliant, independent, athletic, assertive, strong, and forceful make up the masculine scale. Feminine characteristics are measured by adjectives such as yielding, cheerful, shy affectionate, flatterable, loyal, and sympathetic. The androgynous person is one who indicates that both types of adjectives describe him/her. A final category of "undifferentiated" is used to describe people who are characterized by neither masculine or feminine adjectives. The sex-role inventory has been used in a number of studies to show that there are differences among people with differing sex-types. For example, Jones (1979) has shown that masculine students are less likely to interact with preschool children, whereas feminine college students are more likely to interact with them. The range and detail of the behavioral differences specified by the sex-role inventory and other measures of sex-type will no doubt expand as these measures become more refined.

The development of sex-roles

There are a number of generally agreed upon influences important in the development of sex-roles. Obviously, the biological aspects of the person are important and can account for many of the differences among the sexes (Maccaby & Jacklin, 1974). Perhaps more important, however, are the social/cultural influences that exist in the environment of the person. Various contingencies of reinforcement are arranged so that sex-roles are learned. Mass media influences such as television, movies, and books have in the past, portrayed girls to be "sugar and spice" and boys to be "puppy dog tails." Such activity has resulted in two processes operating. First information

194

about what is appropriate for a particular sex is peddled. Second, influences are created that are imitated
by members of the culture. It is in these two ways that
the sex-role stereotypes have been learned and perpetuated
by the culture (Forisha, 1978). Fortunately, many of those
responsible for the mass media have volunteered or been
cajoled to change the content of the information regarding
sex-roles that has been peddled.

However, if one considers the potency of sex-role
socialization that is present in mass media, there seems
to still be a long way to go before androgyny is the norm.
This seems to be especially true when one considers the
role of child-rearing attitudes of parents. Parents who
possess certain sex-role stereotypes directly differentially
reinforce their children for manifesting certain sex-typed
behaviors. Such direct differential reinforced, of course,
firmly entrenches the "appropriate" sex-typed behavior in
the child. Change is difficult.

The future of sex-roles

If it is assumed that sex-role stereotypes are coun-
terproductive to individual freedom, social harmony, and
cultural efficiency; change will still be needed. On the
other hand, there are those who feel that drastic change
of cultural sex roles will result in an unhealthy balance
of "non-home-oriented" individuals. An already-increasing
breakdown of the family (a major device for socialization)
may accelerate. The conservative approach to sex-roles
calls for women to continue as they have for countless
generations, thus preserving the species "natural order."
While this may be a compelling argument to some who have
been reinforced for staying at home, the fact of the matter
is that the contingencies present in modern culture have
changed. And many people have changed in response to those
changing contingencies. The women's movement, sex-dis-
crimination legislation, and individual examples of non-
traditional sex-role behavior (women race car drivers, for
example) have alerted many to the need for androgyny. As
a result, parts of many peoples' "personalities" have been
changed by such consciousness raising. "For the times,
they are a changin'...."

AGGRESSION

Perhaps one of the most startling facts about the

human being is his/her tendency to aggress, to inflict harm on others. This section will discuss the nature and origin of the aggressive characteristics of the human being.

The definition of aggression

First, it is important to define aggressive behavior. Most psychologists include three components to the definition of aggression (Middlebrook, 1974). Aggression can be expressed in any or all of these components. First, there is an emotional feeling component to aggressive behavior. In the definitions of emotion and feeling used in this book, we can remember that emotions refer to the temporary physical changes (autonomic nervous system changes) that occur in response to certain environmental situations. For example, emotion in the case of aggression would be the increase in blood pressure that is experienced when one is frustrated by the fact that a friend has failed to make his/her appointment with you. The feeling part, however, is your self-talk (usually encapsulated so that it appears automatic or "unconscious") about the physical changes that are occurring. So in order for aggression to be present, the emotional and feeling components need to be present. Usually, these aspects of aggression are called "anger."

Secondly, an intent is usually present in the aggressing person. The intention is merely a verbal or cognitive declaration to do harm or inflict pain on the object of the aggression. While it is debatable whether intention should always be part of aggressive behavior, most of what we call aggression is characterized by a maleficent intention on the part of the aggressor.

The third part of aggression is, of course, the act or behavior that does the harm (or intends to do the harm). This behavior may be physical, verbal, interpersonal, indirect, sanctioned by the group, illegal, non-conscious, or deliberate. The extent of aggressive acts in modern life points to the pervasiveness of this personality dimension. This behavior permeates the very mainstream of our culture in the form of business activities, interpersonal styles, and recreational activities. When you think about it, it's no wonder there is as much illegal aggression as there is.

Since people do seem to differ with regard to the ex-

tent that they express aggression (that is, any or all of
the components described above), it can be considered a
dimension of personality. Some people are angry, aggressive, or both much of the time. Others are less likely to
be affected in one of these manners. However, everyone,
at one time or another, can act aggressively. This, as we
shall see, is due to some innate potentials the human
species possesses.

The measurement of aggression

It may be considered a testimonial to the pervasiveness of aggression in modern life that there is relatively
little mentioned in the psychological literature about
the measurement of this class of behaviors. It is almost
as if the existence of aggression is taken for granted, and
it's measurement is not needed. There are virtually no
major personality questionnaires that measure aggression
(Winter and Stewart, 1978). In part this may be due to
the fact that other dimensions of personality under investigation may be viewed as related to aggression. Areas
of research such as power motivation, achievement motivation, authoritarism, and machiavellianism all may be considered aspects of aggressive behavior. There are personality inventories to measure each of these concepts,
but no one device that stands out as the measure of aggressive tendencies. They are, nonetheless, methods of
measuring this class of behavior. Experimental methods
have been used, for example, in which a person is given
the opportunity to inflict pain (electric current) on
another person (Berkowitz, 1970). Various cultural or
social measures of aggression exist in crime statistics.
But, as a dimension of individual difference, aggression
remains an unexplored notion. Future work in this area
of aggression and personality would do well to devise a
personality questionnaire to assess individual differences.

The development of aggression

The point should be made that the lack of a personality measure of aggressive behavior has not held back
research on the topic. Indeed, aggression is one of the
most widely researched topics in psychology. It's just
that most of the work has been in the area of social
psychology in which the situational determinants of
aggression have been investigated. The personality or

197

dispositional aspects of aggression remain to be studied in a direct manner. There are, therefore, considerable data on the origin of aggressive tendencies. Our discussion of those will begin in the primeval forests in which the beginnings of human life evolved. As distant evolutionary ancestory of man lived, died, and evolved, the tendency to behave aggressively was developing as an innate part of these creature's structure. Those creatures who were built to react to environmental dangers and/or harm with aggressive responses were more likely to survive. This can be seen as true because aggressive behavior is more likely to remove a source of danger/harm than is passive behavior. Malott and Whaley (1976) provide an excellent account of how aggressive tendencies became innate. Those creatures who were reinforced for aggressive behavior during certain environmental events, such as the pain of attack, did so because they had nervous systems of a certain structure. Since these creatures were more likely to survive (they tended to be better at doing away with the dangerous things that threatened their survival), they were more likely to reproduce and pass along the structure that made aggressive behavior reinforcing during those conditions of harm. Today, our aggressive tendencies can be seen as a result of this process of natural selection which took millions of years. We have the innate structure that makes aggressive behavior reinforcing during periods of harm, pain, frustration, danger, and stress. (Azrin, Hutchinson, & Hake, 1963). Additionally, since many neutral cues can come to elicit pain, stress, and frustration, aggressive behavior is a pervasive part of each person's repertoire. In this section we'll explore some of the cues that came to induce aggression. It should be remembered, however, that these cues that come to control pain and frustration can eventually induce aggression because of an evolutionary past in which the pain-aggression connection was helpful for survival.

Dread cues

A major type of cue that comes to be operative in people's lives can be called a dread cue. Whaley (1979) states that "dread stimuli (cues) are created when previously neutral stimuli regularly precede the introduction of objects or events characteristically effective as punishers." (p. 129). Therefore, as events, people, places, and other cues get paired with punishment, they became dread cues. If you have had an argument (punisher) or two with your boss, going to work will come to be a dread cue. Dread cues elicit psychological and physiological pain. In the example above, the dread of going to work will most likely lead you to bad talk about your job, your boss, and perhaps yourself. You will experience nervousness, sympathetic nervous system discomfort, and tension while going to work. These behaviors are usually painful. Since pain is present, you are also more likely to aggress. You become jumpy, "short," you lose your temper easily, you may become verbally and physically aggressive. All of this may occur with you never making the connection between your job (dread cue), the pain it cuases you, and your aggression.

Since dread cues can be anything paired with a punisher, we can see that there are many things that can make people more likely to aggress. Financial insecurity, interpersonal trouble, mechanical frustrations, bureaucratic red-tape all can cause the painful dread that can lead to aggressive behavior. In order to find out what makes a person aggressive we may do well to look at what dread cues are present in that person's life. It should also be remembered that the awareness of the person may not be involved in the person at all. Anytime dread cues are present, the likelihood of aggression, direct or indirect, is increased.

Some of the common dread cues that have been investigated are crowding (Shaw, 1973), frustration of various kinds (Buss, 1977) and physical and interpersonal pain (Middlebrook, 1974). Additionally much research has been done on the ways in which people learn to behaviorally manifest aggression. Social learning factors such as parental child-rearing tactics, methods of discipline, parental modeling, and television models provide information about how aggression can be expressed (Bandura, 1969). Thus, when a dread cue is present in a person's environment, these social learning influences will become important in determining how the aggression will be expressed. Some people may displace their aggressive behavior to athletics, others may become verbally abusive to those around them, still others may resort to physical violence. These methods of aggressive expression are learned through socialization influences.

The control of aggression

Changing aggressive behavior is one of the major problems facing the human species. It is a common feeling that unless we find ways to control the aggressive tendencies that exist in the human being, the species may not survive the results of man's aggression toward other men. This section will be a brief discussion of some of the ways in which aggression may be controlled. Some of these methods have been shown to be effective, others are as yet untested. Some of them possess by-products that make their use undesirable or impossible. The need to control aggression, however, will make this topic of changing aggression an important one for a long time to come. (If we survive "a long time to come!")

One way of controlling aggression is through the use of chemical or surgical manipulation. Aggressive people may be controlled by massive doses of tranquilizers. Delgado (1971) describes cases in which the aggressive behavior of animals is inhibited by brain surgery. These methods have, unfortunately, by-products of a depersonalization nature (an overdrugged individual, for example) that make their use difficult.

It is possible to modify child-rearing practices so that parents teach their children more acceptable and less aggressive ways to solve conflicts. Such an approach would take massive education and is time consuming and expensive. Various public awareness programs may make it possible to alert people to the need to control aggression and anger. We may be able to change environmental cues so that there are less props present that encourage aggression. Gun control is an attempt to achieve such a result. Further, by decreasing personal frustration in the form of slowing down the pace of life, teaching people more divergent methods for enjoying life, and making people more responsible to each other rather than being shielded by an institution, we may be able to reduce some of the dread cues that so often lead to aggressive behavior.

Dr. Raymond Novaco has developed, tested, and extensively applied a program of anger control (Novaco, 1975) that is based on the stress inoculation package described in chapter 7 (Anxiety). In this approach the person learns to recognize the situations that make him/her angry

200

(dread cues). Such recognition is the first step in determining the characteristic ways in which the person reacts to anger provocation. By identifying these patterns the person can learn what kind of self-talk causes anger expression to continue. Then the person can modify the self-talk so that the anger is more likely to subside. The entire package has been used for policemen, child abusers, military recruits, explosive adolescents, and athletes. It seems to be a good way to control anger problems and represents a concrete attempt at solving the aggression problem that exists in modern life today.

Aggression: Good or bad?

It is possible that a tendency such as aggression has outlived its usefulness to the species. There is no doubt that aggression was useful to early man. The tendency would not have survived if it were not useful. However, times have changed. Man no longer lives in a physically threatening environment in which physical aggression aids survival. Nonetheless, the legacy remains and man continues to react to pain and frustration by aggressing. The aggression now threatens our survival. At the least the aggression makes life difficult and unpleasant for many of us. This same tendency that once helped our survival now threatens it. Does this mean we should have a race of docile, non-aggressive creatures? No, that, too, would probably be maladaptive. Aggression does seem to motivate the achievement and production that helps us all to survive. The problem, a very weighty one, is to balance the power and the destructiveness of aggression so that man is most optimally served. Once again history will serve as the arbitrator of whether such a balance can be achieved.

SEX AND AGGRESSION: EPILOGUE

We have seen the nature, origin, and function of two important aspects of the human being. Sex-roles develop because of cultural socialization and seem to represent both productive and unproductive stereotypes of people. Aggression was viewed as a basic, innate response tendency in which people respond to painful dread cues. The importance of changing aggression was outlined and discussed.

CHAPTER 10

EPILOGUE: WHERETO THE HUMAN PERSONALITY?

We have considered many of the dimensions of the human personality. Our definition of personality, if you remember, was an integrative one. We looked at personality as the consistent ways in which a person acts across situations, especially in terms of how those patterns of action differ from the way other people act in those same situations. Our search has taken us through the content of personality (from a consistently cognitive-behavioral perspective) and through the methods of experimental personality research. We have described a multifaceted and complex creature. And we have seen from where the creature eminates and how he/she can be changed. Our journey has, by necessity, been biased but, nonetheless, the reader has been exposed to many of the major issues of human personality.

It may be that you leave this journey through the human personality with a mild feeling of incompleteness. Something else needs to be considered in our search. While we have viewed the survival implications of each dimension of personality, the question of the future of the human personality, the individual self-system, still remains. What will happen to this creature, man, who possesses so volatile a system as the "personality?" That query, of course, will continue to be an empirical question. However, it may be possible to look at some remaining issues in human personality in order to orient ourselves to answering the question: Whereto the human personality? This final chapter will try to put the human being together by considering a set of basic characteristics about the creature: love and hope. Science has spent some time attending to these aspects of the human. Perhaps by looking at them we may be able to answer our questions about the future of the individual.

Love

Without a doubt, the aspect of life that is of most interest to most human beings is love. More has been written about love, spoken about love, felt about love, and dreamed about love than perhaps any other human con-

dition. A lyric from a music composer seems to catch the
significance and pervasiveness of love quite well:

> ...Everybody's gonna' tell you it's not worth it,
> everybody's gotta' show you their own pain,
> you may try to find your way up around it,
> but the need for love will still remain
> (Browne, 1974).

Even though love is a major fact of life, there is
really little known about it. One of the reasons there
is so little known about love on a scientific level is
that there are many different definitions of it. Consider some of the following definitions of love. "Love
is the active concern for the life and growth of that
which we love." "When the satisfaction or the security
of another person becomes as significant as one's own
satisfaction or security, then the state of love exists."
"Love means never having to say you're sorry." "Love
is when attachment and caring form a dual feeling of
impulse." "Love is a spirit all compact of fire." All
of these were offered by famous people in the history
of man. Each one is accurate in its own way. But if
everyone is right, what is love anyway? While it may
be true to say that you will know love when you experience
it, as scientists we need some way to measure this pattern
of activity.

A couple of ways in which psychologists have measured
love may be helpful in considering this question of definition. Dr. Zick Rubin (1973) developed the loving and
liking scale in which the person responds to questions
about a particular partner, lover, or friend. For example, "If _____ were feeling bad, my first duty would
be to cheer him/her up," or "I would do almost anything
for _____." are items on the love scale. By using this
scale Rubin has been able to identify many of the important aspects of love relationships. Starting with
attraction and going through to maintaining relationships,
Rubin has mapped out the process of intimacy (See Chapter
6 on interpersonal relationships).

Another method for the measurement of love is the
SAMPLE love scale developed by Laswell and Laswell (1976).
In this scale the respondent answers 50 true-false ques-
tions that can determine the ways in which the person

defines love him/herself. The person receives a score
in each of six styles of loving. Supposedly the high
scores for a person represent how he/she defines love.
The questionnaire is still experimental but represents
intriguing way to study the origin and effects of various
styles of love. The six styles measured form the word
SAMPLE and hence the name of the scale. Storgic love
is a life-long friendship type of love. In this type
the love takes a long time to develop, and it is usually
permanent. It is characterized by interdependence and
trust. Agapic love is other-centered love in which the
love is patient, tolerant, and supportive of his/her
lover. Love ends when the needs of the partner are not
being met. Manic love is dependent and possessive love
in which there is an obsession with the love object.
Love has high peaks and low valleys. Jealousy is part
of this love. When indifference sets in, love dies.
Pragmatic love is practical and sensible. The person
looks for aspects in the partner that insure basic com-
patibility such as values, religious beliefs, career
goals, and so forth. Ludic love is playful, self-centered
love. Love is viewed as a conquest and when the relationship becomes boring, love is over. Erotic love is
romantic love. There is idealization of the love object,
sexual urgency, and a feeling that love conquers all.
Falling in love is very desirable and the loss of a
lover is tragic.

There are some data to show that the SAMPLE scale
relates to other dimensions of personaltiy that seem
to make theoretical sense. For instance, Johnston and
Jaremko (1979) found that manic, ludic, and erotic
scores correlated with sensation-seeking. Further,
Jaremko and Johnston (1979) found that the ludic style
of loving correlated with high self-pre-occupation. Thus
it should be possible to use the SAMPLE love scale to
determine the characteristics of different types of love.

Even though there are ways to measure love, it may
be helpful to look at it in the context of the self-system. It may be possible that the ideal state of the
human personality is love. Certainly many religious
belief systems (e.g., Christianity) have held that love
is the ideal state of the human. On a phenomenological
level, each of us knows that to be in love is a pleasant
state (excluding the uncertainty concerning the permanence

204

of the relationship). And it is fairly safe to say that we spend a good deal of our lives trying to find "true love." Therefore, if it can be determined how love relates to the self, it may be possible to seek love in a more systematic and sensible way. What follows is one way to look at love and the self.

Love can be viewed as the process of stepping outside of one's own self-system into another person's self-system. A famous person once said that we find ourselves by giving up ourselves. If you stop to think about it when you are in love, you are "out of your own self." Such departure from the confines of the self-system seems to have favorable benefits. You don't take yourself so seriously, you feel better about yourself, you have hope for the future, and your outlook on life becomes more positive. This seems to occur because the self-system is a confining experience. By viewing the world from another's perspective, the human personality grows and becomes more competent. In any case, if it is true that love is letting go of the self, it may be possible to "find love" by practical methods that decrease self-preoccupation (Chapter 4). Admittedly the position here is speculative, but it warrants further research and study.

What we seem to be saying is that the human personality, intimatley related to the self-system, is most optimally operative when it"gives itself up." Personal, social and species survival may be best served by the human personality in some way fusing with other personalities. All of this is a highly vague way of saying that man is best served when he/she shows kindness, respect, and attention to other people. The future of the human personality lies in loving (fusing with) each other. Perhaps we should "hang together" or we will all "hang separately."

Hope

Another aspect to be considered when looking at the future of the human personaltiy is the notion of hope. When humans "hope for the future" they seem to display their most effective characteristics. Where does hope come from? How do we insure that people have hope for the future? Dr. Donald Whaley (1979) has presented an elegant and persuasive account of the origin of hope especially as it relates to the survival of the human being. We can learn much about the future of the human personality by a look at Whaley's ideas.

Hope, Whaley maintains, is the single most important ingredient in man's continued survival. Man must have hope in order to overcome the present obstacles that threaten his survival. By analyzing hope as a complex of behaviors that originate from events in our environment, we can see how to make sure that each of us has hope.

There are three components to hope. They correspond to the typology of behavior we have used throughout this book. First, hope is the continuation or resumption of a response class. Hope is hanging in with an activity: finishing school, working at a relationship, or completing a job. Second, hope is physiological responding. Hope is physical well-being. During hope reactions, the person's body is operating in a smooth and efficient way. The parasympathetic branch of the autonomic nervous system is in operation when we are hopeful. It is this physical system that is responsible for relaxed muscles, smooth blood flow, and other aspects of physical high-functioning. Hope is physical efficiency. Lastly, hope is the conscious experience that everything is going to be all right. The person "feels" enthusiastic, "feels" like he/she belongs, and "wants" to continue with the task at hand. It's fairly easy to see that all of these aspects of hope are positive and forward-striving. Hope, therefore, is what we need to insure that the human personality will survive. But from whence does hope come?

Whaley suggests that hope comes from hope cues. In Chapter 9, we used the idea of dread cues to explain the origin of the pain that causes aggression. Hope cues are just the opposite of dread cues. Remember how dread cues come from neutral cues being paired with punishers. Hope cues come from neutral cues being paired with positive or negative reinforcers. Certain things in our world get paired with or associated with reinforcers. These neutral cues then become hope cues and elicit any or all of the three parts of hope. Hope cues can be other people's words, time of day, week, or year, written material, or any other stimulus that consistently precedes the appearance of a reinforcer. Those people who are hopeful and optimistic have many hope cues in their environment. Those not so happy, lack in the hope cues, in fact, they may even have a number of dread cues that elicit dread and its effects.

One of the most important classes of hope cues that exist in modern life is the words of encouragement and compliments given to us by other people. Since this commodity is abundant and cheap, we may be able to use kind words and interpersonal reinforcement as an aid to the survival of the human personality. This is true because modern life is full of instances in which the individual person is asked to perform acts that are unpleasant. In most actions we do, it is possible to see that the long-term consequences of the act conflict with the short-term consequences of the act. Examples abound: smoking in which the short-term consequence is good and the long-term consequence unpleasant; energy conservation, weight loss, population control, education, environmental pollution, and inflationary spending. In each of these the short-term consequences tend to exert more control. As a culture we are, therefore, threatened by the problems that result when we are self-indulgent.

Since we are each asked to practice self-restraint by not polluting too much, not consuming too much fuel, taking care of our bodies, and so forth, our natural tendency to respond to the most immediate rewards is being thwarted. Hope cues, especially in the form of interpersonal cues, can help us to narrow the gap between the short-term and long-term consequences of our actions. As we try to conserve fuel, for example, we can compliment and encourage each other for this selfless action. In this way, the hope cues make it more likely that we will continue the difficult action. Indeed if we support and encourage each other with kind words, many more of us may continue to hang in with the difficulty of modern life. Such a "positive verbal community" would make its members feel and experience all the aspects of hope. The human personality would be more likely to survive. Making yourself more positive results in other people becoming more positive which results in increased chances of survival for all.

This "technology of hope-giving" is not offered by Whaley (1979) as an idealistic solution to distant problems. Rather, the use of the positive verbal community

207

for hope-giving is a workable and effective way to plan enviornments in which people are productive and feel good about it. Each person can achieve the results of hope by encouraging and supporting the others around him/her. Hope, thus, becomes the single most important ingredient in man's continued survival.

While there is no especially good reason for wanting to have the human personality survive (it doesn't seem to matter all that much in the scheme of nature), most of the cultures to which we belong have convinced us that we are worth saving (Skinner, 1974). However, the future survival of the human personality may depend upon two of its most interesting ingredients. If human-kind can learn to consistently transcend the self-systems that engulf its members, and thereby "love" each other, it may just be possible for enough hope cues to be present so that we can continue doing the things that we need to do in order to survive. Hope and love, based on ideals of many religious systems, are reproducible psychological processes. It may be well worth our while to make sure that more of the human personalities that make up our species possess these characteristics. Such a course of action might allow us to survive long enough so that we can find out why we are here.

Let the music keep our spirits high,
let the buildings keep our children dry,
let creation reveal its secrets, bye and bye,
'til the light that's lost within us reaches the sky.
(Browne, 1974)

REFERENCES

Abramowitz, S. I. Internal-external control and social-political activism. Journal of Consulting and Clinical Psychology, 1973, 40, 196-201.

Adler, A. What life should mean to you. Boston: Little, Brown, 1931.

Allport, G. W. Traits revisited. American Psychologist, 1966, 21, 1-10.

Anastasi, A. Psychological Testing. London: MacMillan, 1972.

Arnkoff, D. & Mahoney, M. The role of perceived control in psychopathology. Paper presented at Choice and Perceived Control Conference, Blacksburg, Va., 1978.

Azrin, N. H., Hutchinson, R. R., & Jake, D. F. Painful induced fighting in the squirrel monkey. Journal of Experimental Analysis of Behavior, 1963, 9, 191-204.

Bandura, A. Behavioral modifications through modeling procedures. In L. Krasner and L. P. Ullman (Eds.), Research in Behavior Modification. New York: Holt, Rinehart, & Winston, 1965.

Bandura, A. Principles of behavior modification. New York: Holt, Rinehart, & Winston, 1969.

Bandura, A. Self-efficacy: Toward a unifying theory of behavioral change. Psychological Review, 1977, 84, 191-225.

Bandura, A. The self-system in reciprocal determinism. American Psychologist, 1978, 33, 344-358.

Bandura, A., Adams, N.E. Analysis of self-efficacy theory of behavioral change. Cognitive Therapy and Research, 1977, 1, 287-310.

Barber, R. X. Pitfalls in Human Research, New York: Pergamon, 1976.

Barron, F. An ego-strength scale which predicts response
    to psychotherapy. Journal of Consulting Psychology,
    1953, 17, 327-333.

Beck, A. T. An inventory for measuring depression.
    Achievements of general psychiatry, 1961, 4, 561-571.

Bem, S. L. The measurement of psychological androgyny.
    Journal of Consulting and Clinical Psychology, 1974,
    2, 153-162.

Berkowitz, L. The contagion of violence. In W. Arnold
    & M. Page (Eds.), Nebraska Symposium on Motivation.
    Lincoln: University of Nebraska Press, 1970.

Berschield, E. & Walster, E. Interpersonal attraction.
    Reading, Ma.: Addison-Wesley, 1969.

Bistline, J., Shanahan, F. & Jaremko, M. E. Cognitive,
    behavioral, and physiological aspects of test
    anxiety. Paper presented at Southeastern Psycholo-
    gical Association, Miami, 1977.

Block, J. The Q-sort method in personality assessment
    and psychiatric research. Springfield, Ill.: Charles
    C. Thomas, 1961.

Block, J. Some reasons for the apparent inconsistency of
    personality. Psychological Bulletin, 1968, 70, 210-
    212.

Bonney, M. The normal personality. New York: Guilford
    1970.

Bower, G. H. Scripts in memory for text. Stanford
    University, 1979.

Browne, J. Saturate before using. Record Album, Electra
    Records, 1973.

Browne, J. For Everyman. Record Album, New York: Elec -
    tra Records, 1974.

Browne, J. Late for the sky. Reocrd Album, New York:
    Electktra Records, 1975.

Browne, J. Running on Empty. Record Album, Electra Records 1977.

Bryne, D. Interpersonal attraction and attitude similarity. Journal of Abnormal and Social Psychology, 1961, 62, 713-715.

Bryne, D. An Introduction to Personality. Englewood Cliffs, N.J.: Prentice - Hall, 1974.

Bryne, D. & Clore, G. L. Predicting interpersonal attraction among strangers. Psychonomic Science, 1966, 4, 239-240.

Bryne, D., Griffit, W. & Stefaniah, D. Attraction and similarity of personaltiy characteristics. Journal of Personality and Social Psychology, 1967, 5, 82-90.

Bryne, D. & Nelson, D. Attraction as a linear function of proportion of positive reinforcements. Journal of Personality and Social Psychology, 1965, 1, 659-663.

Bryne, D., & Rhamey, R. Magnitude of positive and negative reinforcements as a determinant of attraction. Journal of Personality and Social Pyschology, 1965, 2, 884-889.

Burgess, A. A Clockwork Orange. New York: Ballentine, 1962.

Buss, A. H. Psychology: Behavior in perspective. New York: Wiley, 1978.

Butler, P. Self-assertion for women. New York; Canfield Press, 1976.

Carr, H. A., & Kingsbury, F. A. The concept of trait. Psychological Review, 1938, 45, 497-524.

Chaplin, J. P. Dictionary of Psychology. New York: Dell, 1975.

Conger, J. The modification of interview behavior by client use of social reinforcement. Behavior Therapy, 1971, 2, 52-61.

Coombs, R. H. Social participation, self-concept, and interpersonal valuation. Sociometry, 1969, 32, 273-286.

Coopersmith, S. The antecedents of self-esteem. San Francisco: Freeman, 1967.

Curran, J. P. Skills training as an approach to the treatment of heterosexual-social anxiety: A review. Psychological Bulletin, 1977, 84, 140-157.

DeCharms, R. Personal causation. New York: Academic Press, 1968.

DeCharms, R. Personal causation choice and control. Paper presented at Choice and Perceived Control Conference, Blacksburg, Va., 1978.

Delgado, J. M. R. The physical control of the mind. New York: Harper, 1969.

Deutsch, M., & Collins, M. E. The effect of public policy in housing projects upon interracial attitudes. In E. Maccoby, T. M. Newcomb, & E. Hartley (Eds.), Readings in Social Psychology (3rd Ed.), New York: Holt, 1965, 612-623.

Dion, K. Berscheid, E., & Walster, E. What is beautiful is good. Journal of Personality and Social Psychology, 1972, 24, 285-290.

Eiseman, R. Experience in experiments and change in internal-external control scores. Journal of Consulting and Clinical Psychology, 1972, 39, 434-435.

Emmelkamp, P. M. G., Kurpers, A. C. M., & Eggeract, J. B. Cognitive modification versus prolonged exposure in vivo: A comparison with agoraphobics. Behavior Research and Therapy, 1978, 16, 33-41.

Eysenck, H. J. The biological basis of personality, Springfield, Ill.: Thomas, 1967.

Eysenck, H. J. Eysenck on Extroversion. London: Crosby, Lockwood, Staples, 1973.

Eysenck, H. J. & Eysenck, S. B. G. Manual of the Eysenck Personality Inventory. London: University of London Press, 1964.

Eysenck, H. J. & Rachman, S. The causes and cures of neurosis. San Diego: Knapp, 1965.

Fenigstein, A., Scheier, M. R., & Buss, A. H. Public and private self-consciousness: Theory and assessment. Journal of Consulting and Clinical Psychology, 1975, 43, 522-527.

Festinger, L. A theory of social comparison processes. Human Relations, 1954, 7, 117-140.

Forisha, B. L. Sex roles and personal awareness. Morristown, N. J.: General Learning Press, 1978.

Freud, S. Collected papers of Sigmund Freud. (Edited by Ernest Jones). New York: Basic Books, 1959.

Freud, S. Instincts and their vicissitudes. In G. Lindzey and C. S. Hall (Eds.), Theories of personality: Primary sources and research. New York: Wiley, 1965.

Geen, R. G. Personality: the skien of behavior. St. Louis: Mosby, 1976.

Gergen, K. J. Personal consistency and the presentation of self. In Gordon, E. & Gergen, K. J. (Eds.), The self in social interaction. New York: Wiley, 1968.

Glass, D., & Singer, J. E. Urban stress. New York: Academic Press, 1972.

Goldfried, M. R., & Goldfried, A. Cognitive change methods In F. Kanfer and A. Goldstein (Eds.), Helping people change. New York: Pergamon, 1975.

Goldfried, M. R., & Merbaum, M. (Eds.), Behavior change through self-control. New York: Holt, Rinehart, Winston, 1973.

Goldiamond, I. Perception. In A. J. Bachrach (Ed.), Experimental foundations of clinical psychology, New York: Basic Book, 1962.

213

Golightly, C., & Bryne, D. Attitude statements as positive
and negative reinforcements. Science, 1964, 146,
798-799.

Gordon, C., & Gergen, K. J. (Eds.) The self in social
interaction. New York: Wiley, 1968.

Gordon, T. Parent effectiveness training. New York:
Peter H. Wyden, 1970.

Gore, P., & Rotter, J. B. A personality correlate of
social action. Journal of Personality, 1963, 31,
58-64.

Guildford, J. P. Personality. New York: McGraw-Hill,
1959.

Hall, E. T. The hidden dimension. New York: Doubleday,
1966.

Harris, F. R., Wolf, M. M., & Baer, D. M. Effects of
adult social reinforcement on child behavior.
Young Children, 1964, 20, 8-27.

Harvey, O. H. Personality factors in resolution of
conceptual incongruities. Sociometry, 1962, 25,
336-352.

Hernstein, R. J., & Loveland, D. H. Complex visual concept in the pigeon. Science, 1964, 146, 549-551.

Holmes, T. H., & Rahe, R. H. The social readjustment
scale. Journal of Psychosomatic Research, 1967,
11, 231-218.

Houston, B. K. Dispositional anxiety and the effectiveness of cognitive coping strategies in stressful
laboratory and classroom situations. In C. Spielberger
and I. Sarason (Eds.), Stress and anxiety, Vol. 4.
Washington, D.C.: Hemisphere, 1977, 205-226.

Hunt, J. Traditional personality theory in the light of
recent research. American Scientist, 1965, 53, 80-
96.

James, A., & Lott, A. J. Reward frequency and the formulation of positive attitudes toward group members. Journal of Social Psychology, 1964, 62, 111-115.

James. W. Psychology: the briefer course. (Edited by Gordon Allport). New York: Harper Torchbooks, 1961.

Jaremko, M. E. Prophylactic systematic desensitization: An analogue test. Journal of Behavior Therapy and Experimental Psychiatry, 1978, 9, 5-9.

Jaremko, M. E. A component analysis of stress inoculation. Cognitive Therapy and Research, 1979, 3, 35-48.

Jaremko, M. E. Cognitive-behavior modification: Real science or more mentalism. Psychological Record, 1979.

Jaremko, M. E. The stress inoculation of heterosocial anxiety. In D. Meichenbaum and M. E. Jaremko (Eds.) Stress management and prevention. New York: Plenum, 1980.

Jaremko, M. E., Hadfield, R., & Lindsey, R. The use of the videotape in the assessment of cognitive tendencies. Behavioral Assessment, 1979, in press.

Jaremko, M. E., & Johnston, T. Self-preoccupation and tendency toward the jealousy response. Unpublished manuscript, University of Richmond, 1979.

Jaremko, M. E., Lindsey, R. Stress coping abilities of individuals high and low in jealousy. Psychological Reports, 1979, 44, 547-553.

Jaremko, M. E., Noles, S., & Williams, D. The measurement of self-preoccupation. Paper presented at the Southeastern Psychological Association, New Orleans, 1979.

Jaremko, M. E., & Walker, G. R. The role of the content of coping statements in the stress inoculation of speech anxiety. Paper presented at the Association for the Advancement of Behavior Therapy, Chicago, 1978.

Johnston, T., & Jaremko, M. E. A correlationa analysis
    of suggestibility, self-preoccupation, styles of
    loving, and sensation seeking. Psychological
    Reports, 1979.

Jones, J. The tendency to interact with preschool and
    sex-role. Unpublished Master's Thesis, University
    of Richmond, 1979.

Jourard, S. M., & Remy, R. M. Perceived parental attitudes
    the self, and security. Journal of Consulting
    Psychology, 1955, 19, 364-366.

Kanfer, F. Self-regulation: Research, issues, and specu-
    lations. In C. Neuringer and J. Michael (Eds.),
    Behavior Modification in clinical psychology. New
    York: Appleton-Century-Crofts, 1970.

Kaplan, H. B., & Pokorny, A. D. Self-derogation and
    childhood broken home. Journal of Marriage and the
    Family, 1971, 33, 328-337.

Katz, A. M., & Hill, R. Residual propinquity and marital
    selection. Marriage and Family Living, 1958, 20,
    327-335.

Kendall, P. C., & Korgeski, G. P. Assessment and cognitive
    behavioral interventions. Cognitive Therapy and
    Research, 1979, 3, 1-21.

Kiesler, C. A. The psychology of commitment. New York:
    Academic Press, 1971.

Kish, G. B. Studies in sensory reinforcement. In W. K
    Honig (Ed.). Operant behavior: Areas of reserach
    and application. New York: Applet n-Century-Crofts,
    1966, 109-159.

Krasner, L., & Ullman, L. Behavior influence and per-
    sonality. New York: Holt, Rinehart and Winston,
    1973.

Kringler, E. Obsessional neurotics, British Journal of
    Psychiatry, 1965, 3, 709-722.

Lacey, J. I. Somatic response patterning and stress: Some revisions of activation theory. In M. H. Appley and R. Trumbull (Eds.) Psychological Stress. New York: Appleton-Century-Crofts, 1967, 14-36.

Lang, P. Stimulus control, response control, and desensitization of fear. In D. Lewis (Ed.). Learning approaches to behavior change. Chicago: Aldine, 1970

Lange, A. J., & Jakubowski, P. Responsible assertive behavior. Champaign, Ill.: Research, 1977.

Langer, E. Rethinking the role of thought in social interaction. In J. Harvey, W. Iches, & R. Kidd (Eds.) New directions in attribution research Vol. 2 Hillsdale, N.J.: Erlbaum, 1978.

Lasswell, T. E., & Lasswell, M. I love you but I'm not in love with you. Journal of Marriage nad Family Counseling, 1976, 2, 211-224.

Lazarus, R. S. Psychological stress and the coping process. New York: McGraw-Hill, 1966.

Lazarus, R. S. Patterns of adjustment. New York: McGraw-Hill, 1976.

Lazarus, R. S., & Averrill, J. R. Emotion and cognition: With special reference to anxiety. In C. D. Spielberger (Ed.) Anxiety: Current trends in theory and research (Vol. 2, New York: Academic Press, 1972.

Leitenberg, H. The use of single-case methodology in psychotherapy. Journal of Abnormal Psychology, 1973, 82, 87-101.

Lefcourt, H. Recent developments in the study of locus of control. In B. Maher (Ed.) Progress in experimental personality research, Vol. 6. New York: Academic Press, 1972.

Lefcourt, H. The readiness to perceive contingencies in specific reinforcement areas. Paper presented at the Choice and Perceived Control Symposium, Blacksburg, Va., 1978.

Levenson, H. Multidimensional locus of control in psychiatric patients. Journal of Consulting and Clincal Psychology, 1973, 41, 397-404.

Linden, E. Apes, men, and language: How teaching chimpanzees to "talk" alters man's notions of his place in nature. New York: Saturday Review Press, 1974.

London, O. H. Interpersonal attraction and abilities: Social desirability or similarity to self? Unpublished Master's Thesis, University of Texas, 1967.

MacArthur, L. A. Luck is alive and well in New Haven. Journal of Personal and Social Psychology, 1970, 19, 316-318.

Maccoby, E. E. (Ed.) The development of sex differences. Stanford, Ca.: Stanford University Press, 1966.

Maccoby, E. E., & Jacklin, C. The psychology of sex differences. Stanford, Ca.: Stanford University Press, 1974.

Mahoney, M. J. The self-management of covert behavior: A case study. Behavior Therapy, 1971, 2, 575-578.

Mahoney, M. J. Cognition and behavior modification. Cambridge: Ballinger, 1974.

Malott, R. W,, Tillema, M., & Glenn, S. Behavior analysis and behavior modification: An introduction. Kalamazoo, Mi.: Behaviordelia, 1978.

Malott, R. W., & Whaley, D. L. Psychology, New York: Harper & Row, 1976.

Mandler, G. & Sarason, S. B. A study of anxiety and learning. Journal of Abnormal and Social Psychology, 1952, 47, 166-173.

Masters, W. H., & Johnson, V. When husband and wife disagree about sex. McCall's, February, 1975.

218

Mausner, B. The effect of prior reinforcement on the interaction of observer pairs. _Journal of Abnormal and Social Psychology_, 1954, _49_, 65-68.

May, R. _Psychology and the human deilemma_. New York: Van Nostrand, 1967.

McGinnis, E., & Ferster, L. B. _The reinforcement of social behavior_. Boston: Houghton-Mifflin, 1971.

McReynolds, P. Changing conceptions of anxiety: A historical review and a proposed integration. In I. Sarason and C. Spielberger (Eds.) _Stress and Anxiety_ (Vol. 3), Washington, D.C.: Hemisphere, 1975.

Meichenbaum, D. _Cognitive-Behavior Modification_ New York: Plenum, 1977.

Meichenbaum, D. & Cameron, R. Stress inoculation: A skills training approach to anxiety management. Unpublished manuscript. University of Waterloo, 1973.

Meichenbaum, D., & Jaremko, M. E. (Eds.) _Stress management and prevention_. New York: Plenum, 1980, in press.

Middlebrook, P. N. _Social Psychology and modern life_. New York: Knopf, 1974.

Mirels, H. L. Dimensions of external versus internal control. _Journal of Consulting and Clincial Psychology_, 1970, _34_, 226-238.

Mischel, W. _Introduction to Personality_, New York: Holt Rinehart, & Winston, 1976.

Novaco, R. _Anger Control: the development and evaluation of an experiment treatment_. Lexington, Mass.: Herth & Co., 1975.

Nowicki, S., & Barnes, J. Effects of a structured camp experience on locus of control orientation. _Journal of Genetic Psychology_, 1973, _122_, 247-252.

Nowicki, S., & Strickland, B. A locus of control scale for children. _Journal of Consulting and Clincal Psychology_, 1973, _40_, 148-154.

Psychology, 1973, 40, 148-154.

Pavlov, I. P. Conditioned reflexes. London: Oxford University Press, 1927.

Phares, E. J. Expectancy changes in skill and chance situations. Journal of Abnormal and Social Psychology, 1957, 54, 339-342.

Piers, E. V. Parent prediction of children's self-concepts. Journal of Consulting and Clinical Psychology, 1972, 38,428-433.

Rachman, S. The passing of the two-stage theory of fear and avoidance: Fresh possibilities. Behavior Research and Therapy, 1976, 14, 125-131.

Rehm, L. A self-control model of depression. Behavior Therapy, 1977, 8, 787-804.

Renshon, S. A. Personal control and political life. Paper presented at Choice and Perceived Control Symposium, Blacksburg, Va., 1978.

Rogers, C. R. A theory of therapy,personality, and interpersonal relationships. In S. Koch (Ed.) Psychology: A study of a science, Vol. 3,New York: McGraw-Hill, 1959.

Rogers, C. R. On becoming a person. Boston: Houghton-Mifflin, 1961.

Rogers, C. R. (Ed.). The therapeutic relationship and its impact: A study of psychotherapy with schizophrenics. Madison, Wi.: University of Wisconsin Press, 1967.

Rogers, C. R. Interpersonal relationships: U.S.A. 2000. Journal of Applied Behavioral Science, 1968, 4, 18-24.

Rogers, C. R. Carl Rogers on encounter groups. New York: Harper and Row, 1970.

Rotter, J. B. Generalized expectancies for internal versus external control of reinforcement. Psychological Monographs, 1966, 80, 1 (Whole No. 609).

Rubin, Z. Liking and loving: An invitation to social psychology. New York: Holt, Rinehart, & Winston 1973.

Sarason, R. G. Experimental approaches to test anxiety: Attention and the use of information. In C. Spielberger (Ed.), Anxiety: Current trends in theory and research. (Vol. 2). New York: Academic Press, 1972.

Sarason, I. G. Anxiety and self-preoccupation. In I. G. Sarason and C. D. Spielberger (Eds.). Stress and Anxiety,(Vol. 3). Washington: Hemisphere Publishing Co., 1975.

Sarason, I. G. Test anxiety scale: Theory and research. In I. Sarason and C. Spielberger (Eds.). Stress and Anxiety, (Vol. 6). Washington, D.C.: Hemisphere, 1978.

Schachter, S. The interaction of cognitive and physiological determinants of emotional state. In C. Spielberger (Ed.), Anxiety and Behavior. New York: Academic Press, 1966.

Schneider, R. & Shiffrin, W. Controlled and automatic human information processing. Psychological Review. 1977, 84, 1-66.

Seligman, M. E. P. Helplessness. San Francisco: Freeman, 1975.

Selye, H. Stress without distress. New York: Signet, 1974.

Shaver, P. Living alone, loneliness, and health. Paper presented at the American Psychological Association, New York, 1979.

Shaw, M. Perspectives on proxemics: Crowding, personal space, privacy, and territoriality. Symposium presented at Southeastern Psychological Association, Atlanta, 1978.

Skinner, B. F. Science and Human Behavior. New York, MacMillian, 1953.

Skinner, B. F. Verbal Behavior. New York: Appleton-Century-Crofts, 1957.

Skinner, B. F. Beyond Freedom and Dignity. New York: Knopf, 1971.

Skinner, B. F. About Behaviorism. New York: Knopf, 1974.

Smith, M. B. Perspectives on selfhood. American Psychologist, 1978, 33, 1053-1063.

Spielberger, C. D. (Ed.), Anxiety and behavior. New York: Academic, 1966.

Spielberger, C. D., and Sarason, I. G. (Eds.), Stress and Anxiety, (Vol. 1). Washington, D.C.: Hemisphere, 1975.

Spielberger, C. D., Gorsuch, R. L., & Lushene, R. E. Manual for the state-trait anxiety inventory. Palo Alto, Ca.: Consulting Psychologist Press, 1970.

Stevens, J. O. Awareness: exploring, experimenting, experiencing. New York: Boston, 1975.

Stone, W. F. Autokinetic norms: An experimental analysis. Journal of Personality and Social Psychology, 1967, 5, 76-81.

Strayhorn, J. M. Talking it out. Champaign, Ill.: Research Research Press, 1977.

Strickland, B. R. Internal and external control expectancies and health maintenance behavior. Paper presented at Choice and Perceived Control Symposium, Blacksburg, Va., 1978.

Sullivan, H. S. The interpersonal theory of psychiatry. New York: Norton, 1953.

Taylor, J. A personality scale of manifest anxiety. Journal of Abnormal and Social Psychology, 1953, 48, 258-290.

Todd, F. J. Covert control of self-evaluative responses in the treatment of depression. Behavior Therapy, 1972, 3, 91-94.

Valentine, V. F. & Vallee, F. G. (Eds.), The eskimo of the canadian artic. Princeton: D. Van Nostrand, 1968.

Videbeck, R. Self-conception and the reactions of others. Sociometry, 1960, 23, 351-359.

Walster, E., Aronson, V., Abrahams, D., & Rottman, L. Importance of the physical attractiveness in dating behavior. Journal of Personality and Social Psychology, 1966, 5, 508-516.

Walster, E., & Presholdt, P. The effect of misjuding another: Overcompensation or dissonance reduction? Journal of Experimental Social Psychology, 1966, 2, 85-97.

Warr, P., & Knapper, G. The perception of people and events. New York: Wiley, 1968.

Watson, J. B., & Rayner, R. Conditioned emotional reactions. Journal of Experimental Psychology, 1920, 3, 1-14.

Whaley, D. L. The origins of hope and dread. Book in preparation. North Texas State University, 1979.

Whaley, D. L, & Malott, R. W. Elementary principles of behavior. Englewood Cliffs, N.J.: Prentice-Hall, 1971.

Wiemer, B. Achivevment strivings. In H. London and J. Exner (Eds.), Dimensions of Personality, New York: Wiley, 1978.

Williams, C. The elimination of tantrum behavior by extinction procedures. Journal of Abnormal Social Psychology, 1959, 59, 269.

Wilson, G. Introversion/Extroversion. In H. London and J. Exner (Eds.) Dimensions of Personality. New York: Wiley, 1978, 217-261.

Wine, J.   Test anxiety and the direction of attention. Psychological Bulletin, 1971.

Winter, D., & Steward, A. J.   The power motive.   In H. London & J. Exner (Eds.), Dimensions of Personality. New York: Wiley, 1978.

Wolpe, J.   The practice of behavior therapy.   New York: Pergamon, 1973.

Worrel, J., & Nelson, C. M.   Managing Instructional Problems.   New York: McGraw-Hill, 1974.

Wyer, R. S.   Self-acceptance, discrepancy between parents' perception of their children, and goal-seeking effectiveness.   Journal of Personality and Social Psychology, 1965, 2, 311-316.

Zander, A., & Havelin, A.   Social comparison and interpersonal attraction.   Human Relations, 1960, 13, 21-32.

Zuckerman, M., & Lubin, B.   Manual for the multiple affect adjective checklist.   San Diego: Educational and Industrial Testing Service, 1966.

Zuckerman, M.   The sensation seeking motive.   In B. A. Mober (Ed.), Progress in experimental personality research (Vol. 7).   New York, Academic, 1974.

Zuckerman, M.   Sensation seeking.   In H. London and J. Exner (Eds.),Dimensons of Personality.   New York: Wiley, 1978, 487-559.

AUTHOR INDEX

A

Abraham, 109
Abramowitz, 104
Adams, 93, 158
Adler, 61
Alberti, 131
Allport, 2
Anastasi, 75
Arnkoff, 103
Aronson, 109
Averill, 142
Azrin, 197

B

Bandura, 56, 58, 90, 93, 97,
    102, 158, 198
Barber, 11
Barnes, 101
Barron, 76
Bear, 26
Beck, 11, 84
Bem, 191, 192, 193
Berkowitz, 196
Berschild, 109, 111, 112
Bistline, 148
Block, 6, 75
Bonney, 152
Bower, 45
Browne, 49, 54, 60, 202, 207
Bryne, 5, 67, 83, 108, 110,
    111
Burgess, 183
Buss, 74, 198
Butler, 136

C

Cameron, 158
Carr, 3
Chance, 88
Chaplin, 125

Clore, 110
Collins, 109
Conger, 30, 31
Coombs, 81
Coopersmith, 76
Curran, 135

D

DeCharms, 105
Delgado, 199
Descarte, 69
Deutsch, 108
Dichoff, 12
Dion, 109

E

Efferaat, 157
Eisenman, 101
Emmelkamp, 157
Emmons, 131
Eysenck, H., 4, 133, 134, 135
Eysenck, S., 133, 134

F

Fenigstein, 74
Ferster, 135
Festinger, 71
Fisher, 65
Forisha, 192, 194
Freud, 7, 15, 32, 183
Fullner, 81

G

Geen, 21, 135, 145
Gergen, 6, 62, 69
Glass, 145
Glenn, 54, 59, 88

Golddiamond, 117
Goldfried, A., 157
Goldfried, M., 156, 157
Golightly, 111
Gore, 104
Gordon, C., 69
Gordon, T., 132
Gorsuch, 146
Grifitt, 110

H

Hadfield, 148
Hake, 197
Hall, 121
Harris, 26
Harvey, 113
Havelin, 196
Heinlein, 130
Hernstein, 42
Hill, 108
Holmes, 145
Houston, 145, 148, 185
Hunt, 6
Hutchinson, 197

J

Jacklin, 193
Jakubowski, 136
James, G., 119
James, W., 45, 69
Jaremko, 12, 13, 66, 68, 72,
    73, 74, 77, 94, 135,
    140, 141, 148, 158,
    159, 186, 203
Johnson, 129
Johnston, 72, 203
Jones, 193
Jourard, 79

K

Kanfer, 71, 72, 82
Kaplan, 79

Katz, 108
Kendall, 148
Kiesler, 81
Kingsbury, 3
Kish, 184
Knapper, 123
Korgeski, 148
Krasner, 153
Kringler, 72
Kupers, 157

L

Lang, 139
Lange, 136
Langer, 45, 139
Lasswell, 202
Lazarus, 19, 142, 145
Lefcourt, 93, 100
Leitenberg, 13
Levenson, 93
Lindsey, 148, 186
London, 110
Lott, 119
Loveland, 42
Lubin, 147
Luschene, 146

M

MacArthur, 101
Maccoby, 192, 193
Mahoney, 21, 102, 103
Malott, 5, 8, 21, 54, 59, 68,
    88, 144, 183, 197
Mandler, 147
Maslow, 7
Masters, 129
Marshell, 81
Mausner, 119
May, 57, 61
McGinnies, 135
McReynolds, 138
Meichenbaum, 19, 65, 140, 158
Merbaum, 159

Whaley, 5, 8, 9, 21, 55, 59,
     68, 117, 144, 183,
     187, 189, 197, 204,
     205, 206
Williams, C., 28
Williams, D., 12, 73, 74, 77
Wilson, 133
Wine, 73, 143
Winter, 196
Wolf, 26
Wolpe, 158
Worchel, 110
Worrel, 132
Wyer, 79

Z

Zander, 108
Zuckerman, 147, 161, 162,
          165, 167

SUBJECT INDEX

A

Active Listening, 132
Aggression, 182-183, 194-200
Anxiety, 12, 18, 39, 138-140, 159-160
Anxious self-preoccupation, 73, 82
Assertion, 131-132, 136
Assumptions, untested, 126
Attentional training, 82
Attitudes, 8, 9, 66-67
Attitudes of Science, 8-11
Attitude similarity, 110
Attraction, 107-113
Attribution, 91-92
Avoidance learning, 152-154
Awareness, 61-62, 65, 70, 83-84

B

Behavior chains, 40-40
Behavioral potentialities, 45
Behavioral practice, 82
Belief, 61
Biological basis of sensation seeking, 171-173
Body language, 49, 121
Body odor, 121
Boredom susceptibility, 165

C

Careful planning, 187
Causal attributions, 92
Chance, 107-108
Classical conditioning, 150-152
Cognitive behavior, 15, 17, 90
Cognitive-behaviorism, 19, 68

Cognitive measurement, 148-149
Cognitive-restructuring, 102-103, 157
Commands, 50-51
Communication, 125-132
Concept, 42
Conceptual behavior, 41-46, 60
Consequences, 23-24
Contingencies of reinforcement, 21-25, 37, 173-175
Correlation, 11-12, 80
Cue, 22, 34-35
Cultural factors in sensation seeking, 175-177, 188-189

E

Emotion, 66-69, 100
Empiricism, 10-11
Environment, 22-23, 173-175
Escape, precluding, 157-158
Existential questioning, 179
Expectations, 124, 127
Expectancy, 88-90
Experience seeking, 164
Experiments, 12-13
Experimental control, 11, 13
External locus of control, 87-90
Extinction, 28-29
Extroversion, 33, 132-136
Eye contact, 121

F

Factor analysis, 77, 93-94
Feelings, 66-69

229

G

Generalization, 102
Good, definition of, 84

H

Happiness, 180
Historicality, 57
Honesty, 130-131
Hope, 187, 204-207

I

"I", 66-67
Ideal self-concept, 70-72
I-E scale, 92-93
Imitation, 57-58, 82
Individual differences, 4,5, 6
Individualistic, 55-56, 61
Information processing, 97
Ingratiation, 112
Initial communication development 113-116
Impression formation, 123-1 124
Integrative approach, 5
Intensive analysis, 13
Internal locus of control,87- 90
Interpersonal Communication scheme, 122-125
Introversion, 132-136
Intuitive control, 88-89

L

Learned helplessness, 91
Locus of control, 87-90
Loneliness, 136
Love, 201-204

M

Make-up, 121
Meaning, 45-46
Measurement of personality, 75, 166-170
Mentalism, 13-17
Modeling, 154-155
Movement artifact, 150

N

Negative reinforcement, 26- 27
Negative self-talk, 34
Neopoleon complex, 80
Not listening, 128-129
Nouns, 50

O

Operant conditioning, 25-26, 29
Operationalism, 15-17
Optimal level of stimulation, 162-163

P

Parental influences, 78-80
Passive aggressopm. 127-128
Performance accomplishments, 97-98, 101-102
Perception, 117
Personal evaluations, 110-111
Persuasion, 99-100
Phenomenological isolation, 60-61
Physical attraction, 109
Physical self-concept, 64-66, 80
Positive reinforcement, 26
Prevention, 159

Psychological self-concept,

Psychopathology, 100-101, 103-104

Psychophysiology, 149-150

Q

Q-sort, 75-76
Qualifiers, 51
Questions of the verbal community 54-56, 78

R

Reactivity, 149
Reading, 48
Reciprocity, 129-130
Reciprocal determinism, 56
Reification, 2-3, 60,62
Reinforcement, 25-26, 111
Relaxation, 156
Realiability, 75, 167
Resignation, 185-186
Resistance to extinction, 28-29
Response class, 37-39
Response differentiation, 30-31
Response generalization, 38
Response interference, 143-144
Response repetoire, 32
Response specificity, 149
Risk-taking in conversation, 116
Reversal of affect, 186
Reward imbalance, 111-112, 128

S

Satiation, 112
Scientific manipulation, 10-11, 16

Self-conceptual behavior, 63-72
Self-consistency, 62
Self-disclosure, 130
Self-efficacy, 90-91, 93-94, 97-100
Self-esteem, 75-77, 79
Self-evaluation, 71, 79,81
Self-management, 81-82
Self-monitoring, 71, 77, 82, 94-97
Self-report, 76-77, 146-147
Self-reward, 58, 65, 71-72
Self-preoccupation,72-75, 77, 82
Self-system, 60-63, 203-204
Sensation seeking, 161-163
Sex, 182, 191-194
Shaping, 31-33
Signal detection, 119-122, 152-154
Situational specificity, 4-6
Small talk, 115
Social activism, 104-105
Social desirability, 76
Social interaction, 14
Social perception, 117-120
Social self-concept, 70
Social signals, 120-122
State anxiety, 145-146
Stimulus class, 39-40, 42
Stimulus control, 33-35, 42, 46
Stimulus generalization, 35
Stream of consciousness, 43-45
Stress inoculation, 140-142 158, 199-200.
Stressors, types of, 144-145
Sublimation, 183-184
Survival, 82-84, 102-106, 159-160, 200
Sympathetic nervous system, 150-151

Systematic desensitization,
158

T

Theories, 6-7
Thinking, 48-49
Thinking self-concept, 69
Thrill and adventure seeking,
164
Three channels of behavior,
8, 138-140
Topography, 23
Trait anxiety, 145-146
Typology, 8

U

Understanding, 45-46

V

Validity, 75, 167
Verbal behavior, 17, 45-59
Verbal behavior types, 47-50
Verbal behavior classes, 50-
52
Verbal community, 15, 17, 47,
52-56, 61-62, 65,
66-69, 72, 78-79, 97
Verbal instructions, 46
Verbs, 51
Vicarious experiences, 98-99
Voice, 121

W

Words, 121-122
Writing, 47